SEARCHING FOR THE REPUBLIC OF THE RIO GRANDE

SEARCHING FOR THE REPUBLIC OF THE RIO GRANDE

NORTHERN MEXICO AND TEXAS, 1838-1840

PAUL D. LACK

TEXAS TECH UNIVERSITY PRESS

This book is typeset in EB Garamond. The paper used in this book meets the minimum requirements of ANSI/NISO Z39.48-1992 (R1997). ∞

Designed by Hannah Gaskamp

Library of Congress Cataloging-in-Publication Data
Names: Lack, Paul D., author.
Title: Searching for the Republic of the Rio Grande: Northern Mexico and Texas, 1838–1840 / Paul D. Lack. Description: [Lubbock]: Texas Tech University Press, 2022. | Includes bibliographical references and index. | Summary: "Recovers the history of a significant regional revolt against the Mexican Republic, presaging other federalist rebellions and the Mexican-American War"— Provided by publisher.
Identifiers: LCCN 2021036715 (print) | LCCN 2021036716 (ebook)
ISBN: 978-1-68283-126-7 (cloth) | ISBN: 978-1-68283-133-5 (ebook)
Subjects: LCSH: Texas—History—Republic, 1836–1846. | Texas—Politics and government—1836–1846.
Classification: LCC F390.L193 2021 (print) | LCC F390 (ebook) | DDC 976.4/04—dc23

LC record available at https://lccn.loc.gov/2021036715
LC ebook record available at https://lccn.loc.gov/2021036716

Printed in the United States of America
22 23 24 25 26 27 28 29 30 / 9 8 7 6 5 4 3 2 1

Texas Tech University Press
Box 41037
Lubbock, Texas 79409-1037 USA
800.832.4042
ttup@ttu.edu
www.ttupress.org

For my family
Children Spence & Brooke
Sister Kathy
Parents (in memoriam) Paul E. and Catherine M.

CONTENTS

ACKNOWLEDGMENTS

RESEARCH ON THIS PROJECT SPANNED MORE THAN TWENTY
years, and I have unfortunately lost the names of many who provided
valuable assistance, including the staff of archival repositories. Thus, I
apologize to those contributors who are not recognized here by name.
Historians typically build on the knowledge, interpretations, and
insights of scholars who have come before, and most certainly that is
the case with the present study. Dr. David Vigness, my professor in his
course on the history of Mexico, provided the first formal account of
the Republic of the Rio Grande in his dissertation. The unrivaled historian of nineteenth-century Mexico, Professor Josefina Vásquez, produced an article on the subject and first correctly portrayed it as Texas
nomenclature rather than a name used in Mexico itself.

Professor Jerry Thompson of Texas A&M International University
in Laredo arranged for a grant at the inception of my research, providing funding for on-site archival investigation in manuscript sources
in the states of Coahuila and Nuevo León. Staff members at the Palo
Alto Battlefield National Historical Park directed me to the digitized
archive of Mexico's war records, an indispensable resource. J. J. Gallegos
sent copies of his archival research, including the Laredo archives, in
an unsolicited act of generosity. Dr. Don Frazier generously provided
the maps for this volume. Professor Alwyn Barr without fail has given
advice and expertise that would define the role of a true mentor.

Friends, family, and colleagues galore assisted on research jaunts
and indispensable personal support in a time of medical convalescence.

They include friends going back to graduate school days, specifically Professor E. James Hindman, who gave great feedback on an early draft and who, along with his wife, Ann, opened their home on several occasions as I mined archives in Austin. Likewise, longtime friends Ben and Missy Pilcher gave sustenance both physical and emotional. An extensive array of individuals from my church supported me with food and companionship during a difficult time in 2019. They include Amy Chay, Linda Andrews, Rev. Laurie Tingley, Lynn Van Natta, Nancy Caspari, Pat Beneckson, Mike and Nancy Kelly, Bill Oliver, Cheryl Van Rensselaer, Amanda Shultz, Dr. Susan Thompson Gorman, and Dr. Randy Gorman. My family, to whom this book is dedicated, endured much and share my pride of authorship.

SEARCHING FOR THE FOR THE REPUBLIC OF THE RIO GRANDE

INTRODUCTION

IN THE YEARS 1838-1840, A REBELLION AGAINST THE CEN-
tral government of Mexico swept over the northeastern states of
Coahuila, Nuevo León, and Tamaulipas (see maps, pp. 16, 36). The
"cause" that enlisted the rebels went by some infelicitous and fleeting names, but most often and most genuinely it simply took on the
expression of what amounted to a catchall slogan as much as a political philosophy: "federalism." In neighboring Texas this conflict in its
latter stages came to be seen as regional separatism under the name,
the "Republic of the Rio Grande." Although the story that began
to unfold in 1838 had its roots in regional issues, it would prove to
be anything but isolated, temporal, or insignificant. Instead, in the
aftermath it shifted the political dynamic toward the conservative,
law-and-order perspective, and by threatening further territorial loss
it stoked the fires of nationalism. The rebellion also produced an array
of characters seen in alternating episodes of valiant and ignoble behavior and included figures of national prominence in Mexico such as
its president (Anastasio Bustamante) and its most effective emerging
military figure (Mariano Arista), along with ideological leaders (Juan
Pablo Anaya and Valentín Gómez Farías) and figures of great regional
influence and still greater personal ambition (José Urrea and Pedro
Lemus). The revolt also featured leaders who were fierce defenders
of their homelands (Antonio Zapata) and cunning self-promoters
(Antonio Canales). From Texas came other prominent players: the
empire-zealous and imperious president of the republic (Mirabeau B.

3

Lamar), glory and adventure seekers (Reuben Ross, Samuel Jordan), and Texas's greatest Tejano leader (federalist Juan Seguín).

This revolt had both extensive and deep roots. The northeastern region in fact had been embroiled in conflict even at the birth of the nation. An uprising in the northeastern region broke out in 1822, the year after Agustín de Iturbide's Plan of Iguala ended more than a decade of struggle against imperial Spain. In Nuevo Santander (soon to be renamed as the state of Tamaulipas), a challenge using the very same methodology as Iturbide's pronunciamiento threatened the fledgling national government. It had the makings of a full-scale regional revolt since Nuevo Santander had been settled largely from neighboring Nuevo León and San Luis Potosí. Issuing a pronunciamiento on September 26, 1822, wealthy hacendado and military chieftain Felipe de la Garza, who ironically owed his position to an appointment from Iturbide himself, launched a movement favoring constitutional government in opposition to Iturbide's monarchical ambitions. De la Garza asserted that his actions followed the political ideology of the region's most significant political thinker and official, Miguel Ramos Arizpe, who would soon take the lead in crafting the first formal governmental system for all of Mexico, the Constitution of 1824. However, de la Garza's initiative did not spread. Although some militias supported his cause, it failed to gain the adherence of either local ayuntamientos or other military leaders outside his province, forcing him to recant and turn himself in to Iturbide, who responded with a full pardon. Subsequently, de la Garza refused to reciprocate and instead soon thereafter carried out the orders of the state legislature to have Iturbide executed. Other efforts by de la Garza to regain and even broaden his influence eluded him, including an interesting plan made with Ramos Arizpe to establish a single large and powerful state comprised of Tamaulipas, Nuevo León, and Coahuila y Tejas, a concept that nonetheless lived on well into the region's future. Discredited nationally, de la Garza likewise lost local influence with the Gutiérrez de Lara brothers and died in 1832 without regaining his stature. This 1822 episode nonetheless echoed forward in sounding cries for regional respect, localized authority, and constitutional government.[1]

To a large degree, peripheral areas such as the northeastern states had their way under the Constitution of 1824, which provided for a structure that elevated the power of the states over a weak central government. This system not only served their regional interests but also had roots in tradition. Mexico had not yet developed an overweening nationalism that might override either local or sectional needs, and Spanish constitutionalism during the late colonial era had provided a form of continuity with provincialism. These factors aligned to produce the loose federal system of the Constitution of 1824, and the fact that its prime architect, Ramos Arizpe, represented Coahuila y Tejas in the Constituent Congress that crafted that document added to the consensus favoring federalism in the northeastern states. Furthermore, distance from Mexico City, where there generally existed little interest in the peripheral areas, only added to the strength of regionalism.[2] In general, the northern region favored liberal rather than conservative ideals, including federalism, which in turn advocated for principles of individual self-determination, social justice, and equality.[3]

The liberal Constitution of 1824 soon faced forceful opposition from conservatives advocating a powerful central government. Historian Michael T. Ducey elaborated on the subsequent dynamic and its consequences: "The Mexican state switched direction every two years between 1828 and 1834 between federalist and populist-leaning governments to centralizing law-and-order administrations. The political whiplash that resulted eroded the constitutional order and heightened partisan tensions."[4] This systemic quarrel produced serious consequences almost immediately. In 1835 the centralists began instituting changes that swept away the authority of the states and threatened the hegemony of traditional local leaders. Constitutionally, under the Siete Leyes (adopted in 1835–1836) the states became departments with officials including the governors and even local prefects in the municipalities appointed by Mexico City and operating seemingly with unchecked power since state legislatures likewise had been abolished in favor of appointed juntas. For northeastern residents the triumph of centralism meant increased burdens of taxation, loss of local control, and no rewards such as suppression of the terrorizing attacks by Comanche and other independent Indians.[5]

Mexico faced a monumental task as it struggled to create nationhood and political order, the absence of which manifested itself in a notorious absence of stability. As historian Will Fowler notes, "The new political order lacked authority, and its legitimacy was constantly challenged."[6] These challenges took the form of repeated threats to revolt, and the method of proclaiming dissent, the pronunciamiento, became an accepted means of bringing about change. Having issued it as a kind of petition to redress grievances, pronunciado leaders often wished to attract external support from others either near or far who might weigh in with their own pronunciamientos of adherence. If one became significant enough, its adherents could then engage in forced negotiations to advance a cause either political or personal, without much further upheaval. Yet, in cases involving long-term or fundamental issues, the pronunciamiento could also produce more extended and bloody consequences.

Thus, the pronunciamiento remained a fundamental part of the fabric of Mexican politics for the next half century. Several factors account for its ubiquity. It flourished in the absence of a well-established tradition of representative government or regular means of expressing concerns and bringing about change. The pronunciamiento typically involved both military and civilian participants, for as Fowler explains: the cause of independence "resulted in the emergence of a politicized army and, to a certain degree, a militarized society."[7] The pronunciamiento involved "a public statement of defiance and/or disobedience, and with the threat of violence."[8] It flourished as an extralegal measure in an environment where the government lacked legitimacy and often appeared as despotic during an era when the concept of nationhood itself had yet to gain ascendancy. Issuing a pronunciamiento could lead to a variety of consequences, from mere public relations as a sign of discontent that quickly dissipated all the way to extended, bloody rebellion, and variations in between. Fundamentally, to use Fowler's expression, the pronunciamiento became a customary means of engaging in "forceful negotiations." As such, it allowed Mexicans "at a time of constitutional turmoil or uncertainty . . . to express and publicize their views, commune with their fellow soldiers, villagers, and parishioners, party late into the night, and advance their careers."[9]

Another omnipresent dimension of the political milieu also fed political dissatisfaction. Local interests typically mattered more than national or even regional needs, especially given the overwhelming rurality that characterized the northeastern states. In fact, in the years that followed Mexico's independence, power to a significant degree rested in the hands of local political bosses. By well-established tradition, citizenship involved a stronger sense of belonging to a community than to the nation, and constitutional towns or municipalities derived authority from a kind of compact that had developed over time between the monarchy and the rural communities, a reciprocity that emanated from an unwritten structure of shared sovereignty. Town councils (ayuntamientos) unquestionably ruled over local matters. Typically, citizen expectations accepted only loose degrees of external control whether it came from state or national authority. Historian Antonio Annino describes a "contest between federalism grounded in provincial states and federalism based on municipal sovereignty." Attempts to alter traditional power arrangements inevitably produced substantial tensions if not outright conflicts, and this fractured political arrangement necessitated bewildering sets of alliances. The power of the ayuntamientos could be disregarded only with dangerous consequences since for those whose lives centered around rural villages, the local authorities mattered most. As Annino concludes: "One point is certain: during the nineteenth century, the center of Mexican political space was located in the rural areas."[10] Historian François-Xavier Guerra thus describes Mexico's political system as "pluralistic" and emphasizes the importance of relationships between local leaders and both their provincial and national counterparts.[11]

This potentially toxic mixture of local, regional, and broader interests, coupled with a structure that placed almost all authority in the states, created a sense in Mexico City that disorder had to be restrained by a more powerful central government. Yet the political situation quickly became even more volatile once the centralists took over in

1834–1835. The changes imposed in Mexico City sparked nearly immediate reactions in the periphery. Regional upheavals against the centralist order included faraway Texas, where a revolt that purported initially to embrace the goal of restoring federalism turned quickly to separatism. In the fall of 1835, a disparate army made up primarily of volunteers from the Anglo settlements laid siege to the centralist forces in San Antonio de Béxar and forced their capitulation in early December. Almost immediately the Mexican government under Antonio López de Santa Anna raised substantial armies to put down this insurrection. They soon crossed the Rio Grande and in February 1836 swept toward locations where armed resistance remained in and around both Béxar and south of there, at Goliad. Under Santa Anna's orders severe retribution occurred against the rebel armies, even as delegates from throughout the province congregated and declared Texas independence in March of 1836. Hastily gathered Texas volunteers fled eastward in the wake of the "no quarter" policy and executions ordered by Santa Anna, who seemed to wield irresistible force given his temperament and the numbers of the centralist forces. Nonetheless, Santa Anna incautiously fell into the hands of the rebels on the battleground at San Jacinto on April 21, 1836, where under threat of death he signed a "treaty" acquiescing in Texas independence and agreeing to a historically invalid boundary claim of the Rio Grande River to its source.[12] Every Mexican administration subsequently refused to recognize Texas independence, but in the tumultuous days that followed this humiliating defeat, Mexican authorities not only failed to win back the lost territory but also faced other revolts carrying the threat of further dismemberment. The very next year after the loss of Texas in 1836 saw pronunciamientos in many other areas in the northern periphery, including Sonora, Tampico, San Luis Potosí, Michoacán, and Zacatecas.

In the following year, 1838, a protracted outbreak occurred in the southernmost geographical extreme of the new nation, the Yucatán Peninsula, where a pronunciamiento of Santiago Imán resulted in the complete secession of the region from the nation of Mexico for over a two-year period. Both fundamental and personal factors contributed to this revolt. Distance (1,150 kilometers from Mexico City) weakened the relationship between periphery and center. Furthermore, the Yucatán area had long been accustomed to virtual free trade with other places in the Caribbean in what historian Shara Ali describes as a form of "autonomous" economic activity. From the inception of Mexican independence, the loose federalist form of government kept tensions at bay since local and regional authority held sway. In the language of Imán's pronunciamiento, the rebellion sought "the re-establishment of the Constitution of the Free State of Yucatán," a not-so-subtle statement that federalism affirmed actual state sovereignty. Localized resentments also contributed to this revolt, the most significant issue being the conscription of Yucatán residents into the army that made the long, winding march to disaster in Texas in 1836. Imán prevailed on the battlefield after he gained the participation of Mayan Indians, and he also found business support because of bitterness about centralist government attempts to increase tariff rates and thus diminish mercantile profits.[13]

Many of the forces that motivated the separatist rebellion in the Yucatán also drove discontent in the northeastern states. Even historians who have concluded that the classic liberal system provided by the Constitution of 1824 poorly suited the new nation of Mexico acknowledge that powerful regionalism underlay it and conclude that a genuine dynamic of nationalism had not yet developed sufficiently to offer any "practical remedies" to the challenge of governing in a manner so as to have order built around a national consensus. Furthermore, in many places local interests sought to free themselves from the long-standing interference of Mexico City, an especially acute fact since politicians in the northeastern states seldom exercised influence on the national scene after the federal constitution came into being.[14] Liberal politics, however widely supported as a matter of principle, faced daunting obstacles in the matter of promoting stability. Mexico as a new nation owed its existence to former royalist army officers who had often converted late to the cause of independence and who retained significant political influence. Many of them also had great regional power but felt extreme skepticism about the viability of the federalist constitutional order.[15] Additionally, hierarchical patterns of wealth-holding nationally meant that economic inequality promoted rule by elites who believed that liberal politics threatened their ascendancy.[16] Throughout the early national period, a powerful pattern of rural unrest created fear of radical upheaval from the classes below.[17] Yet, however strongly the "hombres de bien" might fear excesses by the masses, Mexico found itself struggling without success against what historian D. A. Brading has summarized as "a system of institutionalized disorder," and the early republic could find no answers as it went through forty-nine administrations in its first thirty-three years of independence.[18]

In contrast to national patterns, the northern frontier had greater resources of land than labor, making property more broadly distributed, and thus promoting more widespread political participation. In other ways, too, throughout the states of Coahuila, Nuevo León, and Tamaulipas, in the words of historian Timothy Anna, "sometimes the provincial patria counted more than the national patria."[19] Independence brought a modicum of new wealth and the prospect of economic growth through greater self-determination as the highly regulated Spanish system with its roots in mercantilism gave way to greater laissez-faire. Trade flourished as never before. The new port of Matamoros in the state of Tamaulipas brought commerce from the United States and the Caribbean, and the town grew quickly after 1821 to become the metropolis of the area with a rather cosmopolitan population of over 16,000. By 1837 the state had grown to over 100,000. Urban communities such as Saltillo (Coahuila) and Monterrey (Nuevo León) promoted both themselves and the area through periodic fairs and the spirit of commercial enterprise. Smaller towns along the Rio Grande followed suit and developed in support of ranching and farming economies, with the greatest growth occurring in the ranks of more middle-class ranch owners as opposed to the hierarchical hacendados who ruled elsewhere in Mexico. The villas of the lower Rio Grande and surrounding ranchos had grown in population by nearly 400 percent between the 1790s and 1830, mostly with migrants from Nuevo León. These rude beginnings held out the promise of greater progress, and the quest for municipal autonomy in turn fed support for federalism.[20]

From the northeastern regional perspective, progress from new markets and land speculation translated into support for the states, not the national government. Furthermore, whereas the Mexican economy as a whole declined as a result of wartime destruction and disruption during the long period of the wars for independence, the northeastern states experienced increasing vitality and growth during the 1820s and early 1830s. Much of this prosperity could be traced to an expansion of commerce, mostly with the United States, which in turn pulled the residents of the lower Rio Grande Valley into its orbit as the prospect for liberalized trade became increasingly irresistible.[21] Throughout the new nation a heritage of creole patriotism held sway based on ideas that valued Mexican exceptionalism from foreign influences, but those feelings did not translate automatically into nationalism. Instead, regionalism became a powerful force.[22]

The struggles and failures of the central government of Mexico also produced attitudes of resentment as the desperate nation inflicted burdens of taxation and impressment of goods, services, and manpower, especially as the military buildup passed through the area on the way to suppress the revolt in Texas in 1835–1836 and the ignominious retreat afterward. Essentially, the interests of the northeastern states suffered as the central government-imposed increases in the burdens of government. The leading authority on the history of the state of Coahuila describes the descent of a "terrible depression" there following the 1835–1836 war in Texas.[23] In general, the northeasterners saw their interests neglected by a nation that could not even defend them against the ravages of warfare launched with increasing frequency and fury in the period of 1837–1839 by the "indios bárbaros" (as described in the language of government officials). Comanche raiders, fabulous horsemen and thus virtually immune from retaliation by slower moving soldados from area presidios, ravaged through communities capturing herds of horses, provisioning themselves with livestock, seizing females and young prisoners from among those who were somehow spared, and killing or burning what they could not take with them. Both destruction and depopulation occurred in their wake as this ongoing war shattered the economy of the northeastern states. The Comanche expeditions reached as far south as Saltillo, the capital city of the state of Coahuila. Anglo Texan retaliation against the Comanche enraged "the people," as they called themselves, and they saw no inconsistency in gaining revenge in Mexico for the bloody acts of retribution inflicted by the citizen soldiers of the new Republic of Texas. Thus, a cycle of revenge had infected all sides. Amid this environment of death and devastation, as observed by historian Brian DeLay, mere "abstractions" such as nationalism had but little influence.[24]

In retrospect, these troubles could not have come at a worse time for the nation-state. The federalist Constitution of 1824, with influence and authority in the states and thus closer to the citizens there, had been supplanted by a centralist system in 1834–1836. What followed in rapid order? Humiliating revolt and territorial separation by Texas, increased burdens of government with corresponding deterioration in the security of life and property in the states of Tamaulipas, Nuevo León, and Coahuila, and the prospect of unwanted political interference with commerce in land and goods. Government under the centralist order remained remote and insensitive to local needs. States officially declined to the status of mere departments, appointed juntas replaced state legislatures, governors and other officials derived their position from appointments made in Mexico City, and unelected "prefects" took over as officials in some cases, replacing influential persons from local families of consequence. The centralists also threatened to dissolve militia units. By 1837, in the words of one newspaper, there existed "total discontent throughout the republic with no hope of improvement."[25]

Most especially, disillusionment with centralism had become endemic in the north, where the previous federalist system seemed far superior. In practice, obstacles blocked the advance of the political consensus because, whatever the degree of alienation from the centralist order, the actual exercise of power in the northeastern region still lay largely in the hands of army commanders. They functioned in what one historian calls "virtual autonomy in their respective regions," being "tantamount to provincial autocrats." Often these generals had conservative instincts in defense of the status quo; however, the army did not operate as a monolith but rather as a series of factions.[26] In any case, as the most significant instruments of national authority, the generals became purveyors of policies that produced still more alienation in the region. In particular, the national crisis in the treasury led to efforts to increase taxation, often in the form of forced loans.

Meanwhile, neighboring Texas, while struggling to invent itself in nationhood, also seethed with a spirit of revenge spiced by its own imperial ambitions, thus adding another volatile force to the region. Despite a population of only 40,000 (with about 10 percent being held in slavery and an equal number being Tejanos) at the time hostilities with Mexican authorities began in 1835, a burst of immigration from the United States and elsewhere occurred during the conflict and continued thereafter. Many of those attracted to Texas came as young, single men yearning for fortune or glory. They gave Texas a restless quality and often eschewed the more settled agrarian sections in favor of drifting into the frontier areas to the southwest.[27] In terms of government, the Republic of Texas came under the initial leadership of the military hero of independence, General Sam Houston, characterized in public life by a pragmatic instinct. He had much reason for caution since the government suffered from an empty treasury made no better by circulating paper currency, and it simultaneously faced a multitude of problems. Defense against potential reprisal and reconquest from Mexico, rumors of which circulated constantly, created at a minimum an aura of watchful anxiety.

The frontier areas faced not simply this potential conflict but genuine fighting from resourceful and skilled Comanche warriors, and Houston had no answers for furthering security while facing an empty treasury. Even in the eastern areas nearest to the United States, rumors of Indian-Tejano conspiracy in loyalty to Mexico erupted into open warfare that forcibly evicted the Cherokee and Tejano rebels alike, with Anglo residents appropriating their properties and giving only scant attention to legality.[28] The challenges of governing worsened as Houston's term expired. The presidential election to succeed him in the fall of 1838 displayed a bizarre turbulence reflective of the overall scene: two of the three contestants committed suicide during the election campaign. The lone remaining candidate, Mirabeau Buonaparte Lamar, held undisguised hatred for Houston and all that he stood for, instead embracing imperial ambitions emboldened by a romantic if unstable personality. With its restless, sometimes buoyant but also bitter character, the presence of the Republic of Texas added anything but stability to an already unsettled situation on the northeastern Mexican frontier.

The widespread discontent that had emerged in that region by 1838 represented an important development since a cause that motivates but one segment of the population cannot produce a foundational upheaval. Instead, many scholars agree that several preconditions must coalesce in order to produce a revolution. Both discontent and extensive politicization must exist along with an emerging consensus regarding the illegitimacy of the current government and the existence of a viable alternative to the existing regime. If any of these preconditions has not developed, other and perhaps lesser forms of revolt may well occur, including a coup, a barracks revolt, or (especially relevant to Mexico in its early years after independence) a pronunciamiento designed to force some kind of negotiation with the established authorities. More fundamentally, regional revolts such as this one often had the capacity to expand into something broader and more significant. Historian Will Fowler, the leading authority on malcontents and rebels in nineteenth-century Mexico, also notes that any of these forms of resistance, including a kind of exercise in lobbying, could degenerate into episodes of extended and bloody violence.[29]

The remainder of this narrative will inquire into the kind of upheaval that occurred in the northeastern states of Coahuila, Nuevo León, and Tamaulipas in the years from 1838 to 1840. It will demonstrate that, at various stages, the events appeared as several kinds of struggle, from barracks revolt to attempts at forceful negotiation to a regional revolution that might well separate the northeast from the not yet fully formed nation of Mexico. At some point those involved in these struggles saw their cause as essential enough to risk the well-being of their families and communities along with their very own lives. Whether they clearly understood it at the time, the events in which they were engaged would attain great significance for the future of the entire region and the political entities that battled for it.

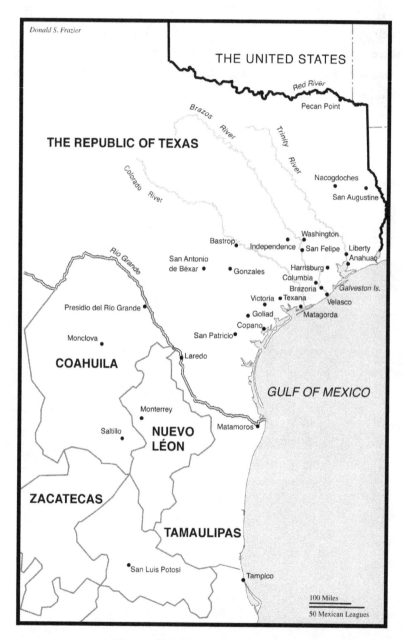

Donald S. Frazier

THE UNITED STATES

Red River

Pecan Point

THE REPUBLIC OF TEXAS

Brazos River

Trinity River

Colorado River

Nacogdoches

San Augustine

Washington

Bastrop

Independence

San Felipe

Liberty

Anahuac

San Antonio
de Béxar

Gonzales

Harrisburg

Columbia

Brazoria

Galveston Is.

Victoria

Texana

Velasco

Río Grande

Presidio del Río Grande

Goliad

Matagorda

Copano

Monclova

San Patricio

Laredo

COAHUILA

GULF OF MEXICO

Monterrey

NUEVO
LÉON

Matamoros

Saltillo

ZACATECAS

TAMAULIPAS

San Luis Potosí

Tampico

100 Miles

50 Mexican Leagues

Texas and Northeastern Mexico, 1838

CHAPTER 1
THE FEDERALIST REBELLION BEGINS

FEDERALIST REVOLTS ALONG THE NORTHERN PERIPHERY HAD a sort of aborted beginning in San Luis Potosí with the issuance of a pronunciamiento on April 17, 1837. It condemned the catastrophic failures of centralism since 1835, blamed selfish aristocratic leadership for the current disarray, and called for a return to federalism. Despite considerable backing by intellectuals and a few army officers including militia units, too few adherents came forward to support the elusive goal of returning to state supremacy along with somehow creating a new temporary general government. The plan failed in no small part because its national objective, essentially returning to a system from the past, could not be attained by a solely regional movement.[1] Thus, in one sense this 1837 episode seems like a missed opportunity for malcontents in neighboring Tamaulipas, Nuevo León, and Coahuila to participate in a wider rebellion. On the other hand, what observers there actually failed to see was the opposite—i.e., a portent of their own future challenges in terms of transforming local revolt not only into a regional but also a national cause. However, in the context of the times optimism concerning the success of rebellion occurred in no small part because revolts in the northern perimeter seemed to break out incessantly. Near the end of 1837, Urrea pronounced again, failed, fled Sonora, but then managed to launch a new uprising in Tampico in October 1838.[2]

Centralist authorities in the northeastern states had no illusions about their challenges as they faced a myriad of regional dynamics. State authorities contributed resources grudgingly, in part because funds, supplies, and manpower would strengthen an army that might well be turned against local or regional leaders and their political allies. Officially, the government's "Army of the North" numbered two thousand in its headquarters at Matamoros, but in practice General Vicente Filisola, at its head, could not muster anything approaching that figure. Further, national crisis divided the army's meagre resources. Just at the time that federalist rebels began to stir in the region, Filisola had to dispatch General Mariano Arista with a large delegation to Vera Cruz in order to deal with the French blockade that had been established to collect overdue debt payments.[3]

At nearly the exact moment that the Army of the North had been divided, a greater internal threat came from the uncertain and fluctuating political views of the regional military/political caudillos. Their ranks included Pedro Lemus and Antonio Canales, who rose in support of Urrea.[4] In terms of the national dynamic, President Anastasio Bustamante dealt with these threats, rumored from the very beginning of his administration, by coyly flirting with the possibility of converting to federalism himself. Yet, pronunciamientos against the centralist regime appeared in one part of the nation after another, signaling widespread upheaval.[5] Government officials, both political and military, wasted no time in recognizing the threat posed by the spread of federalist rebellion. The generals in Matamoros understood the vulnerability of the region and urged all residents to practice restraint. "Unity is essential along with discipline, subordination to your jefes, profound respect for the supreme government and all civil authority, and love and fraternity among all our fellow citizens." Continuing, this published broadsheet signed by Filisola along with Valentín Canalizo, Adrian Woll, Pedro Ampudia, and twenty-one other officers, reminded the public of Indian depredations and the threat posed by "rapacious volunteers from Texas" along with internal enemies of peace and order.[6]

Texas viewed the situation in a similar manner in terms of the sudden weakening of authority in northeastern Mexico. Officials there saw the efforts to reestablish the Constitution of 1824 as good news, if only because it diminished the possibility of renewed efforts by Mexico to reclaim its authority in Texas. Taking advantage of the moment, Texas Brigadier General Albert Sidney Johnston recommended that the Texas secretary of war pursue an accord with the Comanches as good diplomacy to further weaken and check any possibility that the centralists could really threaten Texas.[7]

By 1838, the northeastern states contained an additional source of federalist agitation because the national government disposed of many federalist leaders by exiling them to Matamoros.[8] Cautiously, the exiles communicated to each other a sense of optimism about the prospects of their liberal cause. One of them, former Coahuila governor Agustín Viesca, reported his joy upon hearing that Valentín Gómez Farías had returned triumphantly to the national capital. Viesca declared his confidence in the future of the country based on the assumption that the "disgraceful oligarchy" would soon be replaced with ardent defenders of freedom. "I still of course hope for the strength to carry on," he wrote, "but know that I must remain publicly silent" as an exile. Meanwhile, he bemoaned the fact that the Coahuila government remained in the hands of ignoble Saltilleños. Six weeks later he wrote from New Orleans with satisfaction on learning that defenders of liberty had issued federalist pronouncements in various parts of the nation, including Tamaulipas, and reasserted his faith that the centralists could not "by military responses" succeed in eradicating "the solemn freely made beliefs" of the citizens of Mexico.[9] On the other side, the centralist military leaders in Matamoros continued their publicity campaign, reasserting confidence in the fidelity of the army and deriding the rebels for spewing "hypocritical seductions." The published pronouncement of General Canalizo went on to assert confidence in the "valor" of his troops for upholding the law and for their "constancy" should the need arise to "exterminate the rabble" who always threatened to disturb the peace from Texas.[10]

The late spring and summer of 1838 passed in relative quiet in the northeastern states, but rumors of federalist rebellion elsewhere became widespread by October. Even in Matamoros, the headquarters of the government's Army of the North, potential leaders of insurrection met quietly while under house arrest to establish a potential junta. They waited carefully while expecting outside support, believing that fellow federalist Pedro Lemus would soon be established in control in Ciudad Victoria, the capital of the state.[11] In fact, the movement to overthrow the centralist government had just shifted to Tamaulipas as Urrea, having failed to maintain his government in Sonora, appeared in the nearby port city of Tampico to unite with the federalist forces that landed there under José Antonio Mejia and captured government leaders.

Filisola responded to this news with another broadside written on October 13 and subsequently published in the Coahuila capital on October 27. The commander of the Army of the North reiterated his belief that federalism as a system had failed in previous years and brought about only "disturbances, bloodshed, and desolation." He ridiculed the rebels' claim of having been abused by the government. For all their promises of progress and freedom, their acts would result, according to Filisola, in "the destruction of commerce, agriculture, the arts and industry, and in the end bring about only disturbance of order and peace among families, reducing them to hunger and misery." He characterized the rebel leaders as mere "power-seeking despots. . . . Their grand words of promise are designed to appeal to the desperate and fallen," all the while "cloaking themselves in purity." Furthermore, "this vile act of treason and self-interest aids the foreign enemy and perpetuates his usurped possession of part of our national territory." Rebel leaders speak to us of liberty but bring instead only disorder, anarchy, and an undermining of all that brings good times and prosperity. Filisola proclaimed basic conservative values—true government promotes "order and harmony," whereas "the natural element of the factionalists is that of discontent and disorder." Regarding actions to combat the spread of "vicious and criminal" rebellion, he announced that a delegation from his command under Canalizo had been dispatched to relieve the centralists in Tampico.[12] That same newspaper on December 1 published a letter from the "constitutional" governor in Durango warning against the spread of the rebellion that had begun in Sonora, a tardy message indeed—armed rebellion would prevail in the northeastern states for the entirety of the next two years.[13]

The figure who fired the first words of revolution also had the greatest influence throughout the rebellion. Licenciado Antonio Canales Rosillo headed up a group of rebels and began by issuing a pronunciamiento on November 5 at Ciudad Guerrero, Tamaulipas. Events unfolded in a manner that would occur over and over again, in no small part because of the radically different character traits of the two major leaders: Canales, a man of many words, and a second charismatic leader named Antonio Zapata, a man of action. Seizing the moment, federalist volunteers led by Zapata, direct and bold by comparison to the shifty Canales, forced capitulation of the centralist forces stationed at Mier.[14] By contrast, Canales proceeded to other area military garrisons but attempted to prevail by stealth rather than by force. At Agualeguas he tried to convince centralist officers that he had no purpose in appearing with his army other than to collect supplies in fulfillment of a commission furnished him by Filisola as proof of his intended "submission to the Supreme Government."[15] The centralist in charge of the forces there, Captain Rafael Ugartechea, refused to be duped into turning over anything and ordered the federalist forces to move away or face battle. He also cooperated with Colonel Francisco Pavón but provided unwarranted and thus misleading reassurances to political authorities about the orderly conduct of area citizens and their complete loyalty to the centralist government. Little wonder that Joaquin Garcia, governor of Nuevo León, held out hope that the rebels would accept an offer to avoid any consequences for their treason by quickly surrendering. The governor also asserted that Filisola as commander of the Army of the North had dispatched cavalry and infantry under Pedro Ampudia to move against the federalist "facciosos" at Mier.[16]

By mid-December, Canales reported exactly the opposite outcome in a letter to Mirabeau B. Lamar, president of the Republic of Texas. In addition to a complete victory over centralist cavalry and the fortress at Mier, Lic. Canales detailed federalist triumphs achieved by harassing government forces out of other river towns, successes that soon became complete with popular pronouncements for the liberal cause in Camargo and Reynosa, not to mention claims of a complete military success elsewhere, namely in the crucial port city of Tampico. He asserted that federalism would soon triumph throughout the Republic of Mexico and declared that the people of the interior had also decided "to sacrifice themselves rather than to suffer longer [from] military despotism." He asked that Lamar participate through extending a kind of de facto recognition by suppressing all trade from the river unless the merchants carried passports issued by the federalists.[17] Without fanfare, Lamar quietly agreed, thus ending the strict neutrality of the Republic of Texas as decreed earlier by the previous president, Sam Houston.

Meanwhile, other federalists and their supporters also expressed optimism along with unsubstantiated and thus misleading reports. Gómez Farías wrote buoyantly in late December that "all [of] Tamaulipas has already pronounced in favor of the federation." Some additional leader (likely he had himself in mind) must step forward by appealing to unity and satisfying those who had pronounced—the time had come for justice and patriotism to prevail. On Christmas Day he relayed inaccurate rumors that Canalizo had lost Matamoros, making the town "free" from government control.[18] In the capital of Texas, proposals from even rasher sources presented themselves to Lamar. The vainglorious and ever turbulent Felix Huston wrote on New Year's Eve, requesting authority to raise five thousand men for a Rio Grande expedition against a rumored Mexican-Indian "confederacy" aiming to reconquer Texas.[19]

Clearly, any number of unpredictable twists and turns could transpire in northeastern Mexico in 1839, but the federalists seized the initiative in each of the three states during the first month of the year. The communities along the Rio Grande received orders from newly proclaimed federalist ayuntamientos to prepare lists of individuals capable of taking up arms. Some who did not wish to go into active duty in the local militias sought refuge with their families in San Antonio de Béxar, Texas.[20] The federalist forces took the obvious step of advancing against the vulnerable and valuable town of Matamoros, defended by but a fraction of the dispersed national Army of the North and containing many residents who held federalist sympathies. The centralist commanders had yielded to national needs, weakening Matamoros by sending substantial numbers of troops to suppress rebels under José Urrea at Tampico. At Matamoros the rebels began by attempting to cut all communication by land into the town and by seizing new supplies of foodstuffs, munitions, and medicine intended for the garrison there. They captured and disarmed the unit sent by Filisola to guard the supply line and, in that general's words, "seduced some members of the army" to serve on the federalist side. The commander responded once again with a torrent of words fired off at the rebels rather than in the form of actual military measures:

> Your actions persisted in spite of evidence of the damage they have caused and the dangers posed to the defenses of the country with respect to the barbarians, the usurpers of Texas, and other foreign enemies. You have abandoned your homes and families to the furies of these same barbarians who depredate our property. You have employed your arms and munitions given for defense and used them instead against your brothers and defenders, the soldiers of the Nation. . . . Return to your homes and occupations. Present to the authorities the arms that you seized, and you can be assured that no one will prosecute you. . . . No longer be seduced by sordid suggestions and self-serving ideas. . . . Leave to the representatives of the nation the thinking about what will be the best system of government.

The Filisola proclamation ended with praise for the soldiers who remained loyal "even though they were ill used by those whom they came to help."[21]

The loose land blockade did not humble the defenders; instead, Filisola at last overcame his pacific tendencies and sent out a strong force to attack the rebels at eight o'clock on the morning of January 6. It included four artillery pieces—two cannon and two howitzers—that fired into the rebel lines for two hours while cavalry from both sides clashed over control of grazing lands. The Army of Liberation, as the federalists had begun to call themselves, could only produce two pieces of artillery, but the fight went well enough that one participant believed they had wasted an opportunity to occupy Matamoros. Instead, after five more hours of battle and an assault by government troops (who allegedly outnumbered the besieging forces by nine to one), the rebels retreated, blaming shortages of both munitions and manpower for the missed opportunity. The participant who reported these battle details attempted to maintain a brave front—he insisted that rebel artillerymen would regain their zeal for battle quickly if resupplied with powder.[22] The Army of Liberation found itself instead in a desultory mode, hanging in the suburbs with waning prospects. Never again would the federalist forces come so close to gaining possession of the prize that was Matamoros with its enormous commercial, financial, and symbolic value. Scrambling for supplies became a common theme of rebel armies. Farther up the river at Laredo (state of Nuevo León), the "Division of the Army of Liberation" gathered matériel of war as could be found locally but deemed it sufficient only to serve the company of volunteers there during "the present revolution."[23]

The people in neighboring Coahuila knew little but rumor of the uncertain fortunes of war in Tamaulipas and Nuevo León and found themselves instead energized by the politics of revolution. Claiming itself to be the legitimate authority in accordance with Urrea's plan to restore the Constitution of 1824, the "Constitutional" Ayuntamiento of Monclova endorsed federalism in a public meeting and took measures to spread the news of its actions. The speeches and resolutions of this January 19 gathering reflected ideals of liberty. Coahuilenses there confirmed "with great affection" their determination to return to a situation where "free men can congregate together again" and "voluntarily sacrifice for their country" in efforts to "restore our sacred rights," which had been squandered by "ungrateful children" and lost for the last three years. Specifically, the meeting rejected the centralist system "or whatever other blight may annoy the Nation," in favor of the "happy Era" to come when

> The free man no longer has to live in fear, and the state provides the security in which mankind may seek truth and knowledge for all. . . . *Viva the Independence of Mexico. Viva the Federation. Viva the Constitutional Charter of the State sanctioned on the 11th of March 1827. And Viva the esteemed D. José Urrea, General in Chief of the Army of Liberation.*[24]

Within the week, the political rebellion spread from Monclova (long-time rival to Saltillo as capital of the state) to other area communities, including Candela fifteen miles east, and then Lampasos another sixty miles away, and still farther eastward to towns on or near the Rio Grande, including Gigedo, Morelos, Guerrero, Nava, Santa Rosa, and San Fernando. At least in the case of Candela, the revolution did not triumph unopposed. Prominent rancher and public official Manuel Sánchez Navarro told the story in great detail. It began when longtime federalist Manuel Musquiz appeared at the Sánchez Navarro residence on the night of January 22 with a letter from his brother Ramón telling of the federalist takeover in Morelos. The Musquiz brothers asked for voluntary assistance in bringing about the same result in Candela, provided a copy of a letter they had intercepted, and asked that Sánchez Navarro turn over other correspondence. In the words of Sánchez Navarro, "With the most difficult exercise of restraint, I made my displeasure evident to them. . . . I resolved [instead] to be the first casualty, that I would consent neither to accede nor to second their cause." Although unarmed, he recalled, "I maintained myself firm as a rock" in resisting their demands.

Sánchez Navarro then "assisted my [like-minded] compadres in braving the dangers they faced," as the scene shifted to a building on the public square. He found there a room completely full of people "resting on their weapons in a mood of great silence" as the "principal citizens" entered one by one to be interrogated. He answered with questions of his own. "They responded that they planned to pronounce in favor of the federal system, seconding the actions that they knew" had occurred in Monclova and elsewhere. "With the greatest maturity and politeness that I could attain, I replied that I neither could nor should consent because I had solemnly sworn to guard and promote adherence to the Constitutional Law formed by the central government that ruled us. Further, that I stood for obedience and fidelity to the superior authorities on which that system depends and that without express orders from them . . . any such actions that are committed are detestable crimes."

The federalists then announced that he would be replaced in office, and the principal speaker for them "concluded his lecture in a rejoicing spirit shouting with all the others *viva la federación.*" By voice acclamation the meeting endorsed the principle of representative government based on a draft from Lampasos that had previously been adopted in Morelos and a "plan" from the army at Santa Anna (Tamaulipas) to reestablish a federalist system. The participants in this revolutionary gathering elected new regidores (magistrates) and a procurador (solicitor) before inviting Sánchez Navarro to attest to all their actions and to join with them. "They repeated this invitation two or three times until the last time they stated that anyone who refused to participate had received ample chances" to agree to basic moral values and good intentions. The meeting concluded with the participants in this junta signing the pronouncements and declaring that any who refused had but one more day to do so. And then "with many vivas a la federación" the meeting concluded by "a great demonstration of firing off guns, music, tolling of bells, and strutting around the plaza and the streets." To the governor, Sánchez Navarro pleaded that he simply had no power to prevent any of these acts of rebellion. The following day an official of the Ayuntamiento came forward again, and there ensued a renewed "battle of words." Sánchez Navarro sent his notes on the revolutionary proceedings to the governor of Coahuila by trusted messenger rather than the mails, reminding his superior that nothing could be done to stem the tide but by armed force.[25]

Federalist ayuntamientos in Gigedo and Nava also adopted pronouncements in the next few days, with the latter town reporting that "everyone in the corporation favored this move of returning to 'popular government.'" Its resolutions declared the reestablishment of "the Department of the Rio Grande" making Monclova the state capital. It urged the acceptance of federalism in all other villas of the region and added the forlorn "hope to see all of this done in a peaceable manner."[26] The rebels in Guerrero certainly knew that "the cause of the people" could not triumph without conflict as they made plans in cooperation with Camargo to unite with Laredo federalists in taking possession of armaments there. "This order is to be complied to without losing a single moment," declared "Constitutional Judge" Rafael Uribe.[27] Cooperation among the villas had become an essential tactic. The ayuntamientos of Gigedo and Guerrero sought to act in concert with other villas in organizing for future military and political needs, including

naming a new federalist jefe político. Guerrero took measures to establish a mounted armed guard for maintaining "public tranquility" and
"to sustain the federal system" against those guilty of "sedition" by
refusing adherence to the Plan.[28] In Santa Ana de Nava meetings
occurred to restore officials who had served previously, i.e., before the
centralists abolished local democratic institutions. The public meeting
under the "new restored federalist constitutional order" asserted that
the local ayuntamiento would act "in accordance with the laws of the
general congress and the congress of Coahuila and Texas established
in 1834," including election of a new governor. While boldly pledging support for the new/old local authorities, those in attendance also
engaged in wishful thinking, declaring that "this is a peaceful place
which desires fatherly treatment from the government of its father-
land." Hopes for a nonviolent revolution appeared to dissipate almost
overnight. José Lozano Benavides refused to accept the role of interim
governor of the state of Coahuila and Texas, citing the fact that federalism had not yet triumphed nationally.[29]

With consensus but not unanimity achieved, the federalists soon
faced a military problem. Participants in an unusual midnight meeting held in Guerrero on January 29 wrestled with what to do about the
permanent army stationed in their midst, which had "refused to march
away." It concluded that a force of fifty federalist volunteers would take
possession of the garrison and its ammunition, given that the soldiers
had refused to evacuate voluntarily. The villa avoided what seemed
like an inevitable clash when military commander Pedro Rodriguez
caved on February 1 and brought the entire garrison into obedience
to the Plan. Soon federalist officials made preparations for a new army.
Santana Penalbes, "Alcalde to the villas of the Department of the Rio
Grande," sent out a call from the jefe político for reestablishment of the
militia. Penalbes noted that, whereas previously there had been but one
squadron in the entire department, "there are many more men under
arms since the establishment of the centralist system," thus necessitat-
ing the creation of what he called "a respectable force." He established
an ambitious goal: two squadrons of seventy-five men each would
form one company, and two companies would be a division. Based on

a population census, Nava and Gigedo were to supply one company, Rosas another, and the combination of Guerrero, Allende, and Morelos the third, thus totaling 450 men under arms.[30]

Centralist officials in Coahuila set out to stem the populist tide of federalism on the field of battle as opposed to focusing on the revolution in politics. Governor Francisco Garcia Conde in Saltillo summoned what forces he could and placed them under unified command in the form of Colonel Domingo Ugartechea, who prior to gaining these reinforcements could muster but 130 infantry and cavalry at Monterrey, the nearby capital of Nuevo León. These government forces faced larger numbers of rebels, perhaps six hundred men, most of whom came from former presidial companies led by Severo Ruiz (operating under the authority of Urrea), who advanced against Saltillo on January 21. Ugartechea managed to enter the Coahuila capital even while a battle raged there. Though his combined force barely exceeded half the rebel numbers, he moved swiftly, catching federalists under Severo Ruiz off guard. The federalist commander then divided his forces, whereas Ugartechea and Garcia Conde managed to unite their commands. Ugartechea attacked both wings of the federalist forces, enveloped one of them, and left the rebels completely dispersed and in disorder. As President Bustamante later recalled, Ugartechea did not press the attack against the "fugitives" from the federalist army, sparing them from further bloodletting "because they were, as the great expression goes, Mexicans after all." At any rate he reported that the rebels nonetheless suffered 120 casualties, including sixteen deaths, whereas the centralists had only six fatalities and six more wounded. This victory in Saltillo left the Coahuila capital under centralist control while some federalists, including Pedro and José Lemus, found a quasi sanctuary in the rival city of Monclova.[31]

The loss of Saltillo in January set back the rebellion but hardly killed it. The federalists at that point had at least in theory a unified command and expectations of coordinated movement. "Liberator and General in Chief José Urrea" placed Pedro Lemus over the third division of the Army of Liberation, giving him responsibility also for the "frontier companies" operating in the Matamoros area of Tamaulipas.

The federalists there hoped at least to intercept goods needed to supply the war efforts.[32] Although one of the centralists, Nuevo León governor Joaquin Garcia, still expressed hope on February 16 that swift action arresting the rebel leaders could thwart the entire rebellion, two days later he learned that Lemus and his command had begun a march toward Monterrey after they left Saltillo. The governor then urged centralist forces to intercept the federalists before they reached the Nuevo León capital.[33]

Instead, the centralists, with Valentín Canalizo taking over for Filisola in Matamoros, remained too weak, isolated, and irresolute to attempt an offensive, and the new commander only added an extra dose of timidity to the mix. His background being more political than formally military (he hailed from a prominent Monterrey family friendly with Santa Anna), Canalizo seemed by nature to prefer inaction to the risks of battle.[34] Beleaguered Coahuila governor Garcia Conde wrote to President Bustamante on March 2 in a troubled, perhaps even panicked state of mind over unsubstantiated rumors:

At this moment I have just received from one of my outposts information that Pedro Lemus with his forces is . . . [but] six leagues away from this city [Saltillo], intent on invading it. This situation occurs with me being out of money and without hope of being joined by even one additional soldier from anywhere to assist the heroic forces of the battalion of Defenders. . . . [It would be] a pleasing prospect [if we were able] to present a defense that severely punishes the enemy and gives the country a day of glory. But it will be disgraceful should these be the only forces at my disposal without even the slightest contribution from the supreme government. [If so], the revolution could become an incalculable force and could place the country in great danger. If such were to occur I accept none of the responsibility.[35]

The Mexican president from the Tamaulipas capital of Ciudad Victoria responded quickly, as he explained to officials in Mexico City on March 4, but without sufficient force to provide much balm for Garcia Conde. Though he believed the false reports that Lemus and Canales had united with one thousand men seeking victory in Monterrey, Bustamante had dispatched only meagre reinforcements. They included one hundred men moving toward Saltillo from the

San Luis Potosí command of Mariano Arista, an unspecified number from Benito Quijano heading toward Linares with artillery support, and vague promises of additional reinforcements. He urged Garcia Conde to coordinate with Quijano in making Linares a government stronghold.[36]

That same day on the political front in Monterrey, the federalists made their boldest move yet. With support from the local garrison, Manuel M. de Llano, on behalf of the "Government of the free and sovereign state of Nuevo León," issued a printed circular announcing that the "President of the United States of Mexico" had declared the "reestablishment of the popular representative government adopted in the year 1824." That system had been "disgracefully [and illegally] dissolved," even in the face of unanimity among all the states, with terrible results, including the loss of "territory sacred to all Mexicans." The current regime ruled only by naked force via "enormous perse-cutions" that undermined the welfare of the people, including the improper administration of justice, leading to what amounted to the triumph of "profound chaos and anarchy." The circular asserted that the ayuntamiento of Monterrey had reconvened, declaring a return to "the federalist order" and naming de Llano as interim governor.[37] Even two weeks later news came from Saltillo dispatched to Mexico City in anything but an optimistic spirit. The rebellion had not been confined to Monclova but had spread to all parts of the frontier. Lemus, claiming authority derived from the state of Coahuila, had forces that vastly out-numbered those loyal to the Supreme Government, and they appeared to be congregating in Saltillo. The correspondent urged increased pres-sure on Bustamante to dispatch additional reinforcements from San Luis Potosí.[38]

Neither the Supreme Government nor the federalists could muster sufficient numbers to gain a decisive advantage, and during the entire month of March 1839, the momentum shifted back and forth with-out favoring either one. The situation became even more complicated because Lemus and Canales engaged in secret peace talks with represen-tatives of the Supreme Government. Centralist colonel Pedro Ampudia fielded a proposed armistice by Lemus but did not reply affirmatively until March 27. The basic idea involved mutual retreat, but negotiations never reached a conclusion, even though all centralist commanders except Canalizo signed off on the concept. The Ampudia letter also suggested—with no real details–that Antonio López de Santa Anna had assisted in bringing the two sides together.[39]

Whatever role the mercurial former president played, it was President Bustamante who agreed to guarantee terms that included a vague (and highly inaccurate) assertion that the aims of the federalists had in fact been achieved.[40] The peace accord broke down without notice or fanfare by either side, perhaps because it became public. Indeed, news reached all the way to Mexico City and appeared in print on April 9 with an assertion that Lemus had agreed "to terminate his part in commanding the revolution." The newspaper celebrated, prematurely as it turned out, giving both Ampudia and Lemus credit for saving their country from further destruction.[41]

This dalliance revealed how leadership divisions and challenges hampered the rebel cause. If Canales suffered from excessive timidity on the battlefield, Lemus lacked energy, resolve, and full-fledged commitment. Though he talked of a planned reunion with Ruiz in Saltillo, Lemus could hardly make war while simultaneously engaging in serious peace talks and so decided to suspend his military activity. At the same time, he also sought aid from Monclova, leaving the entire situation in flux. The federalist political chief could do little more than spread the news that everything still hung in the balance. He reported that the federalists had placed themselves in a sound defensive posture in Saltillo, which led to "an immediate and voluntary suspension of hostilities by [their] opponents in order to arrange to resolve our differences if possible without further effusion of blood." In reality, with Lemus irresolute and considering peace, Saltillo remained under centralist control, and the federalists dispersed, as much by inaction as by decision. Both sides seemed quite comfortable with delays. For his part Lemus provided only irresolution, unsupported optimism, and platitudes. So that "federal institutions would not suffer any deterioration," he pledged to be vigilant in restoring "good order." He then retired to a refuge in the federalist stronghold of Monclova before returning to threaten Monterrey.

The federalists in Tamaulipas, Nuevo León, and Coahuila believed at the time that Urrea still campaigned against San Luis Potosí, and that Mejia controlled Tuxpan near Tampico. The hopes of the rebels in the northeastern states thus rested on the assumption that reinforcements would soon arrive fresh from triumphs elsewhere.[42] They had no way of knowing that such assistance would never materialize because the optimistic "news" from Mejia and Urrea actually consisted of false claims of decisive federalist victories.[43]

Centralists in the region attempted to keep each other informed about regional developments. In a letter to his counterpart in Coahuila, the governor of Nuevo León acknowledged the obvious, that federalist takeover would remove him from office, and despaired because his administration relied totally on the support of two hundred badly armed and poorly supplied men who remained loyal to the government. They faced federalist forces numbering 650, bent on sacking the city "to pay themselves for their work and for the expenses of their expedition." Whoever gains Monterrey will be made "the owner of this department," as Coahuila governor Garcia Conde asserted, and the consequences of such a loss would be that the "anarchists" would fulfill their visions, destroying order and "sacking the population."[44]

On March 17 Nuevo León governor Joaquin Garcia published a circular imploring support for government forces under Pedro Ampudia against Lemus and the federalists. "Nuevoleoneses," he wrote, if you support peace and social order you must assist in resisting the "scandalous" invasion against this department by Lemus, "acting under the false claim of bringing protection." Instead, he "leads a platoon of men without order, without subordination, and without discipline." So far, no form of self-restraint had deterred the thirst for evil displayed by the federalist rebels,

> not the energetic tactics of defense brought on by their attack, nor the suffering inflicted on the people, nor consideration of national public opinion, nor the desire for peace and tranquility that characterizes our entire Republic, nor the fear of attracting retaliatory war from the general Government, nor the sad and lamentable consequences [of their aggression], nor the previous experiences of misery and devastation undergone in the Department of

Tamaulipas. . . . These are the evils that come with those who call themselves liberators. They cause people to abandon their homes, they rob our most precious properties, and they bring about in all places terror and loss of security. . . . They bring nothing less than the undoing of the Republic into the abyss of dissolution and death.

"Fellow citizens," he concluded, "if you wish to be happy, resist this seduction." The uprising did not promote the federalist system but rather "only the triumph of self-interest." Activity that undermined public order threatened to destroy the "nervous system and the soul of every government." "NUEVOLEONESES," concluded Garcia, "rally to the cause of restoring constitutional order as supported by the forces of the Supreme Government. . . . I am committed with all my being to repel these malicious invasions and to restore the rule of government . . . [along with] complete and lasting peace."[45]

Devotion to the government cause notwithstanding, the governor privately reported his numerous concerns to authorities in Mexico City, citing the dim prospects of restoring public tranquility. He believed that Lemus remained far stronger than the centralists even before adding reinforcements rumored to be on their way from Texas. The governor described his administration as virtually helpless since he had no caballada and not even a single real to pay loyalist soldiers. The threats to peace had increased because "salvajes" from the frontier depredated throughout the region. Garcia defined the state of affairs in his department as nothing short of pure "anarchy."[46] Actual news rather than hyperbole-ridden pleas for support revealed no greater clarity— Ugartechea himself wrote conflicting accounts of both minor successes and frustrating failures. On March 19 he announced to national officials that the centralists had restored order to Salinas, but three days later he acknowledged that Canales and "his brigade of thieves" still operated with impunity since the government had no horses to mount a pursuit of any kind.[47]

The view from outside the region cast no greater clarity on the likely outcome of the wars in the northeastern states. From the south in Mexico City the Ministry of the Interior did nothing more than label the federalist uprising in Coahuila as "disgraceful."[48] To the east the Republic of Texas officially kept its hands off, while actually allowing Tejano volunteers to join the ranks of the federalist forces in Saltillo.[49] Naturally, the Lamar administration and others considered how to take further advantage of a Mexican nation distracted by civil war. Specifically, expansionists saw the opportunity to define the Texas boundary to include all of the former state of Coahuila and Texas.[50] Meanwhile, the federalists in Coahuila busied themselves ineffectually in ongoing efforts to consolidate their authority rather than answering in meaningful ways the pleas from their military to send reinforcements of all kinds—not surprising since the federalist generals seemed to pursue peace as ardently as victory.[51] Thus, the month of March ended in a strange stasis, with the federalists having lost clarity of purpose and neither side even managing to take advantage of the undeclared truce to strengthen their prospects going forward.

What, in summary, had occurred during this opening chapter of the struggle for power among the states of Coahuila, Tamaulipas, and Nuevo León? Clearly, it began in adherence to pronunciamientos elsewhere in expectation of growing into a movement that would expand both geographically and politically, and within these states the federalist rebels swept away much of the apparatus of the centralist system. Yet, it slowly became evident that comparable activity had actually dissipated elsewhere, even among contiguous or nearby places where the first salvos of rebellion had sounded. Furthermore, those who derived their authority from the central government of Mexico held on even in a beleaguered and nearly besieged manner. Although eventually federalist caudillo Pedro Lemus attempted to negotiate some kind of resolution, if only in the form of an extended truce, President Bustamante along with centralist governors in Coahuila and Nuevo León refused even to budge in the direction of a federalist restoration and instead fought on, albeit without themselves being able to put down the rebellion. Neither did any of the major centralist military figures come over to the federalist cause, nor did any leader propose a lasting negotiated outcome. And so the fight continued as a full-scale regional revolt led and supported by ardent believers dedicated to their cause and faced with shrinking options. Most certainly, rebel gritos of 1838 among the northeastern states had struck a responsive chord and gained devoted followers who gave way grudgingly, persisting in fact longer than anywhere else in Mexico. The remainder of the story will reveal that, in the end, the outcome not only disappointed the federalist ideologists but had quite unintended and in many ways tragic consequences for the region.

THE REPUBLIC OF TEXAS

Río Grande

San Antonio de Béxar

Gonzales

San Fernando de Rosas
Nava
Morelos
Allende
Presidio del Río Grande
Goliad
Aldama
Lampazos
Monclova
Candela
COAHUILA
Laredo

Guerrero
Mier
Camargo
Monterrey
Reynosa
Cadareyta
Matamoros
Saltillo
China
Linares
NUEVO LÉON

ZACATECAS

Ciudad Victoria

SAN LUIS POTOSÍ
TAMAULIPAS

GULF OF MEXICO

San Luis Potosí

Tampico

100 Miles

50 Mexican Leagues

The Northeastern Mexican frontier, 1838

CHAPTER 2

ELUSIVE VICTORY: THE FEDERALIST WARS IN APRIL-MAY 1839

THOSE WHO REPRESENTED THE CENTRAL GOVERNMENT TRIED to put on a face of confidence to stave off growing evidence of their desperation. Temporarily deficient in the ways of the sword, they turned instinctively to a war of words, where control of the printing presses gave them an advantage. Still secure in the Tamaulipas capital of Ciudad Victoria, Governor José Antonio Quintero issued a verbal attack on rebel demagogues for conducting a civil war against their brothers in neighboring San Luis Potosí and Nuevo León. "We must not be seduced by those who with arms in their hands, driven by personal ambitions" have deserted the sanctuary of the law. Whatever faults the government might display at the moment, he argued, it continues to seek reconciliation, defense of national honor, and the kind of security that can only come from orderly conduct. The future rested with the conservators of the status quo. "Victory, make no mistake, will soon crown our valiant forces [who are] extinguishing civil

war, restoring liberty under the law, securing respect of the individual, and protecting private property."[1]

No amount of bombast could obscure the fact that the governor had
much to worry about. The federalist forces under Pedro Lemus controlled access to the capitals of Coahuila and Nuevo León, and their
counterparts on the coastal areas to the south, Antonio Mejia and José
Urrea, held Tampico and also claimed victories sufficient to give them
momentum. The leader of the central government responded with both
actions and words, but he lacked decisiveness and confidence and could
not inspire those qualities in others. In February, President Anastasio
Bustamante announced his intention to leave the national capital
and take command of the northeastern front. But he did not arrive in
Tamaulipas until near the end of April, and once there he held back
from actually leading any forces in the field. Rather, he surrounded
himself with a sufficient escort, placed this unit between the front in
Tampico and the beleaguered capitals of Coahuila and Nuevo León,
and issued orders. While this position seemed reasonable enough, it
soon became evident that he remained ignorant of enemy positions or
intentions, deficient in actual control of the essential matériel of war,
and uncertain as to the course of action to take. His quasi paralysis led
to speculation as to his motive. Perhaps what passed as uncertainty only
obscured a duplicitous scheme—some suspected that he leaned toward
converting to the federalist cause. In fact, the rebel military leadership
also gave off signals either of duplicity or a waning commitment to fighting. Near the end of March, Lemus engaged in correspondence as to a
possible armistice proposed through centralist general Pedro Ampudia,
and Canales used the lull occasioned by this initiative to leave the field
as he set off in pursuit of Comanches.[2]

Those who knew Bustamante at all recognized this hedging and
cautious behavior as simply part of his character. His entire life reflected
a susceptibility to changing his mind. Born fifty-eight years earlier of
Spanish parents in the state of Michoacán, he first chose seminary studies in Guadalajara before switching to medicine in San Luis Potosí, and
then entering the army to fight on the loyalist side. His excesses centered on personal matters (as shown by a pudgy body, a reputation for

scattering illegitimate offspring in his wake, and an inclination toward seeking advice from religious rather than political sources) as opposed to public extremes. In the realm of politics, Bustamante preferred to swerve and to keep his options open. He switched to the cause of independence to follow Agustín Iturbide, a staunch conservative. Two years later Bustamante became politically active and rose to become vice president in the liberal Guerrero administration, which positioned him to ascend to power following a coup in 1829. He and Santa Anna replaced one another as president twice in the 1830s, and Bustamante had been serving in that capacity for two years when he temporarily stepped aside in February of 1839 to take over command of the government forces, a role he would play for four months before returning to political office. Despite his ideological swerving, as president, Bustamante pursued a conservative course of advocating for order and standing against populist excess.[3]

He did not, as rumor had it, unite with Urrea, but neither did the president bring clarity or direction to the government's cause. In his defense, part of Bustamante's confusion reflected sheer uncertainty as to the strength or movements of the rebel forces. Following a federalist victory at Tuxpan by the unit commanded by Antonio Mejia, Bustamante fretted that this force might head toward Matamoros rather than joining other federalists in Tampico. Thus, his orders to Valentín Canalizo—to unite with Mariano Arista's brigade and advance to the relief of Tampico—were quickly reversed, leaving Canalizo at Matamoros and Arista partway between the two ports so as to assist the one in greatest need.

In part these shifting plans reflected another reality—Canalizo behaved in such a recalcitrant way as to border on outright insubordination. Receiving information (actually false rumors) from the ministry of war in Mexico City as to Mejia's intentions to move north to join Lemus, Canalizo justified his stationary behavior at Matamoros. The fact that the ministry provided intelligence to the field commanders in advance of informing Bustamante further undercut the president's authority. Meanwhile the Coahuila governor pleaded for more support because his rebel rivals in Monclova had dispatched men and supplies to Lemus for use against Saltillo. Bustamante, by contrast, suspected that Mejia, Lemus, and Canales had already united their forces to converge on Matamoros; however, he ordered Arista to stand ready to repel any maritime expedition aimed at Tampico. The president further worried that the rebels had acquired steamboats and other support from Texas or even from Louisiana, giving them clear superiority, so he also issued directives to arm ships and concentrate artillery in defense of Tampico. Elsewhere, he excused inactivity by reason of the scarcity of resources while making empty assurances that relief would come from Matamoros to Monterrey and Saltillo. If superior fretting could be listed as a contribution to the government's cause, then its president provided crucial leadership indeed.[4]

Through all this, Canalizo also issued a torrent of excuses (no funds, inferior horses and bad pastures, probable Texas advances against Mexican territory) to supplement the countervailing advice he received from government authorities in Mexico City. Arista attempted to comply with Bustamante's directives but found himself as a result only starting and suspending marches to Tampico or to points north and east. Back in Saltillo, Domingo Ugartechea also remained stationary amid reports that Lemus had begun an advance from Monterrey to Matamoros. Ugartechea at least made no pretension of an aggressive style, informing the governor that he would move only "when the government has sufficient forces to command respect." But he also displayed a willing spirit, acknowledging that the government had many pressing considerations that left Saltillo without additional reinforcements and promising that preparations had been made to encounter Lemus whenever he should arrive.[5]

One of the greatest potential advantages of the centralists—superior communication and a command system to coordinate movement among the forces dispersed throughout the northeastern states—failed them during April 1839. Even Bustamante had no certain knowledge of the strength or movements of the forces of the Supreme Government in the region, much less of their opponents. By April 26, he had at least made a decision—informing Ugartechea of a plan to bring all centralist forces together at Linares in order to move in concert against the "sublevados" and to restore order.[6] Bustamante had by that time attempted to consolidate because he could foresee government forces being picked off unit by unit, as in fact occurred when Lemus defeated a company of forty men under Rafael Ugartechea in mid-April. The Mexican president then issued a peremptory order to Canalizo to leave his defenses and move toward Monterrey, promising that he would receive reinforcements from General Benito Quijano. Bustamante at last appeared to grasp the pressing need to energize the government armies, heretofore hunkered down and threatened in the largest towns in Tamaulipas, Nuevo León, and Coahuila.[7]

Once again, the Matamoros commander made excuses, not war, and he did so in a tone of scarcely disguised contempt. On April 27 he wrote the president, acknowledging receipt of a letter sent five days earlier. His response, in Canalizo's own words, remained "the same as in my last communication and the one before that"—movement from the defenses of Matamoros could not be safely attempted. With so many of his 1,500 men ill or disabled, he would not risk sending half the defenders on the offensive, thereby leaving his supplies vulnerable to a rebel attack. However, Canalizo acknowledged that the ministry of war in Mexico City had ordered him to comply with the president's commands and agreed to abandon the trenches in the face of "a peremptory order absolving me of responsibility." Without mules and with forage scarcely sufficient for a six-league-per-day cavalry advance, his entire force would be at risk should it be divided.[8]

Meanwhile, Lemus and his federalist supporters remained in control of the capital cities or access to them and threatened to advance in Tamaulipas. They had the potential to become stronger. The civil leaders of the revolt continued to mop up their earlier gains, and they took advantage of the lull in fighting to conduct a brisk trade with Texas for badly needed supplies. As a result, local federalist authorities enlisted individuals who provided horses and escorts, thus enabling ammunition and even artillery to get to the state federal capital of Monclova for possible use at other points. A newspaper in faraway Mexico City acknowledged that rancheros from the countryside provided horses, conducted damaging raids, and generally supported the federalist cause.[9]

Federalist spirits in the villas of Coahuila received encouragement from the rumors of success against centralists farther south. In early April the jefe político of the department of the Rio Grande distributed copies of reports via Lemus regarding the victory at Tuxpan. Described as a "complete triumph," the news indicated that soldiers shouting "Viva la Federación" had carried out a vigorous battle resulting in the capture of prisoners of war, mules, horses, carts, ammunition, and other supplies.[10] From there rebel leaders seemed to have a choice among several viable strategies—focusing on Tampico, moving south against even richer Vera Cruz, heading inland toward the national capital, or, of course, marching in a northeasterly direction to invest Matamoros.

Even within the states of Tamaulipas, Nuevo León, and Coahuila, centralist authorities operated from only sketchy information and unclear strategy. Leaders of the national government feared that Lemus held back only in anticipation of a combined movement involving his norteños and the soldiers under Urrea and Mejia. Both sides even sought to avoid skirmishes, as evidenced by a nonaggression accord between the federalist commander and Pedro Ampudia, who headed a detachment of centralists out of Matamoros. Only a single clash interrupted this mini armistice during the entire month of April, a federalist victory against Rafael Ugartechea's cavalry at the villa of Serraldo on the twenty-second. Domingo Ugartechea, in command of centralist forces with the governor of Coahuila, then pulled back to Saltillo, as Lemus in turn concentrated his command in nearby Monterrey. Bustamante seized the opportunity by occupying Linares, the spot on the road from Matamoros to Monterrey vacated by Lemus, giving the scattered centralists a possible place to unite.[11]

This period of watchful waiting extended into May as both sides weighed their potential for decisive victories against the risks associated with defeat or the possible depletion of scarce resources. The centralists continued their commitment to their strongholds and regrouped while maintaining their options of reinforcing government armies to the south or launching coordinated movements in the north. Bustamante made certain that his spies remained in the field and justified the continued lull by noting that his men lacked supplies and could hardly provide for themselves from "a countryside in which there are no resources."[12]

The centralists still made good use of their no-risk resource—the press. From Ciudad Victoria on May 4 Bustamante, in his capacity as "president of the republic and general in chief of the Army of Operations," published a broadside for supporters in the northeastern states. He wrote in a tone of almost obsequious civility regarding his "sacred" duty of restoring public order. The supreme government had conferred unrestricted authority on him, Bustamante declared, but it acted from the most paternalistic of motives and with every intent of exercising the greatest clemency. He disputed the cause of the rebels: "Liberty is of no value if it does not emanate from reason, law, and personal security." The "ingenious agitators" behind this disturbance had brought on a disgraceful civil war, undermining internal peace in a manner that no patriot could countenance. Mexico should not behave with adolescent violence or be swayed by turbulence driven by personal ambition. "Are the misfortunes of our country to be interminable? Will we never sacrifice our individual interests in consideration of society in general?" Bustamante concluded by urging all those who had taken up arms to return to the sanctity of their homes and families in the knowledge that those who did so would not be "pursued or molested in any manner whatsoever." He offered the dictum that the only fruit of revolution would be more evil in the form of increased vulnerability to the nation's enemies in Texas and the plundering of "barbaric" Indians. The Victoria newspaper echoed these views throughout the month.[13]

Using a different form of communication, the federalists developed a mirror image of centralist propaganda. They reminded the people that their cause had triumphed throughout the northeastern states except in the political stronghold of Saltillo and the fortified town of Matamoros, both of which had been surrounded and appeared ripe for the fall. Through communiqués to lesser officials of the state government and then on to the councilmen of the various communities, the federalist governor of Tamaulipas, Bartolomé de Cardenas, propagandized about all the reasons for optimism. He reviewed the progress in restoring legitimate popular institutions of local government and in coping with the few pockets of centralist resistance. Cardenas urged other officials to function from principles of disinterested justice and thereby offset the "enemies of our tranquility and progress." He also foresaw continued favorable prospects on the military fronts.[14]

Pursuant to his own no-risk strategy from his post on the Rio Grande, Lic. Canales remained active in scheming rather than fighting. In early May he wrote to his adversary in Matamoros, General Canalizo, with alarming news of Texas designs on Mexican territory. A Texas force had begun operating around the Nueces River, an area claimed by these notorious aggrandizers in violation of Mexican sovereignty. Canales asserted that all political differences dissolved in the face of a common enemy and brazenly requested that the centralists share their equipment and ammunition so that he could remove this stain—a proposal so extraordinary as to create a puzzled speculative exchange between Canalizo and Bustamante. Could this offer by federalist Canales be serious? Or was it intended merely to create a diversion to support a maritime campaign against Matamoros? Perhaps Canales intended simply to cover up his own recruitment of Texas adventurers.

After a few days of reflection, Bustamante responded. For a second time he canceled his peremptory orders to Canalizo for a combined movement of centralist forces to the main road from Matamoros to Monterrey. Instead, Bustamante directed that a few spies be dispatched to the Nueces to check on developments there. Of course, the commander of the Matamoros garrison had been desperately avoiding a major movement for weeks anyway and made a blustering reply to the rebel leader about receiving reinforcements. So the Canales letter had the effect that the centralist armies did nothing, but continuing that passive strategy may have been the centralist intention all along.[15]

And once again Bustamante's procrastination worked for him. While he contributed a flurry of words and countermanded orders, events elsewhere improved the government cause in northeastern Mexico. The rebels from the south, rather than setting sail to invest Matamoros, suffered a major setback at the hacienda de San Miguel Lablanca near the Tampico–Puebla road on May 3 at the hands of General Gabriel

Valencia. This event ended forever the threat posed by Mejia, who suffered a quick execution by firing squad. Urrea somehow managed a more lenient fate, being dispatched to captivity in Mexico City. The newspaper at the Tamaulipas capital found these outcomes especially comforting because Mejia "had occupied a special place among these evildoers," and it predicted that the events would prove "a fatal blow to the rebellion."[16] The loss of Tampico, a traditional federalist stronghold and source of both revenue and supplies, undid the federalist insurrection as a national movement.

After announcing this triumph on May 10, the Mexican president conferred with two of his northern commanders, Quijano and Canalizo, regarding strategies for defeating the rebels in the northeastern states. Bustamante then departed for Tampico five days later. His parting words included both the promise of pardons to those who laid down their arms as well as threats that "the sword of justice will be applied to those who persist."[17] Neither the president's actions nor his words provided meaningful support or comfort to government leaders in Coahuila and Nuevo León since their capitals remained in the control of the rebel forces or seriously threatened by them. Further, Bustamante misconceived the nature of the rebellion, asserting that the "contagion has been spread from one town to another by the seductions of the ringleaders Lemus and Canales."[18] In fact, the groundswell of federalist support from the substructure in the villas of those states provided a strength that the government forces did not have: namely, a potential for voluntary increases in manpower, provisions, and matériel of war. By contrast, the Mexican president acknowledged the centralist decline in morale because of the absence of affordable supplies sufficient even for subsistence. In Saltillo the meager centralist army did not even gain potential reinforcement from other forces in the region. Although Bustamante had ordered Canalizo to advance with artillery and troops to do battle against Lemus for Monterrey, the Matamoros garrison instead persisted in maintaining its stationary and safe haven from actual warfare.[19]

Lemus and the federalist army by contrast had momentum and for the first time a clear plan, made better because the centralists remained confused even as to which capital city he intended to attack.[20] In mid-May he dispatched three hundred cavalrymen from his force of 1,200 to chase the centralists under Quijano from Linares back in the direction of the coast. The centralist unit had 310 men, but that number included between forty and seventy musicians and other noncombatants. Their forces had dispersed themselves and their ammunition dumps throughout the town of Linares in a manner that suggested anxiety about their own strength and the potential for social disorder. Given these signs of weakness, it came as no surprise that Quijano gave up Linares without a fight. This movement cleared the state of Nuevo León of all the forces of "the illegitimate government of Mexico," in the words of one federalist. Rumors also came into the rebel camps regarding desertions that had weakened the Matamoros garrison. With no real threat of centralist reinforcements coming to the aid of Saltillo, Lemus turned to fight the enemy there, defended by only three hundred men of suspect morale under Domingo Ugartechea and Governor Francisco Garcia Conde. Both the centralist forces and the general population had suffered from a scarcity of provisions for weeks prior to the actual rebel attacks, and its commander knew of the dim prospects of any aid from Bustamante or other commands. Ugartechea believed that their dispirited condition forced many area residents to submit or ignore their obligations to contribute to the defense of the city.[21]

Government eyewitnesses provided a melancholy account of the fate of Saltillo. The rebels arrived on the outskirts of the city on May 22 in numbers three to four times greater than the defenders' and in a mood ready for hard fighting as a prelude to reaping the spoils of this political, cultural, and economic center. Lemus occupied the high ground around the city without resistance since their inferior numbers tied the defenders to their barricades. Civilian curiosity seekers quickly got a glimpse of what might be in store for them as the rebels opened fire indiscriminately before launching an artillery barrage against the parish church occupied by the centralists. On May 23, the first day of battle, the cannon of the attackers fired an estimated four hundred rounds, helping them to seize San Juan church and gain the works controlling one half of the city's plaza.

Lemus ordered continuous small-arms fire, and his successes emboldened him that night to abandon any thoughts of gradually squeezing the lines. The centralists held some favorable positions, including the tower of Santiago church. This placement gave them a decent enough field of fire to make it hot for the rebels if the attack lost its punch. Given that possibility, Lemus decided to peel off one-fourth of his army for an assault aimed at penetrating the defenses. Seeing their fate sealed by this movement, a centralist unit beat the rebels to the punch. However, the centralist attack against a gun emplacement bogged down when a turncoat official betrayed the action at its inception. As a result, a relentless battle occupied the entire day of May 24. Near nightfall the federalists achieved another tactical success by occupying a key rooftop overlooking the plaza. Centralist commander Ugartechea had survived a similar kind of engagement three-and-a-half years earlier as another group of rebels used these tactics against his fixed positions in San Antonio de Béxar, Texas. In that case he had capitulated with the bulk of his command and returned to avenge the humiliation with Santa Anna in February 1836, in an engagement that became known as the Battle of the Alamo. In Saltillo, Ugartechea suffered a different fate. A sniper's bullet fatally struck him as he walked through the plaza amid the descending darkness of the early evening.

On the ground the federalist attackers placed themselves behind a makeshift line consisting of piles of woolsacks, from which they kept up a steady fire varied by feints of retreat. From there they launched a bayonet assault that achieved such success that cries of revelry arose portending victory, but another pocket of centralist defenders delayed that outcome for a short time. Early on the morning of May 25, both sides pulled away from hard fighting to prepare for the final decision. The federalists suspended their attacks in favor of what a government source described as burning, looting, rape, and "general wickedness." What they could not rummage for themselves in the city, the soldiers found readily available in terms of forage and foodstuffs supplied by the surrounding countryside. In stark contrast the centralist garrison ran out of supplies at noon and could only hope for relief from patriotic Saltillenses. These locals also informed the defenders of the imminence of renewed hostilities.

In this perilous context the governor gathered the leaders of all the defending units. They discussed several daunting realities. Many of Ugartechea's command had been holding on out of respect for his leadership—they now seemed unreliable. Indeed, the battalion commander announced that he had lost sixty men to desertion already that morning. The governor heard further that the artillery commander had secretly entered into negotiations with the rebels. The head of the commissary effort announced that supplies had become insufficient for even another day, and the fighting had exhausted almost all the munitions. The governor presented the option of leading a suicidal assault, but some argued against that notion on the basis that such a move would only increase the spirit of vengeance against innocent civilians. The strategy that emerged from this centralist conference involved some sort of feigned retreat and fake truce talks in the hope that a delay might restore morale. Even this wishful thinking evaporated when one of the commissioners sent to conduct truce talks inadvertently revealed the defenseless nature of the plaza, information that led the rebels to resume firing. At that point the garrison imploded in a dispute over a cache of government specie, the cavalry pulled out, and the last seventy soldiers abandoned their barracks in irregular and ignominious capitulation.

Governor Garcia Conde in some manner joined the ranks of those who got away and moved toward San Luis Potosí, busying himself with gathering whatever remnants of the army he could round up. The centralist governor believed he had had some success at least in denying control of additional roads to the rebels.[22] Though grasping at straws, this claim did make a valid point—the centralists had suffered significant blows in losing both the Coahuila and Nuevo León state capitals, but they still had armies in the field. To those who rallied behind Garcia Conde could be added a similar force headed by Quijano and Ampudia, commanders who had chosen to live on to fight another day. In Matamoros the largest army, though inert under Canalizo, still controlled the most significant city in the state of Tamaulipas. That fact provided Bustamante no solace at all. Though still ignorant of the fate of Ugartechea, the head of the Supreme Government wrote a direct condemnation of Canalizo for failing to provide for the defense of the state capitals despite having the greatest manpower and most abundant supplies.[23] Others with equal logic could have cited Bustamante's own weakness in terms of energy, focus, and overall leadership.

Still, if brought together under one command, these centralist forces would be stronger than any army the rebels had yet put in the field at any one time under any one leader. Before leaving the region, Bustamante actually had provided for unity of centralist command. Following a personal conference with Quijano and Canalizo, the president appointed Mariano Arista to lead all the operational forces of the central government in the northeastern states. The new commander had compiled a recent record of successes in restoring Tampico to government control.[24]

Even as they triumphed at Saltillo, the federalists could scarcely afford the luxury of celebration. The loss of Tampico indisputably represented a turning point in the rebellion in that federalism thereby became a regional movement confined wholly to the northeast. As such it retained popular support but without advantages in matériel of war. That reality in turn meant that the rebellion had to have cohesive leadership and a common vision for whatever measures would be required to sustain the cause. The rebels entered the summer months in high spirits, but could they go it alone? Or would they have to seek support from other places?

CHAPTER 3

THE REPUBLIC OF TEXAS AND THE FEDERALIST WARS, 1838-1839

THE PREREQUISITES FOR FEDERALIST SUCCESS, SPECIFI-
cally cohesive leadership and a common vision as to how to sustain the
cause, evaporated almost overnight following the great moment when
the rebels forced the capitulation of Saltillo. Lemus may well have
unwittingly spread the seeds of opposition to him by the leniency he
displayed toward the surrendering government forces. The villas del
norte received word of the victory and celebrated with renewed "vivas a
la federación" on June 1, 1839, but they also heard the easy terms of the
peace accord. Centralist governor Garcia Conde agreed to retire from
the capital within six hours of reaching the agreement, with each member of his entourage keeping his personal arms while the government's
army surrendered all artillery, ammunition, and remaining armaments
before exiting the plaza. Soldiers and officers alike received guarantees
against "retribution for their political views," including any loss of
property. Lemus promised further to remain in a defensive position

and to vacate the federalist trenches simultaneously with the centralist withdrawal. Thus, the government forces lost the place but little else, not even being forced to disband.[1]

Though these terms may have prompted suspicion of Lemus, a more significant disruptive factor lay in the political conduct of the federalist commander, namely his peace talks with Pedro Ampudia. The peace accord broke down in April without notice or fanfare by either side, but it also went public in a way that damaged Lemus, with indications that he had agreed "to terminate his part in commanding the revolution."[2] That language made it seem as if Lemus had sought his own personal safety at the expense of the federalist cause, even though he went on to renew the offensive and capture Saltillo in late May, perhaps the most significant federalist victory ever achieved.

Understanding why Lemus alone came under suspicion as a traitor to the rebel cause had to do with his accuser, the other major federalist leader, Antonio Canales, who had also engaged in negotiations with Ampudia. Bustamante himself named both Canales and Lemus as having "solicited the beginning" of conversations aiming to end their revolution in exchange for clemency.[3] Furthermore, the schemes of Canales continued even as the proposed armistice broke down. He sent a letter to Bustamante expressing regret that "for the past six months we have been considered enemies." However, there remained significant political differences between the two sides, presenting thereby an indisputable sign of willingness to parlay further. The president sent centralist general Canalizo a copy of the Canales message with a stern warning against any further political correspondence with him. Perhaps Canales, with a vulnerability at least equal to that of Lemus for pursuing peace negotiations, decided to strike first in making accusations of disloyalty to the federalist cause. Further, Canales had cleverly couched his overtures in the context of his widely publicized (but stillborn) campaign against "los bárbaros," thus wrapping his pursuit of armistice in offsetting news quite appealing to all norteños. Furthermore, public descriptions of the Lemus peace initiative couched it not as a mere armistice conversation but as one of surrender and obedience to the Supreme Government.[4] In any case, even in the midst of his Saltillo victory, Lemus faced rumblings of leadership discord. The centralist paper in Ciudad Victoria carried reports that the rancheros who followed Canales had made threats against Lemus and speculated that he would be lucky to escape their vengeful clutches on charges of having betrayed them.[5]

The replacement of Lemus also became more likely when the other two-thirds of the nationwide leadership triumvirate succumbed— Mejia died at the hands of a firing squad following the loss of Tampico while the government imprisoned Urrea out of the region (in Mexico City). Thus, Lemus stood alone, and suddenly he could no longer find a secure location anywhere. Clearly, he had outworn his welcome in Saltillo. The Supreme Government's account indicated that he had exacted a forced contribution in excess of six thousand pesos to reward his "thieves and evil doers." Bustamante claimed to have heard from firsthand witnesses regarding events surrounding the federalist withdrawal: "As the [federalist] rabble passed through the streets, the people shouted 'Death to Lemus! Death to the thieves!' All of them set out not to fight but rather to plunder."[6]

Lemus searched for support elsewhere beginning on June 21, when he withdrew from Saltillo, the location of his hard-fought victory, in favor of Monclova, the federalist state capital. There he found not more support but heavy competition to his leadership in the form of both Zapata and Canales, who brought along yet another challenger, federalist ideologist Juan Pablo Anaya. These three proceeded by charging Lemus with "treason," alleging that he had been bribed. The conspirators forced him not only to relinquish command but also to take flight while the remaining federalist forces turned to Anaya.[7] In doing so, the federalists made a commitment to seek external aid, for Anaya held a document from Manuel M. de Llano, the official empowered by the government of the "free state of Nuevo León," conferring authority to "negotiate, contract, and utilize the financial and military resources that he deems to be required . . . for the well-being of the Country." It went on to authorize contracts "with the government of Texas and North America" or with appropriate financial institutions.[8]

The federalist leadership crisis seeped down to the local level. Some of the remote areas easily shifted loyalties. For example, from his head-quarters in the villa of Nava, the political chief of the department of the Rio Grande issued a dispatch acknowledging orders from the governor in Monclova in favor of Anaya, who nonetheless remained philosophi-cal and timid in the exercise of power.[9] On July 22 he wrote to Valentín Gómez Farías deploring "the divisiveness that has begun to occur," and reaffirming his commitment to the goal of restoring the Constitution of 1824 and "la reforma" in general. In terms of national leadership, Anaya deferred to Gómez Farías as the person with the greatest capac-ity to "defend the nation in a spirit of dignity, restore the public good, and recuperate the rights of the people." Perhaps, as Anaya concluded in a flourish of wishful thinking, a resurgence of the correct "public spirit" could end the suffering that Mexico continued to endure.[10] In many ways Anaya served as the perfect stalking horse for Canales. With Lemus discredited and Anaya away conducting diplomacy, no one stood in the way of Canales as he rose to command of the rebel forces in Coahuila, Nuevo León, and Tamaulipas.

In fact, his machinations had been too easy. Scarcely more than a week after Anaya wrote to Gómez Farías, support for Lemus reasserted itself through endorsement by a junta in Monclova, and on August 3 Canales asserted that Lemus had disavowed an earlier agreement to yield his position. The military forces of the frontier villages, according to Canales, stood firmly committed to Anaya.[11] At Villa Aldama the very next day, Zapata and forty-five of his followers signed a document formally absolving them from following Lemus and swearing fealty to Anaya instead, also promising a renewed commitment to the "cause of Liberty." They further declared that Lemus had earlier acknowledged his unworthiness for command in a separate pact with Canales. The document went on to charge Lemus with abusive behavior toward officers and soldiers in the First Division of the Federal Army, "shame-ful" treatment of Anaya and Canales, and conduct as the tool of José Urrea. The agreement ended with a sweeping allegation that Lemus had engaged in other "criminal" acts of disloyalty to the revolution and asserted that "the people" supported the new leaders. It also served as a kind of loyalty oath, pledging renewed zeal "to live free or die." Leaving no detail unattended, the document contained the signatures of all the officers in the division as well as representatives of the sergeants, corporals, and general soldiers.[12]

On August 8, this time in Mier, Canales added a lengthy affirmation, again authorizing Anaya as "senior General" of federalist forces to enlist all manner of resources during his mission to Texas and the United States. Typical of the embellishments of Canales, this "full faith and credit" letter reiterated the constitutional context for a revolution designed to replace the "sad" interlude of rule by naked force that had undermined the actual legal construct throughout Mexico since 1834. "A thousand patriots," he wrote, "have been tragically sacrificed to the fury of armed rule for [supporting] a noble cause" and resisting a government that closely resembled that of the Spanish monarchy of the past. A "fire" animated patriots from the frontier and still burned among the elected representatives of the people. As if to reassure potential supporters outside Mexico, this legal document contained phrases such as: "the tyrants will not castigate us."[13] A week later in Guerrero, Jesús Cárdenas joined in the chorus of support, claiming authority based on a "free vote" of the people that made him political chief of the department of the North of Tamaulipas. As "the only legitimate authority actually recognized under the federal order," he set forth justifications of the Texas initiative and argued that the cause had nothing to rely on other than the "firm resolve" of its supporters who swore "to die before succumbing to despotism." Otherwise, they would have to fight "without sufficient resources," thus justifying the solicitation of external aid.[14]

For the federalists this leadership crisis came at a truly vulnerable time because the centralists by June 1839 had the ability to focus on the northeastern states, and they quickly gained other advantages as well. Bustamante went southward to reclaim his presidency, thus giving the government exactly what the federalists found themselves in the process of losing—unified military command. The president left behind a gift to the suppression of the revolt by naming Mariano Arista as "Jefe de la primera ejercito de Operaciones en el norte." Whereas Canalizo and

Bustamante seemed to outdo each other in procrastination and excuse making, Arista began to act with decisive and sometimes ruthless intent. On June 7 he published an order from Santa-Ana de Tamaulipas requiring everyone holding weapons or munitions to hand them over to civil authorities, the sole exception being arms for self-defense in the hands of those who had "earned the confidence of the authorities as to honorable conduct and [thus who] present no public danger."[15]

Arista could also speak softly when the occasion arose. On June 17 he issued a circular to his "fellow citizens" of the department of Tamaulipas, calling attention to his successes in bringing the war in Tampico to an end "without further effusion of blood." He claimed that his past actions gave evidence of "my desire for peace, happiness, and the well-being of my compatriots. . . . I prefer to use reason, persuasion, and demonstration of the evils brought about by revolution" than to resort to relentless war. He repeated the familiar government theme that the rebellion had been driven by selfish men who plundered the poorest. Those "who have nothing other than their miserable dignity" had nonetheless been "robbed scandalously by rebel leaders." Patriots in current control of the government promised reforms and could be trusted, so in that way Mexico would cease being "devoured by anarchy." The costs of revolution had been vast—destruction of property, new taxes, and the loss of tranquility. He ended with a promise: "I will demonstrate proof of my tolerant and conciliatory nature; I will also take pride in bringing about security for all and in safeguarding the liberty and property of all the citizens." Arista's words may have mattered to some of the centralists, but he did not actually assume command in the field in the northeastern states for several months, leaving the timid Canalizo to carry on in his usual desultory manner.[16]

Others kept up the propaganda campaign. An editorialist wrote on June 8, "Although the revolutionaries promised abundance, prosperity, rivers of gold and silver," they had actually brought only "desolation, immorality, assassinations, [and] robbery." He also made the case for merciless suppression: "When some are treated with clemency by the government, others take their place to prey upon our peaceful citizens." As to the philosophers whose calls for freedom inspired the revolt, they were now "elevated" to their ultimate aspiration, joining the ranks of "the ferocious Attilas and Robespierres. What we need is the sword of an executioner," and fortunately the times had produced such a great man who would bring peace to the land in the person of Mariano Arista.[17]

Still, actual reassertion of centralist control took most of the summer. Federalist influence receded first in Tamaulipas, then in Nuevo León, and finally in Coahuila, hanging on doggedly in the remote villas del norte on or near the Rio Grande. Nuevo León had weaker rural support for federalism, so political activity focused on the state capital of Monterrey starting in late June 1839. The centralist governor, Mateo Quiroz, published a public appeal on the twenty-third, calling for all citizens to support the government in reestablishing a "spirit of peace" in the effort to restore the constitutional order.[18] The centralist military regained control of Monterrey and pledged its support to the legitimate departmental government; in this manner all of Nuevo León resumed its loyalty.[19]

Fierce frontier independence from external authority required relentless attention from centralist politicians, who also seemed slow to recognize their opportunity to take control again. Outside of Saltillo, the federalists continued to operate the civil government into the summer of 1839. On July 1, jefe político Eugenio Fernandez ordered the ayuntamiento of Guerrero to form new military companies of citizens "who love federal institutions." He also urged local authorities to arrest and jail insolent people who spoke against the "sacred cause," especially in public meetings, and to suppress both clandestine trading and thievery.[20] In simultaneous counteraction the centralist governor of Nuevo León presented himself as the interim chief executive in Coahuila, and military authorities openly expressed their intent to march upon Monclova and the villas del norte, but shortages of funds and supplies retarded actual movement.[21] At last an expedition dispatched by Canalizo departed from Monterrey,[22] moving swiftly enough to capture Monclova on August 11 without facing substantial resistance. The leadership quarrels among the rebel forces meant that different units fled separately and in disarray, making them easy prey. Even the normally tepid Canalizo moved into action as he shifted headquarters to Villa Aldama, where Canales and Zapata just days before had adopted their resolution rejecting Lemus. Government troops under Canalizo held a position close enough to other centralist forces but away from the action. He asserted that from his location he could block attempts of the federalists to reconcentrate, and he ordered a vanguard under Col. Francisco G. Pavón to pursue the federalist remnants supporting Lemus even as they ignored Canales and Anaya.

Word of these centralist advances rapidly spread panic among federalist authorities to the east all the way to the Rio Grande. In Nava, the jefe político sought to rally and unite with other federalists from Rosas and Guerrero. At some point early in their expedition, centralist supporters at or near the Rio Grande arrested federalist leaders Severo Ruiz and Mauricio Carrasco. Many local officials soon denied any voluntary support for the rebellion, claiming that they had been forced to oppose the authority of the Supreme Government, had "taken up arms" only in desperation and in accordance with orders from outside their communities, and now regarded the federalist efforts as "futile." Nature contributed to the mess that the federalist cause had become as torrential rainfall made it impossible to travel quickly and to move or protect the prized artillery that gave courage to the rebel troops.

Pavón reached the main body of the federalists at Loma Alta during a deluge on August 17, taking prisoners, capturing armaments, and managing to force them to flee without battle the next day. What Canalizo referred to as the federalist "rabble" essentially withered away without much additional pressure from government forces, and Pavón moved to a place only six leagues from the most remote, northeasterly federalist outpost of Laredo.[23] The fate of the pitiful remnants under Lemus remained still undecided. He managed to get them to the Rio Grande, only to find the river so swollen with rapid currents that he could not effect a crossing. Instead, Lemus sought additional munitions from a stash at Villa de Rosas on August 19. Lt. Manuel Menchaca, with only forty loyalists, then proceeded to thwart Lemus, who ludicrously boasted of leading a force of one thousand and made what Menchaca called one thousand threats against any who refused to join him. The centralist lieutenant remained unintimidated, augmented his force with the help of the loyal alcalde, and made his way to Guerrero in search of munitions. Soon, he discovered Lemus with a band of fifty rebels attempting to commandeer boats to cross the river and forced their surrender on August 21. By August 24, Menchaca reported that his small force had been joined by other "patriots" from Nava, Morelos, and Rosas sufficient to gain control of the entire river valley, including the town of Guerrero, and he repeated his plea for reinforcements.[24] By the end of the summer, the forces of the Supreme Government had regained control of the villas del norte, signaling the collapse of federalism in all the northeastern states.[25]

Pavón issued orders on August 21 to restore all civil authority to the hands of the centralists. For his part Canalizo remained headquartered in Aldama during the decisive week of August 18–25, asserting that he had insufficient transport to pursue the guerrillas under Anaya and Canales, who managed to make their way to Texas. Canalizo busied himself by issuing public notices to the restored governor of Nuevo León and taking credit that the Supreme Government had brought peace at last to the rebel strongholds in Coahuila and the villas of the Rio Grande.[26]

Although agents of the Supreme Government began to take civil rather than further military action, some skeptics in Matamoros, Ciudad Victoria, and parts of Nuevo León expressed doubt that the strife had actually come to an end. *La Brisa* gave "thanks to the heavens if this is the last bloodshed to water the unfortunate soil of Mexico!" but followed with words of doubt. "Will the divine sun of peace never shine on our country? Always fighting—brothers against brothers?"[27] On August 31 a "Nuevo Leones" published a letter in the neighboring state of Tamaulipas to castigate the evils of the rebellion but also to warn against complacency: "Despite the victories of the Supreme Government here, the enemy is obstinate. . . . All should be preparing for the common defense," or "the unjust aggression of these rebels will be repeated, bringing to all the places they touch misery, desolation, extermination, and death."[28]

If that dire prophecy were to come true, the federalist cause would have to regroup, but this time it needed external support in order to do so. By contrast, the centralists faced only slight military duty in mopping up throughout the northeastern region. Canalizo reestablished his headquarters in Monterrey, from where on September 4 he dispatched a detachment to Monclova under José Miñon to eliminate any further threat from the rebels and to sustain order. Canalizo repeated that all who recanted would be allowed their freedom so long as they assisted in providing resources to government troops.[29] A week later he issued more elaborate "measures . . . to assure peace and tranquility." He ordered centralist officials to record the names of all those who "are known to be in conformity" with the Supreme Government and then to provide for their potential enlistment in auxiliary forces so as "to deter the guerrillas," thieves, and others who might provide assistance to renewed federalist uprisings. He ordered that these measures be carefully applied to the river towns such as Mier and Laredo, places that he suspected might be the next federalist rallying points, even though he predicted that Matamoros would become the major target. To provide an illusion of additional security, he announced that units from Matamoros would march back and forth up the Rio Grande as far north as Laredo, but he requested the establishment of command posts in other likely targets such as Reynosa and Camargo, "which have been the principal ones pronouncing for disorder" previously. At the very least, these measures might succeed in disrupting communication among various rebel forces, and he reiterated that "we must remember that Matamoros always has the greatest appeal to the revolution." Canalizo concluded by lecturing civil officials that their "fullest cooperation" might well determine the outcome of renewed hostilities.[30]

By the end of September 1839, an aura of confidence enveloped the supporters of the Supreme Government in the northeastern states.[31] On September 30, downriver in Matamoros *La Brisa* hedged its position on present and future policy. Although affirming its support for ending reprisals against former rebels, the newspaper also warned "that the day will return when the Government renews its rigor and proceeds to bring down the terrible sword of the law on the heads of the delinquent."[32] Previously the newspaper in the capital of Tamaulipas had published other good news for the centralist cause, namely its victory at Tampico. With confidence it predicted that the combined might of forces under Canalizo, Quijano, and Mariano Arista "must produce the effect of liberating our brothers in Nuevo León and in the Villas del Norte," not from the federalists alone but from "the ferocious hold of the Colonists and their collaborators." This sullying of the federalists by associating them with norteamericanos occurred even before Anglo Texans actually arrived on the scene, obviously reflecting feelings of deepest apprehension.[33] As an editorial in Ciudad Victoria exclaimed: "¡¡Ay, the Texans!! Ay, for us all if these pirates should advance beyond the Rio Bravo [Rio Grande]! All of our properties will be divided up, and we will be thrown from our lands . . . while their slaves do the work that produces the fruits from our fertile country."[34]

From the onset of the rebellion in the northeastern states, this "Texas question" posed a multitude of thorny issues. During the administration of President Sam Houston (1836–1838), the policy of Texas toward Mexican affairs had been cautious and defense-minded. The possibility that another military expedition would cross the Rio Grande aiming to reconquer the new republic always stood as the dominant concern. Accordingly, Houston made no aggressive moves but rather attempted to assure strict neutrality with regard to the internal affairs of Mexico. On June 13, 1838, his secretary of state, R. A. Irion, distributed a circular to all borderland counties in order to provide ways that "our friends from the frontier may have leave to trade from the Rio Grande to the town of Bexar." These regulations emphasized that traders who came there would have to turn over weapons, horses, and mules for the duration of their stay and could not legally purchase any "arms or ammunition." Regarding potential trade initiated from Texas, the guidelines forbade travel from "west of the Nueces without orders from the Government." Finally, the policy provided that these regulations should be translated for the benefit of "the Texian citizens who do not read nor understand the English language."[35]

By the onset of the Lamar administration (which assumed power in December 1838), the realities of mercantile enterprise had eroded these neutrality policies. People and their goods from the Rio Grande moved to and from the Nueces area as well as Béxar. Some of those involved had lived in these communities before being displaced by war and revolution in 1836, so in effect they simply returned home. On the other hand, some Bejareños with strong federalist principles headed south to serve in rebel armies and to support the war with horses and trade goods. Merchants in Texas expressed delight that those who came to sell or purchase goods did their dealings in specie. Since this commerce produced profits all around, the government of the Republic of Texas set out to legitimatize it with a proclamation from Lamar in February 1839, based on authority provided him by Congress. It stated that all traders should have "passports" from federalist authorities, a provision that in effect extended de facto recognition to the rebels.[36]

Other voices saw a danger in choosing the wrong side. The most influential paper in the Republic of Texas, the *Telegraph and Texas Register*, judged it a mistake if "our citizens . . . embroil themselves in the internal dissentions of Mexico. . . . It is [to Texas] no longer a matter of importance whether Federalism or Centralism prevail in Mexico." The editorial went on to remind readers not to place trust in people from the country responsible for the Goliad massacre of 1836. Instead, Texas "detests and distrusts both [sides] alike and such is her present situation, that she fears neither." Texas interests required it "to remain a quiet spectator" while Mexico weakened itself in civil conflict. The editor ended with a statement typical of the boisterous rhetoric of the day: "Texas, like a youthful Hercules, is waxing stronger and stronger, and already evinces the workings of a giant's power. If wise, she will at this time husband her strength, in order that she may, when the hour of trial arrives, be enabled to bear up against it with inflexible firmness."[37]

Thus, Anaya stepped onto Texas soil at an apparently propitious time. The young nation had not yet suffered chastening setbacks, and it had an intensely nationalistic president with a ravenous appetite for the politics of adventure. Anaya arrived with yet another letter of support, this time from Tejano José María Carvajal (also spelled "Carbajal") who reviewed again the main theme that might fuel Texas support, namely that the federalists merely continued what Texas had started in 1835 with its resistance to the centralist regime in Mexico. Naturally, Carvajal also reiterated Anaya's broad authority and promised that the rebels would remain under arms "until the tyrants are castigated and the sacred rights of the people are firmly assured."[38] He attempted to pave the way with a letter to family friend Luciano Navarro in Béxar who, since he did not know Lamar, forwarded it as a confidential communication through Col. H. W. Karnes on August 9.[39]

As the federalists and the centralists both clearly understood, the Republic of Texas would be sorely tempted to involve itself in Mexican affairs in order, at the very least, to gain recognition of its nationhood. Complications abounded, starting with the quite spurious claim of the Texas Republic to the Rio Grande as the boundary. Undoubtedly, the temptation to abandon neutrality increased as the outcome of the civil wars remained unclear, and many held that Texas had a far better chance of gaining recognition if the federalists prevailed. In March 1839 diplomats actually expressed optimism because the federalists "professed to entertain the most friendly sentiments toward this [Texas] Government." One assertion even held that unofficial correspondence from the rebels treated Lamar in a manner that amounted to de facto recognition of Texas independence. On the other hand, the president expected (hoped actually) that official negotiations with Mexico City on the topic of recognition would "accelerate," and if so Texas support for the federalists would most certainly derail that possibility.[40]

Outside the official government circles in Texas, the most vocal opinions about the war came from newspapers, especially the *Telegraph and Texas Register*, which published reports from Louisiana speculating that federalism, while it would not succeed nationally, might lead to separation by the northern states since "there is [a] vast difference of ideas, habits and interests between" that region and the interior. "The population of the northern provinces [is] more industrious and moral"; it is "much less averse to a union with strangers"; resources are abundant; and "the geographical position [is] extremely favorable to commerce."[41] On August 14, 1839, the same paper asserted that the federalists had presented a proposal "that Texas should form an alliance" with the northern states that "had determined to declare their independence themselves." The *Telegraph* opposed any such union and favored neutrality, but it professed optimism about the prospects of the federalist cause in the north.[42]

All these speculations from Texas essentially reflected ignorance of the situation in the northeastern states. For example, none of the federalists there had publicly advocated for anything resembling secession from the Mexican nation.[43] However, the solicitation of support from Texas represented a turning point in the rebellion. As it turned out, what the federalists gained in Texas would result in a fundamental shift in the character of the conflict in northeastern Mexico. When war returned, it would be fought by Anglo Texans as well as Mexicans, and the new norm would thereafter be filled with unprecedented acts of brutality and vengeance.

CHAPTER 4

A NEW WAR, SEPTEMBER– DECEMBER 1839

IN TEXAS ANAYA FOUND AN ENVIRONMENT OF UNCERTAINTY.
Rumors swirled, and attitudes toward the federalist movement reversed themselves repeatedly. Minimally, a consensus among residents of Texas favored whatever measure promised to thwart the threat of reinvasion since the new republic struggled to marshal resources sufficient to protect its frontiers. But specific steps involved risk as well as reward. Overt support for the rebels might lead to a government more favorable toward recognition of Texas independence, but committing to the wrong faction could easily backfire by fueling the considerable sentiment in Mexico favoring heroic measures of reconquest.[1]

San Antonio resident C. Van Ness urged Secretary of War Albert Sidney Johnston to give a favorable reception to Anaya in light of his "useful and noble service to his country. . . . Now I can but think is the golden time to strike at our enemy, and by taking prompt and affective [*sic*] advantage of the means and aid offered by Gen. Anaya, . . . the administration will secure the glory of having accomplished the peace & Independence of Texas."[2] The *Telegraph and Texas Register* concurred. It lauded the disinterested patriotism of Anaya for his bravery beginning with the wars for independence and also for his military service in the United States alongside its defenders in the War of 1812. He had suffered greatly for having "espoused the cause of the people and liberty, during his whole public career" against the same forces of tyranny that Texas had overcome just three years earlier. Unfortunately for Anaya, the paper also introduced a dimension of the federalist wars that caused him much trouble, describing his ultimate goal as nothing less than "establishing a new Republic out of a portion of the Eastern States of Mexico."[3]

Anaya gained everything short of official recognition and formal intervention by the government of the Republic of Texas. He claimed satisfaction with his reception in the new Texas capital of Austin and then moved on to seek more than verbal support elsewhere. From Houston the *Telegraph and Texas Register* reported that Anaya had arrived there on September 12–13, having failed to gain "a formal proposition . . . for assistance in behalf of the Federal party in Mexico," but still full of optimism. Anaya "promised stable government over Northern Mexico" and "certainty" of federalist success. Specifically, he sought to purchase munitions based on credit and to recruit troops for his army. The administration of President Lamar rejected any official position of support, as the newspaper explained, because such measures could "embroil ourselves in their domestic difficulties." The newspaper continued: "Our government is [too] young and poor" to be anything but "a quiet spectator . . . our prosperity should not be jeopardized by an interference in their quarrels." Suggestions that Anaya might find a more favorable reception with the Texas congress than the cabinet went nowhere, and he simply professed gratitude for his "many friends" in Texas and hope for greater support still as he continued his journey in the United States.[4]

Before leaving, Anaya wrote an open letter to the editor, eschewing polemics while seeking to correct misstatements previously attributed to him. He absolutely denied an intention of separatism and reasserted his goal "to re-establish the Federal constitution of 1824." He also vehemently disavowed any intention to appeal to the Texas congress over the executive branch and asserted that he had been treated well by

President Lamar.[5] As if to avoid any misattribution, Anaya prepared a formal decree of ten articles detailing his principles. It began with an unequivocal assertion that "every individual who wishes to take up arms or to help in any other manner in the struggle actively underway in the Nation against the so-called Central Government of Mexico will do so under the condition of re-establishing the 1824 federal constitution." In order to advance prosperity based on its bountiful abundance of land and mineral resources, Mexico should abolish all restrictions against "the introduction of industrious foreigners" and their ownership of property. Both military service in the cause of freedom and those assisting with financial support would be paid out of the landed domain. "Any idea of actually dividing the territory of the Republic of Mexico is not permitted," and "the integrity of Mexican territory" would never be compromised by any external interference or by any "pretended Republic of the North." Nevertheless, the northern region with its abundant resources and sparse population had a bright future so long as it dispelled the notion of a separate republic. As to those Anaya sought to recruit in Texas and the United States, they would "benefit from all the rights and privileges of other Mexicans" so long as they "subjected themselves to all the regular orders and military discipline and all laws of the country." He ended by calling for a convention "as soon as it is feasible" to create a provisional government "representative of the Mexican nation."[6]

However patriotic and noble Anaya's words might have been, they mattered for naught amid the realities of seeking volunteers from among the rough-hewn humanity of the Texas frontier. In mid-September 1839, President Lamar received an alarming report concerning disorder in the region of the lower Nueces and San Antonio Rivers that included Goliad, Victoria, and San Patricio, all communities claimed by both the Republic of Texas and the Republic of Mexico. This area had been disturbed for some time by disputes among Irish, Anglo, and Tejano residents that was made worse by warfare between Mexican soldiers and Texas volunteers in 1835–1836, which left behind a culture of revenge, uncertainty as to property rights, and weak restraints over ever-looming eruptions of violence. Further, the social scene included a new element with a new name that was heard for the first time on the Texas frontier—the cowboy. Texas presidential correspondent H. S. Foote found in this region "a state of things prevailing deeply mortifying . . . rendering the most awful consequences to the Republic. The business of cattle stealing, the robbery of private property, has become an extensive and crying evil not confined to the enemies of Texas. . . . There is a strange combination of marauders along the whole western frontier, composed in part of Mexicans, in part of Comanches, and in part of men claiming to be Texian citizens, who are allied, in order to plunder and devastate indiscriminently [*sic*]."[7]

Lt. John Browne in a letter to Secretary of War Albert Sidney Johnston not only confirmed Foote's report but provided greater detail. "I found [the region] filled by a set of men who have given themselves the title of a *band of Brothers*," scattered all over the country. Although they pretended to steal only "from the enemy," in fact they robbed Texians and had recently killed a party of Mexican traders. A group of the rustlers had confronted Browne as to whether he came as a commissioner of the Texas republic, a question that he skirted, resulting in a bold statement: "The band of brothers wished me to understand that they could defend themselves against any force the Government could send to oppose them." Victims informed him that they would not seek protection from the authorities or take up arms themselves out of fears of retaliation. Indeed, the Texas army itself had become involved with the robbers. He estimated that the gang of cowboy cattle thieves numbered between three hundred and four hundred, and he informed the secretary that Major Richard Roman "intends makeing [*sic*] a descent upon the Rio Grande [to] take Matamoros. His object is plunder; he intends the cow drivers shall be his Troops."[8]

Foote informed Lamar that nothing had been done to check disorder by the troops that had been dispatched under Reuben Ross "for the protection of the frontier." Instead, they chose to enlist in the federalist army. As Roman himself recalled regarding the recruits from Texas, "the most of them [were] what was called Cow boys, with the exception of Ross's Company which were Regular troops—The force was organized—Ross was elected to the Command."[9] A decade later

Lamar described the recruitment dynamic in an obtuse manner: "Anya [*sic*] could make no arrangement with the Govt but he found a ready ally in the Cowboys in the West. These Cowboys were men who lived sort of a lawless, depredating life on the frontier, by driving off cattle and horses from the Nueces, to sell in the interior. The contest which this occupation led to, between them and the Mexicans were bloody & horrible, and furnished some of the unparalleled acts of vindictive retaliation. These Cow-boys assembled in the Nueces, about San Patricio & Tenoxticlan [*sic*], where they mustered about 270 and chose Ross for their leader."[10] If, as Lamar stated, Anaya failed to make an actual formal "arrangement" with the Republic of Texas, the administration without apology or explanation stood aside as the federalists recruited and supplied an army on Texas soil, including the enrollment of "regular" troops of the Texas government. In this manner the Lamar administration engaged in de facto intervention in Mexican affairs.

The Texas auxiliary force wasted little time in joining remnants of the federalist army along the Rio Grande. The centralists, although certainly not lethargic during the late summer and fall months, had not prepared an adequate response to the threat of renewed hostilities. The most distant of the villas del norte, Laredo, remained in federalist hands under Zapata while Anaya and Canales gained reinforcements in Texas. Centralist leadership, both political and military, wrote torrents of orders requiring the war-ravaged communities to provide supplies for their own defense because the government treasuries remained exhausted. Given those realities, their strategic approach suffered from excessive ambition. Since many federalist areas had "recanted their pronouncements [in order] to return to obedience to the Supreme Government," wrote Valentín Canalizo to the governor of Coahuila, units already stationed in the region would be able "to eliminate any threat from the rebels and to sustain order."[11]

Secure in his quarters in Monterrey, Canalizo constructed his concept of "measures . . . to assure peace and tranquility." Military commanders throughout the region were to prepare to enroll "all the citizens who carry arms," so long as the officers gained assurances of the loyalty of these individuals. Care should be taken to maintain these "auxiliary units" in readiness but inactive, "to appear only when there is an urgent need," but they could be used against guerillas, thieves, or hostile indios as called for. He promised to order a force from Matamoros "to march back and forth along the left bank of the Rio Grande to the vicinity of Laredo" and to act in concert with government forces in the river towns such as Mier. "If the rebels do not evacuate Laredo as is expected," wrote Canalizo, all the centralist forces would coalesce to expel them. Additional troops would be dispatched to former rebel strongholds such as Reynosa and Camargo from which they would disrupt rebel lines of communication. As to the real target of renewed hostilities, "we must remember that Matamoros always has the greatest appeal to the revolution and is the principal object to which their little leaders are dedicated." He ended with a restatement of his major hope, which remained but an illusion: only full cooperation among all military and political leaders could "bring about a happy end to the revolution."[12]

Canalizo's musings about defense notwithstanding, his truest wish led him to hope that nothing more would be required because "all the leadership of the revolutionary forces" had given up: "It is clear that they cannot continue their unfortunate expeditions." Such an attitude of complacency, unbecoming a general with a duty to provide for every threat to security, certainly did not make him unique even among others with similar responsibilities. In Saltillo military leaders speculated that the whole gang of rebel leaders, in crossing the Rio Grande, had set out not for enlisting aid from the (unrecognized) Republic of Texas but rather for the United States of the north. From the national capital, the minister of war concurred, reporting that "from various quarters I have learned that the rest of the revolutionaries," including Anaya, Canales, Zapata, Carbajal, and other cabecillas, "have dispersed or crossed the Rio Grande" on their way to the Norte de America, thus "concluding the revolution of those points."[13]

A well-informed resident of one of the river towns sounded a similar note as he attempted to ward off further hostilities. After many years of adventure, military exploits, and political service, Bernardo Gutiérrez de Lara had again taken up residence in his ancestral home of Guerrero. By 1839, he had turned sixty-five years of age, and no one there could rival him as a distinguished Mexican patriot. In addition to acquiring substantial property from his mercantile activities and family holdings in and around his birthplace, Gutiérrez had served on both military and diplomatic missions on behalf of Mexican independence. He had attempted to stage an expedition from Louisiana on behalf of that cause in 1812 and won admiration there by also fighting on the US side in the battle of New Orleans. His multiple forms of service had resulted in his being selected as governor of Tamaulipas in 1824, followed by other regional leadership posts. Gutiérrez had been fully committed to the federalist cause and had recently lent his name in support of Anaya's mission in the United States. Since no other area resident had as great a claim to long-term patriotic zeal, his credibility should have lent weight to his views when, on October 22, he warned Zapata about the danger of external meddling in Mexican affairs. Gutiérrez urged the rebellion's most ardent warrior to end the war in favor of returning to family, friends, and home in Guerrero.[14] Zapata did not heed this plea and remained committed to any and all measures needed to sustain the revolt. For Zapata words meant less than action, and through the latter he would soon reveal the depths of his commitment to the federalist cause.

Zapata certainly did not stand alone, but the situation along the Rio Grande remained fluid, as nearly all observers agreed. Some centralist military and political officials in the villas del norte themselves noted that the aftermath of the previous months of civil discord and military conflict still provided ample challenges even for those who believed, as José Lasaro Benavides explained to the Jues de Paz of Guerrero, that "the revolution [is] concluded in this area." Reconciliation remained incomplete in that many citizens continued to struggle with each other to reclaim disputed property that had been seized by one side or the other.[15] The most vigilant of the military officials stationed there, Col. Francisco G. Pavón, reported to recently appointed Nuevo León governor J. de Jesús Davilo y Prieto on October 7 that he had published an edict designed to restore order and that it had been well received by the public. "The major part of the citizenry of these places have returned to their homes and renounced their support of the revolution." He had installed new officials loyal to the government. "There are only a few remaining who still have their arms in their hands and even they are acting in a docile and obedient manner. It is my belief that they will let go of their bitter emotions that produced [such] a disastrous revolution, return to their homes, and occupy themselves in assistance to their families that for some time were abandoned."[16] Residents of the villa of Mier had already voiced their rejection of the rebels because of their rumored enlistment of foreigners from Texas to the cause of revolution.[17]

Pavón also knew that he still had his hands full and then some. He had already written to Canalizo about reports that "colonists" from Texas would reinforce remnants of the rebels and threaten to overwhelm him in Mier. The general in Matamoros minimized the threat and urged Pavón, in effect, to buck up. No further reinforcements could be spared, and Canalizo had established a line among the river towns to intercept the rebels should they come and to give effective warning. "My view" is that the "fears" that Canales has renewed the offensive "are not credible any more today than yesterday, because they do not have" the required resources. In any case, the general continued, reserves in Monterrey remained available to counter any renewed rebel movement, though he admitted to a shortage of resources.[18] Such assurances without support provided Pavón no comfort, but Canalizo's bravado deceived others. *La Concordia* from Ciudad Victoria reported the existence of Canalizo's cavalry operating all along the left bank of the Rio Grande. This phantom "frontier line" would "scatter the remnants of the revolution," and soon "well-being" would return to all of Tamaulipas and Nuevo León. "Peace, rest from heavy labors, a return to the legitimate behaviors of concord . . . all of this is now available under the legal constitutional order."[19]

The anxious Pavón also took one other initiative. From Mier on October 12, he approved an attempt by Rafael de Lira to lure Canales with an offer to negotiate an end of hostilities, not an outlandish concept since the rebel leader had previously engaged in such scheming. The de Lira letter argued in favor of bringing *"peace and happiness for this unfortunate frontier,"* stressing Pavón's perception of "a revulsion toward continuing this conflict among all the villas here." Although he lacked actual authority to make a final deal, Pavón asserted support from Canalizo and outlined generous potential terms. The offer extended to Cárdenas, Zapata, and anyone else who wished to abandon a cause that had failed everywhere else in the nation. Pavón promised that the government would refrain from castigating any federalists for their political views, that he would assist in locating lost relatives, and that he maintained a willingness to take other measures as needed so that the rebels could "provide for the welfare of your families." The offer elaborated on one point for emphasis—none of these terms extended to the "Texas adventurers and vandals." Continued "support for these robbers must cease and you must not tolerate their crimes any longer." The more evils that Mexicans suffer, the happier these Texans become, he urged. They wish to see "Mexican blood poured out in torrents." They sought to extend their boundaries farther into the territory of Mexico, utilizing assassination and any other means to bring about distress and thus to pave the way for their takeover.[20] Pavón reported accurately about war weariness among the villas del norte. On October 13 a public meeting in Mier denounced "the evils that the revolution has produced among this population." It resolved further support for the existing system of government and denounced Canales for enlisting "foreigners of the Texas colonies" in the rebel cause. In order to demonstrate overwhelming support for these resolutions, the meeting invited citizens to sign the document—seventy-three did so.[21]

Pavón's pleadings as to his vulnerability and shortage of supplies and manpower gained a more favorable response from regional political and military authorities, though verbal support, fretting, and promises from Monterrey politicians did not provide what he needed. Nor did reports that other leaders also lacked troops and munitions help to improve morale.[22] Finally, Pavón remained in the dark as to the actual whereabouts of the invading forces. Some reports of troop movement occurred, but such warnings went to places other than Mier. Instead, Guerrero judicial official José María Salinas sent the Coahuila governor a copy of his public notice about the coming of renewed warfare. He indicated that "spies" had spotted a large body of invaders under "the vaunted Zapata" coming south from Laredo, causing area vecinos to fly from their homes. Salinas expected nothing but cowardly behavior from this army and ascribed its intent more to pillage than to a resumption of hostilities in favor of the federalist rebellion. Here again, Pavón knew enough to be concerned, but he had complete responsibility for the so-called frontier line without specific details as to when and where his preparations should concentrate.[23]

On the eve of renewed battle among the villas del norte, hundreds of miles to the east in Houston, Texas, the *Telegraph and Texas Register* provided more accurate and detailed information than the Mexican commander had at his disposal. The invading army consisted of remnants from "the standard of Federalism," a group of (Carizo) Indians from the area around Mier, the cowboys from the Nueces region, as many as eighty volunteers recruited in Houston, and a company of Texas regulars under Reuben Ross. The newspaper exaggerated their numbers (this force amounted to nowhere near 1,800 as it claimed) and disparaged their character, describing the men as "civilized, half-civilized, and savage—all pretty well armed and with considerable ammunition," but without artillery. The newspaper also only half accurately described the mood of the invaders, ascribing to them a "desperate adventure for the reduction of the whole Rio Grande country to the standard of Federalism," a misconception in asserting that political principle played such a big role among the Anglo Texas volunteers. The *Telegraph* added that the soldiers of this army had "an account to settle with their opponents," though it failed to identify a legitimate origin for this spirit of revenge. As to an excuse for Ross's abandoning his post, his men had become "impatient and could not be kept from desertion," and after all, his orders provided considerable discretion as to how exactly he would act "*for the protection of the Western frontier.*" Most interestingly, the paper had a specific and accurate understanding of the initial tactical objective of the invaders—they would begin with an attack at the villa of Mier.[24]

Both sides left accounts of the military events that transpired, and together they provide a fairly detailed narrative. Pavón from his vantage point in Mier operated blindly as to the exact disposition of the enemy, rumored to have crossed the Rio Grande somewhere to his north. To learn more he sent a cavalry unit in that direction on a probing mission; had he heard back, his alarm would only have increased.[25] The army that had gathered in Texas under Canales in mid-October had advanced 1,100 strong to the great river without significant delay, choosing the area around the town of Guerrero as a place to cross in two contingents, one north and made up mostly of Anglo American recruits from Texas, with the remaining majority south of town. They had been joined by remnants of earlier battles led by Zapata who had stayed behind during the recruitment expedition. At some point Canales objected to the regulars' display of the flag of the Republic of Texas, thus setting in motion a series of running quarrels that beset the motley army for the remainder of its service.

As planned, the "Americans" came into Guerrero from the north first, before daybreak, and dispersed the garrison, reputed to number somewhere between 200 and 320 under the old warrior/politician and former federalist Bernardo Gutiérrez de Lara. The attackers found the Mexican commander soon after he fled in full dress uniform, wading in the river, made him a prisoner, and disfigured his uniform. Gutiérrez escaped further persecution because he had sons serving with Canales and had also fought in the War of 1812 with relatives of Ross. The plan of attack worked perfectly in that members of the garrison who fled southward fell quickly into the hands of the other wing of the invaders—essentially the centralist army at Guerrero provided no resistance. Seizing the initiative, Canales placed the "Americans" in the lead and immediately sent the whole army off southward against Mier.

Ignorant of the events at Guerrero, at this same time Pavón had reached a point of desperation regarding the critical shortage of food and other provisions. On November 1 he left the town of Mier and moved farther south in the hope of making contact with a supply train from Matamoros, knowing that it had an insufficient escort. Simultaneously, as he exited the villa, units of the invaders from the opposite direction came up from a short distance away in the middle of the night after a forced march. Hearing that the villa had been deserted and sensing the vulnerability of Pavón's entire army, the rebels rested only a short time before pushing forward, entering the town just after dawn. Only a few miles farther south they found the centralists under Pavón in sound defensive positions ready for battle. At noon the rebel forces clashed with the rear guard of the centralists and quickly attacked its flanks. The rebels occupied a ditch and rested there while under both artillery and small-arms fire. The battle quickened in the afternoon as each side tried to organize assaults, neither army gaining a decisive advantage in intermittent hand-to-hand and disorderly fighting.

The "American" volunteers noted bitterly that they had done most of the heavy work as Canales positioned himself in the rear. Pavón's men charged repeatedly against the norteamericanos, who felt hard pressed enough to call for assistance from Canales. One or two hours into the fighting he came up but stayed out of range, as they recalled later, doing nothing other than to have his buglers sound the charge while dashing to and fro in the woods. In contrast, the gallant Zapata galloped forward and even attempted to direct the counterattack, to no avail because of language differences, so their advances remained irregular. Zapata also expressed disgust at the "cowardice" of Canales. The fighting occurred amid a dense chaparral, with dust and smoke obscuring the advantage gained by the rebels, who fell back to their original position in a ravine that afforded protection from the government's artillery, from which location they also turned back an infantry assault. The invaders countercharged and laid down effective rifle fire allowing them to hold their positions until the next morning.[26] At night Pavón moved his forces to still higher ground in the wooded area and began to contemplate his choices. Hungry, thirsty, and short of ammunition, the centralists lacked even superior knowledge of the terrain, but soon Pavón faced a more fundamental problem when his muleteers deserted in wholesale fashion, further depleting his supplies and spreading dissension in the ranks.

On the morning of the second, he decided to parlay with Canales. Pavón had the disadvantage of desperation and little to offer, but Canales of course had a proposal—if the suspension of hostilities could be extended, the rebel leader would dismiss the Texas contingent of his army. He sought in return nothing short of command of all the government forces of the villas del norte. Pavón (without authority) accepted this offer, but while he was engaging in this quasi-comic intrigue away from camp, his cavalry unit returned with really bad news. It had failed to make contact with any supply train, information that plunged the centralist army into further despair. Still hoping that he had a deal to suspend the fighting, Pavón broke camp and headed out under a civilian guide, who took the army on a circuitous route away from the road, marching single file with the cavalry in the rear in what amounted to a vain attempt to protect the ammunition. Word came from Canales to the government forces that hostilities would resume; to make matters worse the centralist army found itself traversing terrain cut by deep, barely passable ravines. Throughout the engagement the rebel army had commanded all the watering holes, and the government soldiers had gone without drink for thirty-six hours. When Pavón's command finally came upon some additional ponds, they bolted for them in disarray even in the face of enemy fire. Colonel Pavón then had no functioning army with which to fight and thus surrendered.[27] He had no way of knowing how close the "Americans" in the opposing army had come to quitting the fight and returning to Texas, so great had become their disgust for Canales. Pavón offered his sword as his army stacked arms. All the officers received "paroles," but an estimated four hundred soldiers remained as prisoners before accepting the offer to change sides. The rebels had suffered only about twenty casualties compared to 120 on the centralist side, including eighty-five deaths.[28]

The engagement south of Mier, sometimes referred to as the Battle of Alcantro, ended the hard fighting for the remainder of 1839 as the rebels moved slowly in contrast to their earlier pace.[29] News of the disasters at Guerrero and Mier spread rapidly among government leaders throughout Tamaulipas, Nuevo León, and Coahuila, as did speculation about the next targets. A debilitating and ongoing theme emerged too, one that accused rebel soldiers of brutal and vicious behavior toward innocent civilians, including women.[30] In Matamoros, Canalizo issued a pronouncement to his army confessing that he had erred in assuming that peace had come to the region and expressing shock at the outright treason of Anaya, Canales ("an ignominious ingrate"), and Zapata for recruiting norteamericanos and even fighting under the Texas flag on

Mexican soil. Canalizo declared that the conflict no longer concerned political differences but instead amounted to a defense of property and indeed even national independence. The army must have tired of his bravado by then, made worse since as commanding general he offered no real insight into the next object of the invaders nor their size and strength.[31] The governors of Nuevo León and Coahuila, soon learning about events along the river, exchanged messages indicating that the invaders, numbering between eight hundred and twelve hundred, had fallen back to the town of Mier and speculating that both Matamoros and Monterrey would be attacked next. Equally disturbing, reports circulated that federalists in Monterrey had gathered, shouting gritos of rebellion once again and proclaiming the expected appearance of the rebel armies. The centralist leaders in the capital renewed their efforts to put military preparations in order, rounding up provisions and committing to joint operations.[32]

News spread with equivalent speed to Texas, where the Houston *Telegraph* praised the "Texian adventurers," predicted the fall of Monterrey and Saltillo, and speculated that the next of their "conquests" would be Matamoros. This "apparently rash and imprudent expedition may eventually terminate in the downfall of the present Mexican dynasty," gushed the newspaper.[33] *La Brisa* in Matamoros found an easy scapegoat and made a demand for inquiry into the performance of Pavón, believing that "mysterious maneuvering" and not force of arms had led to his defeat. His effort to lure Canales to the side of the government tainted Pavón with images of duplicity and a lack of patriotism. The paper then attempted to outdo Canalizo in hyperbole: "Our properties, the fruits of the labors of our entire lives, are threatened by rapacious and ambitious foreigners" who seek possession of our "fertile countryside where we were born and which we have cultivated with our own hands and fertilized with our own sweat. . . . We will concentrate all our resources and forces to fling back to the other side of the river a few knaves who have come to insult us." Rather than submit, Mexicans would unite and "go to Texas and regain the beautiful province from the usurping domination of the pirates who occupy it."[34]

The alcalde of the port city added his own diatribe in the form of a November 8 circular directed to his "fellow citizens" and provided a glimpse into how the wealthy and powerful viewed the social origins of the rebel soldiers. Throughout these times unemployment ran especially high among the mestizo population, who then frequently found livelihood as something akin to soldiers of fortune.[35] Jorge López de Lara reflected a conservative perspective in describing the rebels as "a few unnatural [and infamous] Mexicans" who commenced again their "ignominious activities" at a time when order, law, and constitutional reform offered so much hope. Worse still, of course, these "bandidos" solicited the assistance of our outright enemies who reopened the wounds of the recent past. These "horrendous criminals," by making common cause with "vile adventurers" from Texas, had in effect awarded that republic a form of legitimacy and now sought the separate, independent status of another part of Mexican territory. They should all be driven east of the Sabine River (which signified the Texas boundary with the United States). Those who united "with such villains are not Mexicans. We do not share a common blood with such as these." All patriots must step forward in defense of "the integrity of Mexican territory."[36]

Canales, having paused at Camargo, south of Mier, could not resist replying to all these allegations; he attempted to clarify his intentions in an eleven-point proclamation of his own. Under the title "General in Chief of the Federal Army," he acknowledged that continued resistance to the "so called Government of Mexico" could easily be construed as socially irresponsible for prolonging the "horrors of civil war." In that context, the prologue continued, those who fought for the "cause of the people" of the "three States of the frontier" had come together to articulate their views. The proclamation began innocuously with a claim that any and all governments could endorse—security of the frontier came first. From there the document moved in the opposite and more truly revolutionary direction by declaring that all those who opposed the cause would lose their property and that during the time when the rebels overthrew the existing government, power would pass directly to Canales himself as general in chief. Support for the centralist authorities amounted to assistance provided to the "enemies of liberty," and those holding government positions must "recant" in favor of transferring power to the federalists. Everyone had to choose immediately between the current regime and the revolution—those who failed to embrace the "cause of the People" beginning three days after publication of this pronouncement would lose their opportunity to do so. Citizens had to make declarations of support in an "open and unambiguous manner" or be considered opponents of the cause of liberty. The proclamation also called for the establishment of national militia units and envisioned a new government for the three states (Coahuila, Nuevo León, and Tamaulipas) soon but at an unspecified time.[37] The following day Canales added to his justification for continuing the revolution, emphasizing the failures of the Supreme Government to provide security for the frontier residents against rampaging Indians.[38]

Unfortunately for those who marched with Canales, these words did not spark aid of any kind from anywhere in the northeastern states. Only one place gave evidence of supporting the rebel cause. An official of the national government while on a mission of chasing "indios bárbaros" found that he could not enlist additional support because citizens in the Cadereyta area remained committed to federalist principles.[39] Some federalists expressed optimism about additional recruits coming from the villas del norte,[40] but the rebels had no means of publishing the Camargo proclamation, and no new federalist gritos rang out in any of the three states. Canales also yielded to his irresistible attraction to debate, replying to a letter from Canalizo and detailing additional complaints against the national government. Cheekily, the rebel commander charged the centralists with "placing us at the mercy of the Texans, as well as ignoring frontier security and trampling the rights of the people." The government's own policies created this revolution, he concluded.[41] Canales in effect wasted time on argumentation instead of making more decisive military movements of the kind that had carried the day at Guerrero and Mier. Impatient with this inactivity, his army began melting away. Ross and some of his regulars headed back to the Texas capital, arriving there on November 15.[42] The centralists remained securely hunkered down in both Matamoros and Monterrey and spent their days tinkering with fortifications and shoring up the morale of their troops while the invaders dawdled. Tamaulipas governor José Antonio Quintero in the state capital railed against the seductions of the invaders in a circular to his fellow Tamaulipecos on November 15, but he reflected a spirit of optimism regarding the prospects for restoring "peace and order."[43] Fellow governor (of Nuevo León) J. de Jesús D. y Prieto also remained unruffled as he discounted reports that Anaya would make a maritime move to invest Matamoros.[44] On December 11 *La Concordia* in Ciudad Victoria published a letter calling for everyone to "abandon the spirit of party" and declared that the current national government was "known to favor the interests" of Tamaulipas.[45]

The invaders moved in such a desultory manner as to provoke no alarming reports even regarding their exact whereabouts, though officials knew of continued activity on the Rio Grande and issued orders to intercept forces that might threaten the capitals of Nuevo León or Coahuila. The governor in Monterrey nevertheless expressed certainty that the next major scene of battle would indeed be Matamoros.[46] That expectation did materialize, in no small part because of a major shift in the centralist military effort as a new leader came to the fore with plans to end the resistance altogether. The government in Mexico City at last released Mariano Arista from the other duties that had delayed his arrival since his May 1839 appointment as commanding general of the Auxiliary Division of the North. Shortly after taking field command in December, he had demonstrated a new, more spirited style, letting it be known that "half-way measures" of defense would not suffice.[47] Above all else a man of action, under the guise of a conservative pronunciamiento opposing military and clerical reform, in 1833 Arista had led his army on a circuitous march from the south, skirting Mexico City via forced loans and impressed supplies until it reached the mining district of Guanajuato. There he seized in excess of 100,000 pesos from a British silver mining company and forced an additional "loan," with the entire proceeds distributed in part to his followers, while keeping a sufficient amount to finance a temporary exile in the United States. Notably, Arista brazenly denied making any personal gain and did in fact come down somewhat consistently against the breakdown of social

order.[48] In contrast with the waffling Canalizo, who had been the leading centralist military figure during 1839, Arista brought an aura of
reckoning both in manner and activity.

The new commander lost little time before joining in the denun-
ciations of the invaders. He wrote to the inhabitants of all three
northeastern states in a proclamation issued from Saltillo after he had
inspected the other two state capitals. Arista sounded familiar themes
but in a decidedly confident manner. He came on behalf of the Supreme
Government to "protect your homes" and "to inflict punishment on
the traitors" headed by Canales. They "are not federalists. **They are
thieves! They are barbarous Indians!**" Their real leader, the clever,
"indolent," "nefarious" traitor Juan Pablo Anaya, had ingratiated himself with and duped Canales. The invaders came without resources
or a sense of honor. In Mexico they attracted only "the most ignorant
rancheros" pursuing not principle but plunder and would not be con-
tent until they had taken all the land and forced its residents beyond
the mountains. The steadfast great majority of citizens would support
Arista in shouting "the terrible cry of **war to the death**." He had come
"on behalf of humanity so that you will not become victims of this
most treasonous and treacherous invasion. . . . **When a People rally
together, it is strong and invincible**. You have but to wish it and this
band of assassins will disappear like smoke blown to the north."[49] [bold
text in original source]

With this publication Arista returned to Monterrey amid reports
that the rebel army under Canales intended to move quickly, had indeed
occupied Reynosa, Cadereyta, and other river towns, and arrived
within a league of Matamoros.[50] The invaders had operated along the
Rio Grande for over two months without a discernible setback—but
also without taking the major prize, Matamoros.

Furthermore, the rebellion during these last months of 1839 had
lost its way in political terms. Zeal for federalism did not manifest itself
as it had during earlier stages, and the most populous places, including the capital cities of Coahuila (Saltillo), Nuevo León (Monterrey),
and Tamaulipas (Ciudad Victoria), as well as the most significant port
town (Matamoros), all remained in the hands of the centralists, albeit

insecurely should they face focused and determined threats from the rebels. Such a possibility, though, was withering away as segments of the invading federalist forces gave up and returned to Texas while others whiled away their time, harboring a spirit of discontent. The loss of military initiative in the days immediately following successful attacks against the river towns made it difficult to sustain morale or a sense of purpose. The primary leader, Antonio Canales, had already placed intrigue in pursuit of his own interests above advancing the original political cause of restoring a federalist government, amid innumerable suggestions that plunder replaced principle among his followers as well. More worrisome still for the rebel cause, the decision to recruit volunteers from the Republic of Texas, the acknowledged enemy of Mexico, while understandable given the scarcity of declining resources, gave off a scent of treason. Their entry also made the rebel forces even more combustible, given their rowdy character and ambition for either glory or plunder or both. Finally, though the rebels could be excused for an absence of prophetic insight, they had no way of knowing that they would more than meet their match in the person of Mariano Arista, who had replaced the irresolute Canalizo and would soon become well known as "el tigre del norte."

CHAPTER 5

TEXAS AND THE "REPUBLIC OF THE RIO GRANDE"

FOLLOWING THEIR STRIKING SUCCESSES AT GUERRERO AND Mier in November of 1839, the rebels encountered once again first a sag and then a disaster. And once again the same factors accounted for their ruin. Rivalry for leadership and its inevitable consequences—namely deterioration of the strength of the army, loss of singleness of purpose, and thus delays, squandering of momentum, and doubts about their prospects—all bedeviled their fortunes. The rapid movement that had served them so well at Guerrero and again at Mier just seemed to fade away. Furthermore, during those battles Zapata had become disgusted with Canales, and for some unstated reasons the volunteers from Texas voted out Ross, who soon set off for home along with other failed candidates for leadership roles and a significant number from the ranks of the Anglo Texas contingent. One report had them bound for Austin to raise additional troops, but malcontents such as these could hardly be expected to produce more support.[1]

Initially, the prospects for rebel success seemed quite favorable. The invaders encountered no resistance as they moved first to Camargo, then to Reynosa, and finally to within striking distance of Matamoros by December 6. The rebels encamped, entrenched, and sought to lure the centralist defenders out into an assault in the open, expecting an attack at any time. After two days Canales dispatched his cavalry and succeeded in driving enemy pickets back into town. On the morning of the ninth, another mounted force, composed equally of Anglo Texans and Mexicans from the villas del norte, launched an attack against a battery consisting of three pieces of artillery and one hundred defenders, but it retired after only fifteen minutes because of anticipated centralist reinforcements from the city that did not actually materialize. The cavalry then rode around the outskirts hoping to lure the defenders into battle, but without success.[2] Officers of the Supreme Government considered this action (led by Zapata) as their victory, but so far the rebels at least held together. Two of them reported that "the greatest harmony prevailed amongst the Anglo-federalists and Mexicans, and we are happy to say that the volunteers from east of the Rio Grande have conducted themselves with the utmost propriety since they have been in the Mexican republic." However, these two former participants contradicted themselves regarding the supposed unity among the besiegers. "The Anglo-federalists who were at Matamoras [sic] would have attacked the place if their force had been five hundred men, without the aid of the Mexican federals and with a strong probability of success."[3] In fact, neither the defenders nor their superior officers elsewhere in the northeastern states felt significantly threatened. Canalizo consistently displayed very little aggressiveness, but during the previous year he had worked assiduously to perfect the defenses of Matamoros.

Furthermore, Canales soon lost his boldness. Sources from within Matamoros convinced him that the centralists could not be successfully assaulted, estimating that they marshalled as many as 1,800 troops. A narrative left by one of the invaders from Texas recounted other reasons for the timidity of the invaders. According to Anson G. Neill (sometimes given as "Neal"), Canales would not take action without consulting his horoscope, doing battle only if his divination produced the image of a "warlike bird or animal" as opposed to a lamb or a dove. In any case, the invaders suffered what Mariano Arista on December 13 described as a defeat at Matamoros.[4] Canales became alarmed about a potential attack by a much superior force and on the sixteenth "stampeded" his men (in the words of Benjamin F. Neal) in a forced nighttime march onto the Monterrey road before eventually encountering the enemy. The rebels hastily threw up a breastwork in anticipation of a "close engagement" but received long-distance cannon fire instead, with neither side coming into view of the other. Canales used four cannons captured from Pavón to reply in kind, and the centralists moved off toward the capital city of Nuevo León the following day. The rebels followed and occupied the town of Cadereyta, ten leagues from Monterrey, on December 26. Meeting no resistance there, Canales moved his army again, taking up positions outside the capital city, where they withstood fire from a heavy mortar that did no damage.

Officials of the Supreme Government never felt threatened by the rebel forces outside Monterrey. From the perspective of the government, Nuevo León governor J. de Jesús D. y Prieto expressed complete confidence for two fundamental reasons. First, he argued that the composition of the besiegers would compromise their chances. The governor's sources persuaded him that the enemy had the character of a rabble more than an army, being composed of "criminals and other profligate men who in order to elude punishment for their deeds have taken refuge among the enemies of the Nation." Secondly, Prieto informed his counterpart in Coahuila that Mariano Arista himself now commanded the government forces in person. The governor wrote that Arista's plan of operations would "give the enemy a certain and decisive blow."[5]

Yet, for a while the centralists seemed no more decisive than their enemy. When both infantry and cavalry did emerge from town to offer battle, Canales refused to be baited because he believed that Arista had kept a strong force in reserve. Remaining once again a safe distance from the firing along with his "American" bodyguard, the rebel commander finally committed Zapata's cavalry against a similar unit of the defenders. Zapata quickly routed the enemy, Neal recounted, because "his very name was sufficient to do this." However, both sides lost men and horses to desertion. In the midst of the fray some of the besiegers who had formerly served with Pavón's forces made for the city in order to join again the side of the government, and they laid plans unsuccessfully to return and betray Canales. When this plot failed to materialize, the rebel commander nonetheless had enough and began a retreat toward the Rio Grande with Zapata's cavalry serving as the formidable rearguard and the only steadfast unit amid "the utmost disorder and confusion." Canales, "terrified out of his wits," according to Neal, traveled sixty miles before he halted in a mountain town but without his guard of North Americans, who had fled back to Texas. In relative security Canales retired to east of the Rio Grande in the vicinity of Guerrero.[6] Other witnesses and participants added details and largely affirmed the basic outlines of the story as told by Neal but without the benefit of hindsight or the same bitter recrimination. Canales actually received some praise for his commitment to the cause and his efforts to provide for his troops.[7]

Other area rebel forces did not fare well either. Arista reported that on January 7, 1840, government forces commanded by Juan José Galan, though numbering no more than one hundred, fought off an attack led by "El Faccioso" Francisco Vidaurri at the head of 270 men carrying rifles as they entered the villa of Gigedo. Galan inflicted a dozen casualties and remained in possession of the town at the time he informed his superiors of the engagement.[8] With excessive optimism the newspaper in Ciudad Victoria declared that Canales had at last been defeated and that the underlying conflict between centralists and federalists must end, if for no other reason than to head off the threat of a Texas takeover. The cycle of depredation emanating from the decrees of the "so-called Chief, General of Generals or other titles taken on by Canales" had concluded. "The Guerrero genius has exited from this country. The movement leading to this barbarous tyranny has reached its end."[9]

In Texas enthusiasm for intervening in the affairs of the northeastern states of Mexico had waned as well. Perhaps the most astute observer there to summarize events or to render a forecast, José Antonio Navarro from Béxar, wrote to an unnamed "public representative" in the Texas capital, relaying news that had come from individuals "of consequence" on the Rio Grande. Well connected with both Anglo Texas and Mexican friends, politicians, and business associates, the forty-four-year-old Navarro certainly wrote from a position of great knowledge and authority. His analysis bears repeating verbatim:

A large chain of circumstances and a combination of late events in Mexico, render it impossible that [Mexican] troops are coming [to Texas] . . . in a regular invasion—for a considerable number of Federalists forces are yet scattered about through the States of Tamaulipas New Leon & Coahuila. But I do not in the least doubt that the triumph obtained by the Centralists over Vidauri [*sic*] near the Rio Grande, and the retreat of Canales from Monterrey where he was defeated by the Government troops under General Arista, have inspired the Centralists with the bold idea of invading Texas, or at all events of coming as far as this City, where they think they can triumph with ease and reap heavy booty—

General Arista has about 1500 men this side of Monterrey—Canalizo has 1000 in Matamoros and at the intermediate points there are about 2000 men—You will see that these forces are insignificant for an invasion—but sufficient for a sudden blow—a blow perfectly in accordance with the character of such Generals as Arista & Canalizo who act without system, or foresight & regardless of consequences—But the blow o[n]ce struck & we, broke up & perhaps slaughtered, will take but little pleasure in the revenge that may follow—I trust that the [Texas] Government will take immediate steps to relieve us from our threatened & dangerous position.[10]

He may have underestimated the shrewdness of Arista and most certainly exaggerated the likelihood of a "blow" against Texas of any kind, given the state of war weariness and wariness in Mexico. At the same time Navarro stated accurately the desperation of the rebel cause. Others in Texas argued for an end to support for Canales. His offer of ample pay and a share of the booty made the editor of one newspaper incredulous at the naivety of any future recruits: "Who would not enlist under such a chivalrous hero, inspired by such patriotic motives? Go ahead, ye loafers. Here is a chance for an overflowing purse or—a dungeon. Go ahead, and let your motto be, 'Neck or nothing.'"[11]

Canales chose this unlikely moment—a time of defeat, demoralization, and waning prospects—to turn toward politics and not just to the mundane either. Instead, he and some followers declared the birth of a new nation, what many historians refer to as "the Republic of the Rio Grande."[12] As a concept, the potential for a separatist nation had been bandied about for some time, but prior to the last days of 1839 mostly outside the boundaries of the Republic of Mexico and by individuals with one common attribute—none of them were Mexicans. The first mention of creating a new republic occurred in August 1839, in the form of a letter to the *Telegraph and Texas Register* from "the Louisianan." In a rambling manner he disparaged public political sophistication in Mexico but called for a convention to achieve two major and related outcomes—a separate nation for all the northern states extending from Tamaulipas to the Californias, and recognition of Texas independence. This correspondent also misidentified Anaya as the agent promoting such a scheme.[13] Even before that letter actually appeared, the same newspaper reported that Francisco Vidaurri y Villaseñor as the federalist governor of Coahuila had proposed northern separatism and alliance with the Republic of Texas. It claimed that the cause of an independent northern nation would move forward with or without Texas support and further observed that the northern rebels had no choice but to pursue their own way because federalism had failed as a national movement. A week later the same paper asserted that sources in San Antonio had reported that "the states of Tamaulipas, Coahuila and Nuevo León have DECLARED THEIR INDEPENDENCE OF MEXICO!" and sent agents to negotiate with the government of Texas.[14]

Canales certainly had the capacity to combine simultaneous political and military maneuvering, as shown previously when he paused his descent down the river toward Matamoros on November 10, 1839, to clarify the goals that underlay his war making. At that moment he declared that the "cause of the people" centered around reestablishing the "federal system," the means for which would include an interim grant of authority to the "general in chief" (himself). Although unclear as to how the popular will would be ascertained, Canales stated that one of the final steps would subsequently be the creation of a "Government . . . for these three states." Thus, he had muddled the purposes of the rebellion. It had become a return to the past (federalism) that somehow opened the way for a new paradigm (a separate government for Tamaulipas, Nuevo León, and Coahuila).[15] Two days earlier Matamoros alcalde Jorge López de Lara charged that the "vile" rebellion had two "ignominious" goals—recognition of Texas independence and "pursuit of the independence of yet another precious part of Mexican territory."[16] At the national level government officials concurred but went further, ascribing the renewed rebellion to a plot by the most bitter enemies of Mexico. As the minister of the interior wrote on November 26, 1839, "The adventurers of Texas intend to form a new Republic in Mexican territory."[17] Actually, some of the veterans from Texas later asserted that they had an even more ambitious goal. From the moment the "cow-boys" enlisted, their motive had been, as one stated it: "the union of the Northern States of Mexico, to Texas as one large Indepent. Govt."[18]

Along with its diatribe against the rebels for extending suffering by renewing war and for enlisting inglorious Texans in their ignoble cause of separatism, the centralist newspaper in Matamoros also subjected Canales and his followers to ridicule. "Lic. Bastard D. Antonio Canales" had returned, united the villas del norte, and given Guerrero a new name: "the city of Canales, now established as the metropolis of the new republic of North America." The editor continued, "D. Jesús Cárdenas has been named constitutional governor elected by an absolute plurality of his two brothers-in-law who by right of conquest take on the presidency and vice presidency of his famous republic."[19] Either *El Ancla* had insider information or extraordinary powers of prophecy because it announced (albeit derisively) a new independent republic in northeastern Mexico before it had been declared and also correctly named its president (Cárdenas), secretary (José María Carbajal), and military chief (Antonio Canales), all indeed related by marriage.[20]

It seems unlikely that anyone could have predicted Canales's next move. On January 28, 1840, from Mier where he found refuge following his disastrous campaign against Monterrey and subsequent pell-mell flight back to the Rio Grande, Canales made a proposal to his chief adversary, Mariano Arista. Having been assured that Arista favored measures "to calm our differences" and recognized that our "unhappy country" suffered from repeated changes in its government, Canales announced: "I am disposed to end this war." His brazen approach requested an audience to persuade Arista that "we are not fanatics," as agents of the government had asserted. The rebel leader sought "personal protection and security" and invited his opponent to come forward to the Rio Grande area and see for himself how the people had been "reduced to misery" by Santa Anna's confiscation of property three years earlier as the Mexican army prepared to march into Texas. His rebellion, wrote Canales, stemmed from a common conviction "that nothing could ever be hoped for from Mexico" in the way of restoring the area to its former prosperity. In short, the revolution in the northeastern states had been a reflection of "our desperation," but the country now wanted peace. The offer from Canales ended by proposing an accord to enable a conference between the two leaders.[21]

Arista wasted no time in replying. Writing from Cadereyta, he also minced no words and made no concessions. He found the Canales letter to be nothing short of an insult to the "*legitimate Government* which by duty and by principle I *respect and defend*." He saw the Canales proposal as but another ploy to further the revolution. Arista stated unequivocally that the rebels had no role in setting forth the terms for peace. As for Canales, "you remain a disgraceful traitor to your country and to its interests." Arista made it abundantly clear that he had no respect for his opponent's character: "I know you," he said, therefore to move forward in the direction of peace, "you must be humble, courteous, and governed by reason." Arista would tolerate no further "misleading submission" by Canales, no more "sham" proposals. If the people of the frontier continued to suffer, Canales bore the blame for prolonging a revolution that had no result other than opening the way for further plundering by indios bárbaros and for other forms of anarchy. "Be assured that I understand completely: *you are culpable for the sadness and miseries that you lament. . . .* Why do you have this treasonous agreement with the Texans, enemies of your Country and ambitious for the land that you inherited from your ancestors who inhabited these Villas?" Arista declared that there would be no further exchanges until Canales submitted completely to the Supreme Government and dismissed his foreign contingent.[22]

With no prospect even for a negotiated cease-fire, the separatist agenda moved forward. On February 2 in Guerrero editor C. José Gonzales Cuellar issued a prospectus for a new newspaper defending the principles of the rebellion of the northeastern states. Its byline countered Arista's views of the origins of the conflict, declaring "the governing power of Mexico has opened the door of anarchy and is pursuing it to the point of being devoured." There could be no doubt as to the ongoing status of war and peace—all negotiations for an accord had been denounced by Arista and stood now "closed and without effect." Operating under protection of "the army of these villas" the new periodical would be called *El Correo del Rio Bravo del Norte*. Its editor promised to focus on the evils caused by hostile "savages" and to "make known the state of the revolution on this frontier." It also existed to publish the acts and decrees of the "provisional government" along with communications between its military leaders and the "governing powers of Mexico," should negotiations be reopened.[23] Some seven years later a veteran recalled the pomp and circumstance also associated with this nation-building. According to Andrew Neill, "A Federal Flag was planted in the center of the square [of Guerrero]. The soldiers all marched under it, kissing it as they passed; which was considered as an oath of alligiance [*sic*] to the new Govt.—A great Ball was given in the House of Zapata," though many could not attend for want of clothing.[24]

On February 8 Canales, styling himself this time as the general in chief of the "Conventional Army," wrote to his troops, the "soldiers of the people," expressing gratitude that they had sworn to maintain "at all risks" the "provisional government of these States." Canales assured his men that "the day of tyranny is left far behind." Their enemies wished "to revive old and worm-eaten privileges" as well as to reassert bygone ideas, to "disarm the citizens," and to "undermine" the "natural principles" of liberty and equality before the law." The "groveling policy" of the central government sought to divide and rule, to provoke foreign wars, to protect the "privileged classes," to "depreciate the national income, to extinguish patriotism among Mexicans and to garrison the ports and capitals of the republic, leaving defenseless their frontiers." Freedom-loving people in the northeastern states had launched the current rebellion in the belief that if a "part" of the nation organized promptly, "the others will follow your example. Nothing is accomplished in a minute." "Let us continue with constancy," knowing that small beginnings at other times and places had established successful nations. He ended with a ringing appeal. "Soldiers: let us continue being long suffering and virtuous, let us not forget . . . discipline and subordination, and the happiness of our country will be the reward of our efforts."[25]

If the Canales proclamation held out even a slim prospect of hope, it set forth but one possible avenue to success—a provisional government for the northern states represented the only alternative to submission since the federalist cause had disappeared everywhere else. By example, this union of Tamaulipas, Nuevo León, and Coahuila might encourage other areas to follow. President Cárdenas set out to address the most pressing challenge—to feed, supply, and enroll soldiers in a desperate effort to field an army and thus keep his cause alive. He had begun issuing decrees in Guerrero on February 16, declaring that the people had the right to bear arms "for the defense of their liberty, property, and interests."[26] On the twenty-ninth Cárdenas wrote friends in Texas announcing that he had been "honored" with the presidency of a new "provisional government" for the "frontier," states which had suffered so much "tyranny" in the recent past. He sought to persuade José Antonio Navarro to function as his agent in negotiating a formal alliance with the Republic of Texas.[27]

The next day he offered to commission John T. Price, a veteran of recent engagements, on behalf of what Cárdenas then styled as the provisional Government of the "Mexican Republic, Frontier of the North." He authorized the commissioner to travel back to Texas recruiting fresh volunteers. The president quite optimistically set forth conditions on the new recruits, including length of service (six months), promises of payment, and a limitation on their inclination to overthrow officers by holding new elections. No such actions could be taken except for "legitimate cause" and in accordance with the military laws of Mexico. Acknowledging that any who enlisted would do so on faith that the new government would succeed, Cárdenas provided rules for the distribution of any "booty that may be taken from the troops of the centralists." He stated that all munitions would remain the possession of the rebel government.[28]

Little wonder that critics saw Cárdenas as a dreamer; however, he found some believers when he came personally to the Victoria (Texas) area in pursuit of recruits. No one seemed to notice that the president had changed the name of his government once again, this time to the "Federal Government of Mexico." Otherwise, Cárdenas presented his case in a candid manner. The army of this new "provisional government" had "met with a disaster," rendering its officials "no longer able to sustain themselves in their own country" and now dependent on the "sympathy" of the "Texian government" and its people. He knew how to stir up Texas. The "enemy of the liberal party of Mexico, are the implacable enemies of Texas—they are the same who shed the blood of Texians in the Alamo and at Labahia—they are the same who now wish to reenact those scenes of horror and barbarity—can there be a doubt that Texas will afford auxiliaries against such enemies?" Leaders of the public meeting in Victoria passed resolutions of support and offered many toasts to Cárdenas and his cause,[29] but he suffered some reverses. Navarro rejected an appointment as agent to the Republic of Texas, pleading ill health and other commitments. He also advised that Texas would not likely "intermeddle officially" with Cárdenas in his capacity as "president of the Free Frontier States of the Mexican Republic," but instead would stay aloof from all such "domestic" matters. Navarro stated that Anaya had received this same message during his courtship of the Republic of Texas.[30] Almost on cue, Anaya in a March 20 letter to a US newspaper reiterated his staunch support for restoring the Constitution of 1824 (as opposed to establishing a new, separatist nation) as the only honorable cause.[31]

The centralists within northeastern Mexico gave some attention to the nascent nation-building by Canales and Cárdenas. Arista in early April spread the welcome news that the "revolutionary government" had moved across the Rio Grande to Laredo and farther east to the La Bahia area.[32] Most other reports by the centralists mentioned the separatist government only to deride it. Soon after concocting this "ridiculous government" as if by "volcanic explosion," these self-important "bandoleros" deserted their posts along the Rio Grande and became once again "vagabonds" fleeing for their lives. "Lic. Traitor and the infamous servants who formed the cliques of his dream world" would soon be tamed by the higher powers of the region, assured the editor of *El Ancla* in Matamoros.[33] A few days later this same journal described the constitutional activities coming from Guerrero as merely a "burlesque of dolts," but it worried that some in the outside world reported as fact that the states of Tamaulipas, Nuevo León, and Coahuila had declared themselves independent from the Republic of Mexico and formed a separate government. It traced fictitious rumors to the machinations of Francisco Vidaurri in New Orleans, adding that these ludicrous stories named Chihuahua, Durango, New Mexico, and the Californias as members of an "immense confederation." Apparently, these outlandish reports had reached all the way to London. Certainly, the article concluded, one place could be counted on to embrace such a "grandiose vision"—Texas.[34]

The Matamoros newspaper could not have been more correct, but what it asserted as speculation had already begun to take shape. Of course, the news in Texas as always focused on the prospects of an invasion from Mexico, and some awareness had developed that Texas intervention on the side of the rebels of the northeastern states gave Mexican patriots a powerful rallying cause. By early March Texas meddling had added a new twist in the form of imperial schemes to establish a new "republic of North Mexico," extending beyond the three northeastern states all the way to the Pacific and including in between the departments of Zacatecas, Durango, Sinaloa, Sonora, Nuevo Mexico, and the Californias.[35]

For his part Cárdenas found it impossible even to settle on a name for his cause. In February and March, he referred to himself as president of, simply, the "provisional government," then alternatively, the "Mexican Republic, Frontier of the North," or confusingly, the "Federal Government of Mexico," and, finally, the "Free Frontier States of the Mexican Republic." Strikingly, given his nomenclature struggle, Cárdenas himself never used the term that came into vogue in Texas, first used in publication on March 18, 1840: "Republic of Rio Grande." Not only did the chief executive not use that name, it never even once appeared in print or in script in Mexico, whether by the representatives of the Supreme Government or by the rebels.[36] Instead, citing as sources "some Americans and Mexicans" from Monclova who had witnessed events in Laredo, the *Texas Sentinel* in Austin reported as the "latest news from the West" that a convention had been held to select officials of the new "Republic of the Rio Grande." If such a meeting actually occurred, its participants did not have to travel far to congregate since half those named as officeholders were related by marriage. The Texas newspaper listed the following by position:

President—Jesús Cárdenas, former political chief of the state of Tamaulipas

Army commander—Antonio Canales

Lieutenant Governor—Juan Nepomuceno Molano, who formerly held the same post in Tamaulipas

Delegate from Coahuila—Francisco Vidaurri y Villaseñor, former governor of Coahuila

Delegate from Nuevo León—Manuel Marina del Llano, former governor of Nuevo León

Secretary—José María Carbajal

The story continued with details that bore significance for Texas. The rebel government sought volunteers from Texas and the United States and offered bounty lands as payment in a most generous manner. It intended to finance the conflict by expropriating church property. All this no doubt seemed attractive to residents of the Lone Star republic, but the troubling issue of the boundary promised to undermine any easy accord—the new Mexican republic claimed territory as far east as the Nueces and Medina Rivers. At the same time reports in Texas maintained that the Republic of the Rio Grande somehow intended to include Zacatecas, Durango, Chihuahua, and New Mexico within its limits. More troubling still, the *Texas Sentinel* acknowledged that Mariano Arista, in command of several units, had begun a march to suppress this newest insurrection, with nothing to prevent a reconquest of Texas other than three companies of "Texian troops" stationed west of San Antonio. In fact, the centralists defeated both Zapata and Canales in separate engagements at the end of March (see chapter 7), casting further gloom among the ranks and supporters of the latest rebellion.[37]

From Béxar, Navarro on March 23 took up the phrase "Republic of the Rio Grande" and sought to elicit support by countering the damage done in Texas relations regarding the boundary issue, which he claimed to be "in a more historical sense" than as a matter of current policy. Navarro wrote letters "in favor of the poor Federals of the frontiers of Mexico" and criticized the Lamar administration for "refusing to assist" the rebels, thereby implicitly trusting in "the benevolence" of "the aristocrats of Mexico." "God grant," he continued "that this conduct of our Government may not prove a sorrow to our Texas."[38] Advocates of supporting Cárdenas and Canales quickly attempted to counter the damage done regarding the boundary issue. On April 1 the *Texas Sentinel* reported having seen the newspaper published in Guerrero on behalf of the separatists and praised it for "speaking boldly and fearlessly upon the subject of central usurpation." Further, the "temporary" military reverses suffered by the rebels would soon give way to "ultimate success." Coahuila delegate Vidaurri, now back in San Antonio, chimed in with the assurance that he accepted the Rio Grande as the proper boundary line.[39]

Even if others accepted this verbal accord on the boundary, obstacles loomed regarding relations with Texas. In a letter to Navarro dated April 17, 1840, George Fisher, himself a veteran of many failed rebellions and plots in both Europe and the Americas, spelled out several reasons for caution, despite generally endorsing the would-be republic. "I do not comprehend how Cárdenas can exercise the duties of President of the 'Republic of Rio Grande,' being in the territory of our Republic, vanquished, or dispersed, by Arista."[40] The boundary issue did not easily or quickly go away. A Houston newspaper expressed reservations that troops recruited in support of the war against the centralists would remain for any significant amount of time in Texas lest future claims cite previous right of possession. It viewed the entire enterprise of the separatist government with suspicion, asserting doubts as to whether its leaders would prove "worthy of the enjoyment of freedom and of liberal institutions" and describing the Mexican soldiers under Canales as "miserable" for failing to prevail already. "They are too imbecile, indolent, and cowardly, ever to make good their independence . . . and instead of calling for aid, as they are continually doing, they should be taught that the gods help those only who are willing to help themselves."[41]

These expressions of public opinion reflected the wavering position of the Lamar administration. From his self-styled "refuge" in Victoria, Texas, Cárdenas made his best case for support in a letter to the president of the Republic of Texas on April 8. He began with flattery of the Texas government and its people for their "philanthropic ideas" and asked for permission to stay "for the length of time necessary to arrange the affairs" of his administration. These included "establishment of peace and commercial relations" with Texas and negotiation for "aid in order that this government may resume the war against the government of Mexico." Cárdenas argued that his cause should be supported in light of "the sympathies which unite" his country with Lamar's and "the similarity of the cause which both sustain." His case depended on agreement that the "interests of both countries" promoted mutual support.[42]

Lamar made but little attempt to mold the views of the public. He expressed himself in print in a broadside on March 14, admonishing deserters from the Texas army, including (without stating so directly) those who had fled their posts to join in the federalist wars. He expressed "feelings of deep regret and mortification" for having to confront this issue at all, stating that he intended his warning to substitute for actual prosecution of the offenders who had deserted their posts since the penalty could well have been a death sentence. "Hitherto" no punishments at all had been dealt for reasons of "humanity" and with a view toward "clemency." He concluded with an offer—all who voluntarily returned to duty would be guaranteed a pardon.[43] Lamar left implementation of policy to the diplomats and largely shied away from the public eye on the matter of the separatist government of northeastern Mexico. Officially, according to Secretary of State Abner S. Lipscomb, citizens and soldiers alike must adhere to "neutrality . . . in the contest between the government of [Mexico] and the Federalists," as the president had stated in an earlier proclamation.[44] Lamar also claimed to have disapproved actions by Ross and his command in leaving the ranks of the Texas army to serve in the federalist wars and also disavowed those "Anglo-Americans" who "united with" Mexican rebels in the spring of 1840.[45]

The most detailed if nonetheless evasive statement of the policy of the Republic of Texas came on April 4, 1840, in orders of the office of the Texas war department to William S. Fisher, commander of the frontier detachment stationed at Mission San José outside of San Antonio. Canales and all other representatives of "the Federal forces" should not "be permitted to organize or raise a force within our limits" for use in Mexico. "Protection" would be granted, "but not for the purpose of enabling [Canales] to prosecute the war here, or of preparing to renew it elsewhere." However, should the centralists pursue the rebels into Texas territory, "it will be an invasion of our rights, which we shall be bound to repel, and in such an event, the services of the Federal Army will be expected and accepted, to aid in repelling the invasion—but with the distinct understanding, that [such forces] though directly commanded by their own officers, . . . are under the orders of this [Texas] government." All who might serve in those instances would fight under the Texas flag. To skewer the "neutrality" policy of the Lamar administration even further, Canales "may be permitted to purchase supplies for their subsistence" while on Texas soil, "but unless we are invaded, he cannot be permitted to do more." Regarding even the feelings behind the policy, representatives of the Lamar administration attempted to hedge: "Those courtesies which may be due to Genl. Canalez [sic] and his officers, as Gentlemen, your own feelings will prompt you [Fisher] to assess."[46]

Lamar continued his public reticence on policy toward the separatists of northeastern Mexico throughout most of the year. Acting Secretary of State David G. Burnet on August 9 and the president himself on November 12, 1839, reported to Congress on efforts for the peaceful resolution of differences with the government of Mexico that included sending an "agent" to the national capital. This diplomatic move had no chance of success in that Texas officially sought not only the Rio Grande as the boundary but also its extension from El Paso to the Pacific. Lamar blustered that his patience for diplomacy had come to an end and that he intended to "extort" an agreement by force.[47] When he finally broke his silence specifically on relations with the northeastern rebels, it came as a retrospective near the end of 1840. Lamar made it clear that he had considered outright intervention and war but felt constrained by an empty treasury. Instead, he used "every effort which presented even a remote probability of success by pacific measures" to gain recognition of Texas independence, including direct negotiation and opening trade with "the Northern provinces." On the latter point, it seemed genuinely to escape him that such commerce provoked the Supreme Government because it lured the north into closer connection with Texas and violated national trade regulations. Finally, Lamar touted the utmost "forbearance I exercised when invited to make common cause with the Federal party, while assured of the acknowledgment of our independence in the event of the success of that party."[48]

The fiction of Texas neutrality also became apparent when questions arose as to reverse scenarios, i.e., Mexican support for insurrection by Indians, Tejanos, or slaves in the Lone Star republic. Indeed, Bustamante had ordered that a former Nacogdoches rebel against the Republic of Texas, Vicente Córdova, then in refuge in Matamoros, should be used as an auxiliary to the centralist army.[49] In the eyes of Texas, these acts amounted to simple aggression and justified meddling in the Mexican civil war. Thus, despite all the declarations of restraint by officials of the Texas government, President Cárdenas remained unhindered in his efforts to drum up support for the separatist cause. The practice of hands off regarding the raising of volunteers, munitions, and funding continued in the Republic of Texas throughout 1840. Civil war in northeastern Mexico could not have stayed alive without support for the rebellion from Texas.

In the end, the idea of a separate republic for the northeastern states represented but a phantom flirtation in statecraft. Support came primarily from the Republic of Texas as it latched onto any method of weakening the government of Mexico, at the minimum thereby forestalling actual prospects of reconquest. The more brazen aggressors conjured up aspirations of grand imperial schemes even at a time when Texas could barely sustain its own defense against threats not only from

Mexico but also from marauding Indians. Indeed, the very nationhood of the Republic of Texas hinged on its stubborn persistence through difficult times, restricted by an empty treasury and distracted by equally empty boasts of a powerful future, barely sustainable given the reality of its actual weakness, no matter how compelling to dreamers like its unstable president, M. B. Lamar. The northeastern federalists who conjured up a separate republic for its region had at least the merits of a desperate grasp for some kind of political entity that might catch on and spread amid times of genuine and widespread discontent. They also sounded some of the key notes of Mexican liberalism, including individualism, business enterprise, and even (however faintly) anticlericalism. Yet, in fact by early 1840 the federalist rebels lacked viable alternatives other than to make peace with a national government that had no incentive to cease firing since the rebellion had come so very near to collapse. The fact that these weary rebels held on to their fading prospects during the spring of 1840 and beyond serves as a testament to their commitment and perseverance.

CHAPTER 6

CENTRALIST VICTORIES, SPRING 1840

THE POLITICAL INTERLUDE DEVOTED TO GOVERNMENTAL affairs occurred during a lull in military action. Winter campaigning had resulted in such government successes that the rebels either dispersed or retreated all the way to east of the Rio Grande and farther still into Texas. Mariano Arista took stock of the situation from his headquarters at or near the capitals of Nuevo León and Coahuila and began moving in search of scattered rebel remnants in February 1840. Toward the end of the next month, the greatest prize he could have imagined fell into his hands because he had pressed his advantage and moved steadily east with probes consisting of main bodies of troops rather than just small advance units. Arista's move also benefited from citizen support, but perhaps most importantly, he himself took to the field rather than remaining in more comfortable, urban-based quarters. His presence seemed to embolden officers and men alike. Canales, meanwhile, collected his few remaining veterans and interspersed new volunteers from both Texas and the Mexican frontier as he moved back to west of the great river. Government informants provided repeated and accurate information regarding both his activities and those of President Jesús

Cárdenas among the river towns. Arista absorbed these reports about the "sublevados" and "foreign invaders" and assured Mexico City that this time he would "castigate them severely."[1] He also dispatched a unit to disrupt the "gobierno convencional" headed by Cárdenas.[2]

Thus, though the rebels from the region formed by the villas del norte had fought the Supreme Government for most of 1839, early in the next year they would discover what it meant to face a relentless effort like the one put forth by Arista. President Bustamante later excused previous government armies because of the need to move across large barren areas carrying their own supplies (albeit reduced) with no guarantee of reinforcements. However, he wrote, "no obstacle" discouraged Arista as he moved three different units in coordinated fashion with one purpose—to destroy rebel armies under Antonio Zapata and Lic. Antonio Canales once and forever. Not even a tantalizing note indicating a request for an armistice by the intrepid fighter Zapata deterred the unremitting commitment to military action of the general in chief of the Army of the North.[3] The rebels had to operate in the same spare environment, except that they had reduced baggage since they frequently functioned as guerrillas living off the land. That practice actually meant feeding and supplying themselves at the expense of local residents. With such a goal in mind, on March 23 Zapata came to the village of Morelos at the head of thirty cavalrymen (with a caballada of thirty-eight horses) seeking money, corn, fresh mounts, and other provisions. That place may have been chosen because, as a survivor later recalled, "Morelos was under Central influence."[4] Perhaps the renowned fighter had chosen to raid it for precisely that reason, but if so, he incautiously sealed his fate by accepting a tempting offer from the locals to delay his planned move of joining Canales in nearby San Fernando. His hosts, "offering every hospitality, proposed to kill a beef for his men. He yielded to their kindness, and ordered his men to dismount, saying he would spend [another] day in Morelos."

Zapata then carelessly accepted an offer to turn over his horses for care and feeding, but no sooner had that exchange occurred than he began to take fire from those entrusted with the caballada. Zapata and his followers quickly sought refuge in a house on the corner of the town square. With escape blocked by being separated from their horses, Zapata and his followers soon came under a barrage of small-arms fire from government troops who had been "secreted there" and who outnumbered him by more than twenty to one, once the light infantry under Isidro Reyes joined the eighty-eight-man cavalry unit that initially intercepted the rebels. All of Zapata's men rallied to join him, and together they fought for three full hours, losing four who fell dead inside and three others outside their house. They kept it up, but once "the very last cartridge was expended," they came forward and surrendered. As one of the captives stated to his trial judges, Zapata and his men made "a desperate resistance until he exhausted his ammunition and was made a prisoner without any guarantees."[5]

Arista and his officers also told the story in significant detail. Their forces included enough troops from northeastern presidios to afford good knowledge of the terrain—they became a key factor in attaining surprise. Second-in-command Reyes, at the head of 650 men, had been ordered by Arista to make an exploratory expedition. Zapata's foray had alerted a government cavalry force under Captain Juan José Galan, who moved at double time from his station only two leagues distant and surprised the rebel commander. "Hearing of this situation," Reyes then "came with [his] squadron of infantry from San Fernando," just over a league farther away.[6] Another officer acknowledged that Zapata's men had resisted "fiercely," but that the inspired attackers, shouting "vivas to the government," had seized the opportunity to press their advantage and force capitulation on March 24.[7]

Reyes, who according to Arista had marched six leagues in one day, immediately turned his attention to the rebel army under Canales, who attempted a move from San Fernando to Morelos later that day trying to liberate Zapata. Once again, the actions and motives of Canales came into question from within his own ranks. A veteran of the campaign later asserted that Canales had purposefully held back after hearing sounds of the gunfight in Morelos and moved indecisively because he actually wanted Zapata out of the way. More than one of the veterans indicated that Zapata and Canales had quarreled (again) in the days just before the battle at Morelos, thus suggesting a purpose behind the failure of the rebel commander to effect a rescue. In the deep background another rebel reported that Zapata had once threatened to kill Canales should he quit the cause, adding a further reason behind this widely alleged betrayal. Specifically, according to Santos Benavides, Zapata had earlier promised "vengeance . . . more speedy and terrible than that which you apprehend from the foe" should Canales be bought off or otherwise "abandon the cause."[8]

At any rate Reyes prevailed rather easily against Canales in the evening and nighttime engagement on the day of Zapata's capture but prudently held back from a full assault until the main body of troops arrived, supplemented from units under Ampudia. Arista claimed that these forces had made an incredible march of fourteen leagues at night, despite being encumbered by a large cargo train of mules. He continued, "We found the enemy at 10:00 a.m. [on March 25] situated in a grove of chaparral and protected by 2 trenches." Prior to launching his assault, a messenger arrived with news that Zapata sought an audience. He then "presented the case that an opportunity existed both to avoid further bloodshed and also to have the rebel troops dispatched to the border." "Zapata told me personally," Arista recounted, "that Canales could be turned." Zapata "was quite certain that this whole thing could be settled decisively" if only a rebel representative could reach Canales with a message that his choices amounted either to "surrender or be destroyed."

Arista made a lame effort to negotiate with Canales by letter, but the zealous centralist commander clearly wanted no bloodless outcome, seeking instead a decisive engagement and thus a permanent end to this exhaustive rebellion. So, waiting but forty-five minutes for a peace parlay that did not occur, he arranged his troops for battle, placing his artillery in the center, 120 infantrymen on the left, and 160 cavalrymen on the right for a simultaneous advance under the field command of Ampudia. Arista also had his personal guard of cavalry and another two hundred infantry held in reserve and in charge of Zapata and the other prisoners. The assault commenced at 11:30 a.m. and took only an hour to envelope the rebels despite their determined resistance, inflicting over three hundred casualties, consisting of two hundred killed and 126 made prisoner, with the remnant still in flight follow-ing a three-league post-battle pursuit. Arista claimed "light" casualties but acknowledged suffering an unspecified number of deaths, forty "gravely wounded" requiring care in a makeshift hospital, and several more with less serious injuries. President Bustamante later asserted that government losses approximated those of the rebels, who had the advantage of using rifles from their well-chosen defensive position in an oak grove. The forces of the Supreme Government ended the battle in possession of rebel artillery, flags, munitions, and weapons includ-ing carbines, sabers, and lances. The commander credited the valor and perseverance of his troops for this outcome, noting that they had marched 150 leagues and conducted themselves "as valiant soldiers on the battlefield," resulting in the "complete destruction" of the enemy and paving the way for the "tranquility and integrity" of the frontier. Arista asserted that "we have at last taught" a "convincing lesson" to "traitors who make alliances with the enemies of Mexico."[9] This deci-sive outcome came at a cost, namely the bloodiest day of the entire civil war in the northeastern states.

Arista also had ideas about how to make that lesson as compelling as possible. One of those captured in Morelos with Zapata survived to describe subsequent events. Jesús Barera, who hailed from the towns along the Rio Grande, explained that "Zapata and his men were tied, and kept prisoners until the next day [March 25, the date of the battle at San Fernando]. Ariste [sic] then had an interview with Zapata; what passed between them, I [Barera do] not know, personally, not being pres-ent; but it was generally reported in town and understood that he had proposed to pardon Zapata, if he would join the Centralists—Zapata refused—Ariste then promised him his life if he would lay down his arms and cooperate no further with the Federalists. Zapata still refused, and claimed his right to be treated as a prisoner of war; Ariste told him that he, Zapata, must either abandon his cause or die—Zapata, then told him to shoot him; for he would never lay down his arms as long as he was at liberty.—He was shot accordingly—the narator [sic] was at the time one of the prisoners taken with Zapata, and was confined when he heard the guns fire, that killed his leader."[10]

Another witness, Valentín Soto from Laredo, added that Ampudia had argued against the execution, "but the Regular officers on the frontier all urged death; having great dislike [for] Zapata because they feared him, he having greatly harassed them in his expedition[s]." Arista not only rejected clemency but went further and gave the order to have Zapata's head cut off. Soto explained what happened next: "His head was placed in a cask of brandy, and taken by Ampudia," accompanied by the bulk of the government forces, in a processional as far north as Laredo before moving back down river to Guerrero, where he placed the head "on a pole opposite to Zapata's house."[11]

Arista made no apology for these actions but instead wrote a public justification. Calling the inhabitants of the villas del norte his "compatriots," Arista, still in Morelos four days after the battle, began by announcing that his victories would bring about "the return of order and the conclusion of the long procession of troubles resulting from the crimes of those miserable Whores" who had been posing as leaders. The law, he continued, provided severe penalties for all "those damned rebels" who had destroyed the peace, but especially reserved the "sharpest penalties to be levied against the infamous people who attack" their own country with foreigners. As to Zapata specifically, Arista asserted that for some time there had been a "price on his criminal head" (gruesome pun apparently intended). Some "appropriate castigation" had to be exacted; therefore, "the head alone of this disgraceful traitor has been returned to the city of Guerrero as a warning to all who observe it even a thousand times of the necessary consequences of such transgressions. I hope to the heavens that this warning dissolves the threats to peace and security for the Villas del Norte."[12]

The government newspaper in Matamoros provided publicity for Arista's shocking treatment of Zapata.[13] Military officials elsewhere quickly followed up, sending the Arista proclamation to ayuntamientos and urging public celebrations in cathedrals so that the news would not escape anyone. The governor of Nuevo León chimed in, describing the outcome of the Morelos and San Fernando battles as a matter for rejoicing because it promised to end the "great and incalculable evils" of domestic insurrection. He also committed to complete cooperation in the work of "spreading pacification" throughout the department.[14] From Mexico City came word that the Supreme Government wanted Arista to temper his reprisals by considering the immense pressure that many citizens felt to accommodate to the revolution.[15]

Arista had one other matter that required his immediate and personal attention. If the rationale for Zapata's execution centered around the crime of treason for introducing foreigners into Mexico to overthrow the government, what about the fate of those very same "extranjeros?" One of them had surrendered with Zapata in Morelos on March 24, and another fell into the hands of the army following the battle at San Fernando on the twenty-fifth. Wasting no time, Arista the very next day had foreign-born captives Bennett McNeil and Victor Loupy turned over for trial by military tribunal. The charge read that these two had been "apprehended with their weapons in their hands while resisting the troops of the Supreme Government." Their captors transported McNeil and Loupy all the way to Monclova, former center of the rebellion in Coahuila, a location chosen most likely for the purpose of spreading more shock and awe. If, as Arista wrote on another occasion, Guerrero had significance as the "theater of [Zapata's] misdeeds," then Monclova provided the best stage on which to draw the final curtain on this rebellion.[16]

The trial ascertained that McNeil (a thirty-seven-year-old native of Philadelphia) and Loupy (aged forty-six, from France, by vocation a sailor) had volunteered for the "Texas auxiliary" unit filled totally with foreign "adventurers" and had seen prior service in federal armies at Guerrero, Matamoros, Monterrey, and Talayotes. The testimony of Mexicans who had also served with Canales established that McNeil had performed the duties of a soldier while Loupy served as Zapata's assistant and interpreter. Canales had recruited them in October 1839 in the vicinity of the Nueces River on the promise of receiving twenty-five pesos per month. The Frenchman testified that, far from enacting evil deeds as the government charged, he "believed he was working for the well-being of the country" by fighting for the federalist system. The trial judge, Adjutant General Miguel Blanco, heard testimony from five witnesses and "concluded on behalf of the Nation" that McNeil and

Loupy must "suffer the ultimate penalty reserved for pirates," namely execution by firing squad. The jury of six military officers also heard a plea for clemency from defense attorneys, rejected it, and ordered the sentence to be verified by Arista, which occurred on April 13. After an interpreter had explained the verdict and punishment to the accused the next day, a firing squad carried out the sentence at daybreak on April 15, 1840, in the municipal plaza of Monclova. Arista had played out the drama to the hilt.[17]

Later that month under orders from the Supreme Government, he publicized a sweeping amnesty policy. All those who truly repented of their rebellion would receive pardons. Noting that many who "strayed" had been "seduced" by Canales and other rebel leaders and in light of the "terrible lesson" inflicted at Morelos, Mexico City favored a policy of "compassionate justice," even for those who simply acknowledged the futility of continued resistance. Former rebels had but to present themselves to local civil and military authorities and agree to limit travel and otherwise submit to proper surveillance. The combination of vengeance and forgiveness all came from the same source, the central government, which unabashedly sought to fulfill an enunciated goal of establishing a stronger "national" identity in the northeastern region.[18] Arista dutifully spread these words of assurance, but he also made it clear that nothing guaranteed clemency going forward, even to those who merely "raise their voices against the Government," so none should assume the continued benevolence of the Supreme Government.[19] Civil officials in Nuevo León also informed Arista that the squeamish there had made protests about his severe policies, so the impulse favoring an end to bloodlust resonated with others besides government leaders in the nation's capital.[20]

Once again, voices of optimism spread the news of the ultimate defeat of rebellion in the north and assumed that from the moment the rebels fled the battlefield of San Fernando, "we march united around the Supreme Government in order to save the integrity of our land." "'Honorable'" citizens could now "begin to rest from the continuous hostilities that for the space of 18 months they suffered from a few disgraceful Mexicans led by the blackest of infamy in making common cause with the most ferocious and irreconcilable enemies of the country."[21]

Inevitably, the news of Zapata's fate and the defeat of rebel armies trickled into Texas with a mixture of fact and fiction. On the very day of the battle at Morelos, volunteers who had gathered at Victoria prepared to march to join the rumored concentration of rebel forces in Zapata's hometown. News arriving in San Antonio regarding the "almost complete destruction of the Federalists" held out false hopes about Arista's policy. "Instead of arresting or persecuting in any way such as have aided the Federalists he is forgiving and forgetting. . . . Even Zapata was treated with the utmost politeness and offered the commission of Colonel in the regular service." The author of this letter, C. Van Ness, expected that the imminent arrival of Canales would confirm these reports.[22] The rebel commander and scattered others came instead to the Medina River and to Goliad by April 8, carrying with them quite unwelcome reports both of Arista's vengeance and the likelihood that he would soon follow them into Texas. Lt. Col. William S. Fisher, commander of the Texas troops responsible for the defense of the west, had the dubious responsibility of communicating the terms on which Canales would be permitted to remain in the Republic of Texas. The same issue of the Matagorda paper that provided this information also reported the names of eleven soldiers from Texas who had been killed, including Bennett McNeil.[23]

Canales arrived in San Antonio in early April, as anticipated, and once again, as should have been expected by then, he mixed news with rumor, speculation, and self-justification. He accurately reported the fate of Zapata and claimed to have fled the battlefield himself accompanied by only 120 followers, with forty more having been executed. He attributed defeat to poor weaponry and the absence of ammunition and persuaded the *Texas Sentinel* of his worthiness: Canales and his men "are certainly entitled to our warmest sympathies;" whereas the centralists always could be counted on to "despoil, and incarcerate, and generally conclude by murdering. In fact, the federalists for the last eighteen months, have served as a barrier between us and the enemy. They have been fighting *our* battles, and alone and unaided, almost repudiated by us, have been doing what we should have done." "Being driven from their homes and their families, and having lost their all," they justifiably sought security "within our limits."[24]

Arista's account of the battles at Morelos and San Fernando, published first in Matamoros in *El Ancla*, reached the newspaper in Houston in time for the last edition in April. In this context of increased understanding about the disastrous fate of the rebel cause in northeastern Mexico, Canales informed the Lamar administration that he intended to travel widely in the Republic of Texas to seek "clothing and provisions" for his troops, who had stopped in San Patricio on the Nueces. His letter to Lamar recapitulated the essence if not the details of their conversations in late April in Austin. "The high favours [*sic*] that your Excellency has dispensed [to] me, and the generous reception that has been extended as well to myself as to the troops under my command on entering into the territory of this Republic, shall never be effaced from the hearts of the Mexicans of the Frontier of the North." In the mind of Canales, Lamar had provided "new proof of the interest" that he "has always manifested for our happiness and liberty." What guarantees had come from Canales in order to gain such a favorable reception? "Very soon, when the ties that now unite us to proud Mexico shall have been torn asunder, we shall have occasion to prove" both worthy and grateful.[25] In other words, Canales seems to have affirmed his goal of establishing a separate nation on the northeastern frontier of Mexico in return for, at a minimum, a free hand and endorsement by the Republic of Texas as he went about the task of raising a new army. Lamar then dropped all pretensions of neutrality. At this quite inopportune moment, i.e., at a time when the war had essentially been lost, he committed his nation unequivocally to intervention on the side of the antigovernment rebels. Further complicating his "policy," Lamar announced his decision only in private conversations, as if to shield his actions from public scrutiny.

Meanwhile, support for Canales and Cárdenas in Victoria peaked as well. A champagne dinner produced a standing-room-only crowd, and one of the organizers concluded that almost everyone sympathized with the rebel cause. However, he doubted the potential for organizing a sustainable expedition into Mexico as opposed to a single thrust.[26] The resolutions of the meeting, although expressing support for Lamar's policy of "friendship" toward the "Federal Mexicans," reflected mostly a concern that the president should undertake additional steps to protect the frontier region of Texas against a potential advance by the centralist government of Mexico.[27] In mirror-like fashion, authorities in Mier the very next day sought to establish measures to shield the villas of Camargo, Guerrero, and Mier from "the evils brought on by revolution and war" in general but invasion from Texas in particular. The senior prefect of the department of Tamaulipas promised that all three villas would cooperate in rejecting the "thieves" from Texas, establishing tighter measures for internal security, and somehow providing for a renewal of the "line" of defense along all the river towns.[28]

These reports expressed a new if tacit understanding—the battles in the borderlands no longer reflected civil conflict within Mexico so much as war between the Supreme Government of Mexico and the (unrecognized) Republic of Texas. One outcome had also emerged, without any fanfare, after nearly two years of civil discord in the northeastern frontier. Officials in Mexico, even as they took a hard line against dissent, also acknowledged regional grievances and promised to ameliorate them. The Tamaulipas authority who reported on tighter security measures threw in as an aside the news that the port of Matamoros would be open to trade on behalf of the frontier villas. On April 17 *El Ancla*, a government organ, ruminated on the shame that the entire episode of revolution and civil war could have been avoided had representative government been provided as a legitimate vehicle for popular expression.[29]

By far the most profound reflections came from a major player in the early stages of the rebellion. José Urrea, defeated, disgraced, and imprisoned, produced a remarkably astute analysis of the background and unfolding of the federalist cause. From his confinement in Perote castle, Urrea wrote a long epistle, on April 8, 1840, to another major leader, Valentín Gómez Farías. Urrea declared his continued hope for political reconciliation in the name of patriotism, but nonetheless held firm to his criticism of the centralist takeover in 1834–1835 as the starting place for political dysfunctionality. He feared that not only would the northeastern states seek independence but that New Mexico, Sonora, Chihuahua, and California would follow suit. All these states, of course, had been previously named as future targets for secession by federalists and Anglo Texans. Norteamericanos had very real antipathy toward the capital of Mexico, Urrea wrote, but maintained good relations with notable families along the distant frontier region, an area that had no defense against the "barbaric tribes" that wreaked havoc there with seeming impunity. Meanwhile, the inattentive national government did nothing beneficial but instead made war against the states and set aside the rule of law. Presently, "there is nothing to oppose rule by pure force, there is nothing for people of good will to lean on." Governing authorities had no real program but instead set off in one direction only to fall from power and yield to another party, which reversed policies, and so it went back and forth without advancing the welfare of the citizens of the country. Mexico needed stability above all else, but sadly the forces of disorganization prevailed over and again. Urrea acknowledged his own errors, which he attributed to political "ignorance and inexperience," but he expressed hope that order could somehow be produced out of this anarchy. He offered one idea—if Gómez Farías were to become the leader, Urrea promised that he and many others would follow.[30]

All these melancholy reflections aside, the warfare had entered a new phase by the summer of 1840. Within the three northeastern states, internal support for continuing the conflict had dissipated, transforming the contest from a civil war to a conflict between nations, one that neither side could actually win. Essentially, the republics of Mexico and Texas could launch thrusts into each other's territories to the point that a cycle of retaliation and revenge set in, but they behaved like fighters too accustomed to battle to quit but too exhausted to strike a decisive blow. Nonetheless, the federalist wars in the northeastern states had led to significant change within the region. The central government now benefited from an emergent nationalism, and it put forward an instrument to further that cause in the person of Mariano Arista. By bringing a terrible and swift end to those who dared oppose the nation, he stimulated a kind of national respect based on fear if nothing else.

Furthermore, the desperate rebels, by bringing foreigners into the fray, had inadvertently produced a form of patriotic reaction greater than the political instincts behind the federalist cause.

CHAPTER 7

RESURGENT WARFARE / FINAL DEFEAT

DURING THE SUMMER OF 1840, EVENTS THAT A YEAR EARLIER might have sparked renewed rebellion on the northeastern frontier passed with only a minor disturbance of the peace. Perhaps the distance helped to insulate the region from renewed eruption—the spark of revolt this time came at the very center of the political arena, Mexico City. On July 15 Urrea and Gómez Farías took their private dreams for restoring federalism into a daring public act by staging a coup d'état. Whatever the merits of their vision, the powerful "hombres de bien" in the capital saw instead explosions of terror so frightening that the wealthy and powerful lined up in all but unanimous opposition. The whole affair ended after only twelve days with the old order back in power and rebellion repudiated once again.[1]

News of the coup attempt traveled fast, reaching Tamaulipas and Nuevo León on July 23. In the latter department Governor José María de Ortega called the whole thing a mere "moment of disorder" and urged public calm,[2] as did Mariano Arista from Tampico. The embers of insurrection had become so cool that no one, not even in Coahuila, that traditional hotbed of federalism, raised a grito of support. Even the fact that Urrea and Gómez Farías had named Canales as commanding general of Tamaulipas brought forth no renewed upheaval. Arista had reported an earlier canvas of communities in Coahuila and Nuevo León showing peace everywhere and no doubt took great pride that even in Guerrero, as a local official announced, "public tranquility exists . . . and its inhabitants have no greater loyalty than to the Supreme Government."[3] He seemed only to worry a little while assuring civil officials that he was "preparing to inflict an exemplary punishment on those who dare to express their depraved views by invading our frontiers with their perverse Texas allies."[4] As for the Lone Star republic, word reached there about the coup attempt the same day as did the news that Arista had rallied government supporters in the northeastern region.[5] At Matamoros, too, vivas to the Supreme Government rang out in a special supplement to the local newspaper with bold headlines announcing the triumph of order over the forces of "liberty without license."[6]

Perhaps the July coup became a non-event in the northeastern states because the centralists had prepared actively during the early summer days of 1840, even amid their expressions of confidence that civil insurrection had come to an end. The authorities responded to perceptions of rebel activity with increased vigilance. On May 3, 1840, the veteran centralist general Pedro Ampudia sent out orders from Matamoros reminding officials in Laredo to share news of a possible move by Cárdenas from his recruiting station on the Nueces.[7] Other towns along the Rio Grande reported thievery, possibly from rebel remnants who had dispersed following the battle of Morelos.[8] While still in Saltillo, Arista attempted to normalize impressment activities and thus to eliminate one source of popular discontent and antigovernment feelings. His circular on May 9 set forth compensation standards for civilian contributions to the military, including even for pasturing animals, and he also provided measures to ensure prompt payment.[9] Civil officials in the villas of Guerrero, Mier, and Camargo joined together to provide for greater security against possible renewal of "the evils that anarchy and revolution have caused" during the past year. In five articles of agreement, they set forth measures to improve communication regarding violence, whether coming from "gangs of thieves or forces of sedition including advances by Texans." "Extraordinary mails" should be used to carry news of these kinds of threats, and local officials also established a passport system for implementation "throughout the frontier."[10]

Toward the end of May, Arista sent out a message warning frontier residents about the "seductions" of Canales and other rebel leaders and reminding everyone of the "terrible lessons" of the revolution. He urged patience as the "paternal" Supreme Government continued to implement reforms and to reinstitute the rule of civil law.[11] Arista left it to the political officials to call regional volunteers into active service.[12] Propaganda in favor of the existing system of government for the "ancient Mexican Nation" included reminders that the temptations of the "anarchists and revolutionaries" had only resulted in "doubt and upheaval."[13] Political and military preparations along with pro-government propaganda understandably led to greater confidence that rebellion in the northeastern states had been extinguished, but speculations about the prospects for peace went further. It was claimed that defeat on the battlefield along with subsequent reprisals had taught a bitter lesson in Texas as well as in Mexico. The editor of the newspaper in Ciudad Victoria, for example, expressed doubts that Canales and his combatants would leave their sanctuary in Bejar and even that the "colonists" there would resupply an invading army. Instead, the "adventurers" now cowered out of respect for "the courage and valor of the Mexican troops."[14] Actually, on that very day (July 25) invaders from Texas struck against the centralists at Laredo. But newspaper propagandists could hardly be blamed for their blind optimism since even Arista had joined in, writing, as noted previously, that his "exemplary punishment" would restrain those who might dare to "invade our frontiers with their perverse Texas allies."[15]

Instead, in the wake of the destruction of rebel armies at Morelos and San Fernando and the bitter reprisals that followed, support for Canales in Texas continued and became even bolder and more open. Some of this sentiment occurred among those who believed that Mexican separatists could still prevail. In that case the Republic of Texas could be saved from having to face the full might of Mexico alone and without allies. The *Texas Sentinel* maintained that supporting a few federalists in the northeastern states "would have been highly indiscreet and utopian . . . but it appears to us that these circumstances have materially changed. The Republic of the Rio Grande seems now to possess, or at least to aspire to a real existence." This wishful thinking (that aspiration represented a form of reality) gained support from two other contributing notions—that the new separatist nation had been created "in our very image" and that it consisted of the states "bordering upon our territory and thus most discretely within the range of our example." Offering advice to the administration, the newspaper argued for "active measures" of support for "the establishment of such an empire."[16] A week later this editor elaborated in geopolitical terms. "Diminutive" Texas, he asserted, would always suffer by its location between two immense nations and would function as if "Polandized." By contrast, another smaller nation to the west would relieve Texas of external threats and produce many commercial benefits as a bonus.[17]

Others in Texas supported Cárdenas and Canales because of a staggering combination of motivations. Labeling himself a lieutenant in the Federal Army, John McDaniel urged "the youth of Texas" to seek glory by "shouldering your rifles and marching beyond the Rio Grande and relieving the oppressed" from "the grasp of Priestcraft and Despotism" while accepting the offer of the rebels to give over "their lands, their silver and their gold."[18] The *Telegraph* in Houston urged not only that volunteers should join the rebels in Mexico but also that the regular army should move to the Rio Grande in order to reopen trade with the northeastern states. Such a move might well reenergize the rebellion there, even as Texas itself remained at peace.[19]

In fact, that newspaper formulated ideas that closely resembled the actual policy of the Texas government—essentially one of promoting war within Mexico while functioning as an active bystander itself. As the Houston paper asserted near the end of July, overt engagement in the war in Mexico would be "foolish and expensive. Peace is the true policy of Texas." Only "rash adventurers" favored aggression, even in the form of direct support to Mexican rebels as opposed to providing them sanctuary and hoping that renewed civil war would cripple the central government.[20] Likewise, the newspaper in Matagorda stated its opposition to calls for war. Rather than "formally aiding" Mexican rebels with "troops under the banner of Texas," the proper policy would allow internal discord in Mexico to fester, thus reducing the possibility of an invading force coming to Texas. A more openly warlike posture by the Lamar administration, especially one that placed troops into Mexico, could unite the people there in a desperate struggle that might conclude in the ruination of Texas.[21] Others within the government joined the calls for circumspection. For example, the Texas diplomat in Europe sent Lamar an unqualified plea for complete neutrality as the only policy that had any hope of securing badly needed loans.[22]

In the face of all this advice, Lamar rather remarkably continued to hide his actions behind a wall of public silence. Virtually all his correspondents and advisors came from political backgrounds as ardent provocateurs favoring the bold, extreme stances of what was emerging as Southern nationalism inside the United States. Given that context, the Texas president behaved with more caution than might have been expected. When he finally made an unpublished public address to explain his policy, the president again insisted on his "forbearance" and defended his support of the rebels because they had agreed to recognize Texas independence.[23] Meanwhile, diplomats, informal advisors, and military officials of the administration also spoke of their restraint while actually supporting Canales as he prepared for his next moves into Mexico. A key issue for the administration concerned the continued viability of the rebels. On May 4, Secretary of State Abner S. Lipscomb wrote from Austin to financial and diplomatic representative (and former governor of South Carolina) James Hamilton that "the federalists have been for the moment put down on the Rio Grande, but they are not subdued, and are ready to rise again at the first favorable conjuncture."[24] A month later, writing this time from Galveston, where Canales raised his next army, Lipscomb assured the government's special agent in Mexico City (James Treat) of the prudence of the Texas government. For evidence he cited the fact that the administration had not officially recognized the rebel government nor allowed its flag to be displayed on Texas soil. Regarding the raising of troops for the rebellion, Lipscomb quite simply misled Treat: "We even forbid and used the best influence of the Government to prevent Volunteers from Texas joining the Federal party." He concluded by ordering Treat to inform the Mexican government that Texas "restraint" could not last much longer.[25]

Lipscomb's description could not have been more deceptive. During the months of May and June, Canales, with the complete compliance of the Texas government, operated from his sanctuaries in Texas, making preparations to renew the war in Mexico. He also took care to keep the Lamar administration fully informed, even as to exact purchases that included, remarkably, a steamboat.[26] Writing from his residence in the community where Canales staged his troop buildup, Lamar supporter and confidant James Love informed former Secretary of War Albert Sidney Johnston in Kentucky that the rebellion had persevered through its lowest ebb and still had strong support from "the whole population west of [the] Rio Grande. . . . A general feeling exists with us to aid them, and hundreds of our citizens are [prepared] to give aid to the Rebels. . . . Do not be surprised if you hear before long of the capture of Matamoros. The President is here [in Galveston and] is very much my friend and actually asks advice." If negotiations with Mexico failed to gain recognition of Texas independence, Lamar "must send out the fleet, order out the troops to the Rio Grande, and then away goes Centralism forever."[27]

Personal emissary S. A. Plummer, writing Lamar from farther west in Victoria, added that the rebels encamped there had gained a boost from "the encouragement the Govmt. of Texas has extended to the Federalist[s] . . . [who] will be able to raise enough men, not only to whip the Centralist[s] but the whole Country across the Rio Grande if they desire it." He added an intriguing dimension. "The Feds that I have seen are so well pleased with you, I would not be surprised [if] you were invited over there to take a turn as President after your turn of service here." No documentary evidence substantiates Lamar's personal ambition with regard to leadership in Mexico—much of what he and Canales actually discussed did not get recorded. At the same time, Lamar did operate from visions of grandeur, and the great schemer Canales may have unlocked a key to influence the Texas president.

The rebel general from San Patricio provided an update on his plans to Lamar (in Galveston) on July 21.[28] Later that month Assistant Adjutant G. W. Hockley wrote more cautiously to a captain of the frontier unit regarding the frequency of desertions once again. "It is highly probable that the greater part of the men are endeavoring to join the federal army" and should be apprehended if possible.[29] Johnston arrived back in Texas, specifically in the rebel recruitment center of Galveston. He informed Lamar that he had returned because of "the suggestion of a mutual friend that my services in a military capacity would probably be required. . . . I infer from the tenor of his communication that yr Exclly contemplates a movement against Mexico, under certain contingencies, as soon as the requisite arrangements can be made." He stood ready to serve should he be called.[30]

Johnston had been kept informed through unofficial communications. Love wrote him from Galveston on May 20 that "Canales is here and is surprisingly success[ful]. Arms & some munitions is all he wants."[31] In June Lamar heard from his private secretary, Henry J. Jewett, that the forces gathering in the San Patricio area had enrolled 200 "Americans, & 600 Mexicans [are] embodied, and are expecting reinforcements."[32] Perhaps in order to boost confidence, Canales continued his pattern of exaggeration. Love stated that he had been told by the rebel leader that the "Americans" numbered four hundred in San Patricio and that four thousand Mexican rebels prepared to join the army that departed from there in late July. Meanwhile, Canales left Galveston for the staging area on the Nueces to add his 120 recruits to the fold.[33]

J.M.J. Carbajal, who had accompanied his father-in-law Canales on his mission to seek support in Texas, provided Lamar with more accurate numbers while continuing the pattern of flattery that seemed so successful with the Texas chief executive. On July 27 he forwarded a letter from Canales to Lamar and added further information. The chronically unstable Samuel Jordan, formerly an officer in the Texas army, left as a volunteer in the rebel cause in mid-July with one hundred "Americans" and two hundred Mexican cavalrymen to fulfill his orders to "clear the country" along the Rio Grande, and "take possession of

Laredo," where he would find six to eight hundred pounds of hidden gunpowder. Canales had issued orders to inform Lamar "verbally" that his own movement would then commence on August 15. Carbajal planned to join this force and add three hundred pounds of powder, small arms, and another one hundred men. The rebels also had 7-1/2-inch shells but no artillery piece because the officer in possession of it at the town of Texana was "unwilling to give it up." Carbajal expressed the hope that Col. Hugh McCloud (Texas adjutant general and a West Point graduate) and Col. Henry W. Karnes (commander of a company of volunteers in Texas service) will both "be with us in time" to provide "enough" artillery. Carbajal assured the Texas president that "whatever commands you have for our camp I will bear with pleasure. Your talents and good fortune[,] permit me to say Sir, have now placed you in a situation to immortalize your name beyond the reach of envious and vindictive enemies, of ensuring at little cost the prosperity and happiness of the Country over which you preside, and of making to yourself millions of admiring and greatful [sic] friends in Mexico and all other parts of the world. I am sure you will have in our country at least as many friends as in Texas."[34]

The Texas expedition reached Laredo on July 25 and had an impressive start. The invaders under the command of Luis López and Jordan found a government garrison there numbering only 150 and unaware of any threat. The "American" unit moved against the town and approached the public square undetected at daybreak, succeeding also in threatening the barracks, an action that forced the occupants to flee. López and the cavalry had little success in guarding escape routes, entering Laredo as its erstwhile defenders fled in the opposite direction. As a result, only about twenty surrendered along with ten other casualties (four killed and six wounded). The attackers lost only one man killed. Some of the centralist remnants escaped by swimming across the river or by taking refuge in the dense chaparral on the riverbank, but no disappointment dampened the thrill of victory. López with his cavalry charged into town shouting "loud huzaz and firing off their guns in a great Jubilee," despite having failed to block the enemy retreat, as an Anglo participant reported with disgust a few years later. López sent news of the success to Canales and swore an intention of executing two enemy "spies," citing vengeance against "the vile assassins of our brethren at Morelos" as justification.[35] Officials of the Supreme Government reported this action and speculated as to the next destination of the invaders, but none of their guesses proved correct.[36]

Jordan went back to the Nueces with some of the volunteers to confer with Canales; he returned with orders to advance against Ciudad Victoria, the capital of Tamaulipas. No public expression illuminated the purpose of this expedition. Canales apparently concealed his intentions from his colleagues because he sought to link up with federalists in San Luis Potosí, an objective that his recruits from Texas did not share and would not pursue. The Anglo Texas volunteers made no attempt to hide their objective. As the expedition traveled deeper into the interior, they made it increasingly apparent that they wanted to be paid. Canales joined the expedition tardily and then from his accustomed position in the rear while his brother-in-law, Juan N. Molano, functioned in a kind of shared command with Jordan. Molano repeatedly promised that funds would be extracted from the centralist cities they moved against and thereby kept the Texas mercenaries at bay, but amid an atmosphere of constant and increasing tension. For his part, Molano became disgusted by the impatient, plundering ways of the Anglo Texas recruits, some of whom came from the ranks of the "cowboys" for whom theft had become a way of life well before they volunteered for this new adventure. In due time most residents of the frontier region of northeastern Mexico would come to agree with the views expressed by an editorial from Ciudad Victoria on September 12, labelling the "would-be conquistadores" from Texas as "ruffians."[37]

Jordan had left the Nueces with a force of only seventy before being reinforced at the Rio Grande by Molano, López, and their cavalry. Together they started for the interior under orders from Canales to add more horses at the town of China, although some of the Anglo volunteers questioned a movement into the interior with such a small number (fewer than two hundred), and others doubted the wisdom of relying on López because of his sketchy recent performance at Laredo. Jordan overcame their distrust and set out in search of the horses, but the expedition found none at China, presumably because the animals had been extracted to a neighboring town. And so it went, as Anson Neal later recalled, with "Jordan being lured on from one place to another." Along the way some residents provided information that a small centralist unit could be found hiding in a chaparral, and Jordan forced it to surrender without a fight, capturing muskets and cartridges while adding to their numbers as some of these captives changed sides. Soon they caught up with a herd of really "good" horses, generating more disputation because many of the "Americans" wanted to return to Texas at that point—on the backs of their newly acquired property.

Molano overcame that initiative with a promise—only sixty miles farther inland at Ciudad Victoria, "they should be paid off." Antonio Pérez, "a man well known in Santontio [sic] Texas and not a coward," having failed to persuade Jordan to accompany him and warning against placing trust in Molano, set off for Texas with a portion of the caballada. The main invasion force continued onward to Ciudad Victoria, taking possession of the town, its military provisions, and much more on September 9. The governor and other political leaders had fled only three hours ahead of the attackers under the influence of a former rebel familiar with the Anglo Texans, who "represented the Americans as perfect cannibals & devils." This account continued, with no apparent sense of insincerity by either the narrator or recorder: "The people recd. [us] with open arms and the merchants threw open their stores to the credit of our men." Jordan, Molano, and their followers first collected payment from the citizens before installing a new "federalist" state government, an act accompanied by frequent "vivas." One resident made it clear that, in his words, the "inhabitants of this region" had no choice other than "taking measures to save themselves" from the "conquistadores."[38] The expedition remained in Ciudad Victoria for three weeks in order to "protect" the new regime against the old one, promising free elections and other reforms. The invaders finally left in the face of Molano's report of the approach of a centralist force too large to resist (which actually arrived there under Arista but not until mid-October), and they retrieved a previously spiked artillery piece, advanced a short distance, and occupied a defensive position nearby on the road to Saltillo. By then Molano had received an affirmative answer to his inquiry to Arista seeking amnesty and other guarantees in exchange for abandoning the Texas "adventurers."[39]

Undoubtedly, the invaders tarried in part because they had found bountiful resources in Ciudad Victoria by comparison to anything the countryside had to offer. Furthermore, Jordan had gone on a drunken four-day binge while in the town and had but little taste for anything else. Others among his men stood accused of murder and rape in addition to the charges of drunkenness and plunder.[40] Tensions among the invaders had dogged their journey but increased to the boiling point even among the Anglo Texans, one of whom died at the hands of another (Captain John T. Price), who "drew his pistol and shot him down" over a quarrel about tobacco. That commodity as booty played a role too in the worsening relations between Molano and the norteamericanos. According to one version of the story, the Mexican leader carted up a large quantity that had been appropriated during the trip, intending to use it as partial payment to the soldiers to meet their relentless demands for compensation. When they refused to accept it, Molano had the tobacco burned in Jaumave, a place the Anglo Texans called "Deadman's Town." The residents there all fled at the approach of the invaders, who soon left as well amid quarrels over the proper route to Saltillo. Suspicions about the trustworthiness of Molano escalated, as to both his competence and his loyalty. In fact, this "little man" (as one centralist called him) attracted scorn from many directions. His Mexican opponents also labeled him, variously, an ingrate and a dullard.[41] His promises of extracting payment from the towns along their route repeatedly fell through because, once there, the invaders found each community too poor for such a purpose. After considerable disputation, the invaders countermarched back to Jaumave, which they had left just two days earlier.

Questions arose too because Molano busily wrote and read messages along the way, letters in Spanish, of course, that none of the Anglo mercenaries could read. He insisted that they contained only good news of reinforcements that awaited them ahead and of the vulnerability of Saltillo, which he promised to sack unless paid a bribe of $50,000 for distribution among the men. In actuality, while in Ciudad Victoria he had written to Arista confessing that "our blood boils" at the prospect of continuing the "alliance" with the Anglo Texans, who "always shall be our enemies." He assured the general that both he and López had decided that "from this moment not a single shot shall be fired by this division at a Mexican citizen." His letter asked for terms that included forgiveness of past political expressions as well as agreement that his men could keep their arms and horses so as to defend their families from Indian depredations. He also had the temerity to ask Arista for payments to all the Mexicans who served in the invading force.[42]

The expedition held together mostly because Jordan continued to accept Molano's stories, though this Mexican officer "never recovered the confidence of the Americans." Everywhere they went, the invaders forced at least a sham submission to the provisional government, but they found no support along their way. Disputes over the distribution of arms and ammunition also contributed to the pattern of growing suspicions during a circuitous journey where everything seemed to go wrong. At one point the soldiers found themselves on a road leading to San Luis Potosí, a place where rumor had it that other federalists still fought the government. The Mexicans under Molano first remonstrated about the suicidal nature of that advance, and once the Anglo Texans joined them in opposition, the entire force simply refused to continue, leading to another reversal of routes. The soldiers also had to stop to provision themselves along the way, occasioning further delays and additional, bitter frustrations. As they made their meandering march the invaders passed through at least four pueblos without acquiring any advantage in terms of position or supplies but rather incurring public hostility everywhere they went.[43]

The expedition finally halted under pressure to prepare for battle on grounds known as Buena Vista in the outskirts of Saltillo. Jordan had no way of knowing the full extent of his inferiority in numbers. Not counting those too ill to fight, he had 107 "Americans" in the ranks, and Molano and López added perhaps 120 more; both segments had the advantage of being mounted, though the Anglo Texans had only enough horses for about half their number.[44] They discovered what appeared to be a much larger centralist force approaching them from the direction of the city. This significant disparity in numbers existed in part because during the time after Jordan left the Rio Grande, Canales and his army had failed to make an appearance. Everyone understood that he had planned to trail the Jordan expedition, but Arista sent Isidro Reyes to block any possibility of reuniting with Molano/Jordan, and Canales did not force the issue. One account had the armies under Canales and Reyes marching in virtual unison, "the one making no efforts to escape and the other none to overhaul his enemy," and continuing in that manner all the way back to the Rio Grande. The armies moved in such close proximity that Canales and his men awakened to the bugles of the centralist army morning after morning.[45]

Thus, Jordan operated without any possibility of reinforcement, nor did he know either the intentions or the strength of his opponents, who in fact had been preparing to receive an assault for at least three days.[46] At mid-morning on October 23, Jordan's Anglo Texans and Molano's Mexicans came into sight of a substantial array of what they correctly judged to be both citizens and soldiers. The invaders could not have known that they faced some of the most capable and experienced military men in all of Mexico. Their opponents, under the command of veteran, successful fighters who included General José Cayetano de Montoya assisted by infantry under General Juan Morales and by cavalry under Rafael Vásquez, had chosen a favorable location. Specifically, they held high ground fronted by a valley or ravine. The surrounding area also consisted of rough terrain favorable to making a defensive stand, and neither side wanted to squander that advantage. However, the craggy grounds limited the usefulness of centralist artillery because it could maneuver only slowly and with great difficulty. Jordan attempted to clarify the strength and character of his opponent by dispatching scouts, but he failed to learn what he wanted to know and had to rely solely on his allies for an assessment of centralist strength, which as it turned out just about equaled twice that of the invaders. The government troops numbered about four hundred (half cavalry), not counting the accompanying civilians who lacked all arms and had prepared to fight with clubs, knives, and rocks, if necessary.

129

Indeed, some civilians on the grounds of Buena Vista had already come into contact with Jordan's men and launched verbal assaults, chastising them as robbers.

Having previously gained an agreement that they would function as separate units during the projected engagement, Molano with Jordan's approval moved forward to ascertain whether the Saltillenses had come to buy them off or to fight. He held lengthy conversations under a white flag until nearly midafternoon; Molano periodically reported back to Jordan that their prospects for getting a ransom looked favorable. In fact, as Montoya's battlefield report indicated, Molano and his followers "wished at that moment to place themselves under the Supreme Government" and to abandon the "Americans" in exchange for promises of ongoing protection. The Molano delegation showed the Mexican commander documents from Arista offering these same guarantees. This battlefield conference, as Montoya wrote, "developed a plan to prevent further effusion of Mexican blood."[47]

At the last minute, Jordan intercepted a letter revealing the plan to abandon him in the face of the enemy,[48] but he continued to watch from a distance and saw that, after many delays, the enemy in an apparent show of force made Molano a captive. Immediately after that move, more defenders suddenly appeared than had been previously visible to Jordan. The Anglo Texans as usual exaggerated the odds that they faced, asserting that the centralists had perhaps as many as twelve hundred, but the disparity in numbers was closer to two to one than six to one. That disadvantage quickly grew to four to one because at the point that the full strength of the army of the Supreme Government became visible, Luis López, second-in-command under Molano, rode away from the Anglo Texans to join the enemy, making his intentions clear as he shouted words of loyalty to the Republic of Mexico and death to the Americans. A smaller cavalry unit under José M. Gonzalez also broke away from the invaders to operate alone, neither fighting against them nor joining in the hostilities. When his plan of attacking the defenders' right wing with cavalry became impossible because of these defections, Jordan and the Anglo Texans had no choice but to flee while fully exposed to the enemy or to fight alone on the defensive and with limited munitions since Molano had taken all the reserve ammunition with him.

An attack against them finally came in midafternoon, executed at first by cavalry firing what their commander called their "blazing pistols." The Anglo Texans soon found themselves in a desperate position, almost cut off from their horses. They managed to withstand that threat by charging back to the corral, which was partially enclosed by a rock fence, and then quickly regrouping in a new defensive line once they had secured their caballada. From that position Jordan, urging his men not to fire their rifles and muskets until the enemy came into close range, held out against repeated assaults. They maintained their position even after the government forces finally managed to bring up artillery, which demolished much of the stone wall using grapeshot and canister. Jordan and his followers fought in these close quarters from a house on the property until nearly sundown, losing only five killed to sixty of their enemy. Montoya's account emphasized that he had ordered a retreat out of range to save his men from further damage inflicted by the deadly rifles of the Anglo Texans.

With at least a lull in the fighting and under the potential coverage of impending darkness, Jordan ordered his men to mount up and retreat. Further danger still lurked because some of the men remained afoot, his escape route had been blocked, and his men had to scramble off the road into nearby mountains where, not surprisingly, they wandered aimlessly while occasionally being plummeted with rocks unleashed by angry residents. Jordan's men made their escape after they happened upon a remnant left behind by Gonzalez to guide them away. In fact, they barely avoided a complete disaster. Montoya had dispatched Col. José Juan Sanchez at the head of forty dragoons and Vásquez with seventy infantrymen to stymie the retreat while the bulk of the centralist force returned to Saltillo in triumph. As it turned out, these centralist pursuers also got lost in the nearby mountains. Thus, during the next few days Jordan and his men made their way to Candela, only occasionally harassed by a centralist scouting party, arriving after a five-day journey on October 28, at which point rebel cavalry sent by Bejareño Juan Seguín finally appeared and escorted the retreating men over the last forty miles into Laredo, where they arrived on October 31.[49]

This story of conspiracy and betrayal continued to be told in a cauldron of fact and fiction, with several fundamental dimensions often overlooked. Most importantly, the distinctly different goals of the two parties in this tense partnership drove the Mexican rebels and their Anglo Texas allies apart, and the gap widened as their journey deepened into the interior of Mexico. The norteamericanos functioned as virtual mercenaries rather than true allies, and their leader, Samuel Jordan, possessed a personality characterized by severe excess. The Mexicans under Molano found it difficult to hang on to their waning federalist dreams as the exhausted people no longer responded to forlorn calls for freedom against an oppressive central government. Instead, as Montoya reported to Arista after the Buena Vista engagement, "More and more there is evidence indicating that the inhabitants have formed a fidelity and good feeling toward" the Supreme Government.[50] The residents viewed as a much greater threat the ferocious ways of the invaders, which had occasioned relentless criticism by the centralist press regarding the "heinous marauders" and "vandals" who had plagued the entire region in a "most horrible" manner.[51] These protests cited as perpetrators both the Anglo Texans and the Tejanos under Seguín, who exacted forced loans and evicted residents from their quarters.[52] In a very real sense, the Anglo Americans led by Jordan and the erstwhile rebels under Canales, Molano, and López had ceased to function even as reluctant allies before they reached the battlefield at Buena Vista.

Canales remained in the field, but he had been forced east of the Rio Grande across from Rancho Clareño, on October 17. He made his escape only three hours ahead of General Isidro Reyes after a week-long meandering chase covering more than 130 leagues, sometimes through a virtually impenetrable chaparral.[53] Unofficial negotiations had already begun to end this civil war once and for all, beginning with Arista's October 12 letter to Canales urging him to abandon the "robbers" from Texas. With rather stunning candor, the centralist general stated that Canales had already done enough to establish his reputation, including having unfurled and marched under a flag symbolizing a separate nation. That cause, as Arista made clear, had no chance of success, but he assured Canales of the government's desire for peace above the temptations of inflicting the chastisement that his treason richly deserved.[54] Thus ended the final military phase of the federalist wars amid an enhanced spirit of bitter discord among the rebels, including both its Mexican and Anglo Texas components. Each side viewed the other as malignant and untrustworthy, and that same spirit characterized the attitudes of their governments as well. A conflict that had begun roughly two years earlier amid feelings of political idealism and ethnic cooperation had produced nearly opposite consequences.

CONCLUSION AND EPILOGUE

JORDAN'S RETURN TO TEXAS SET THE STAGE FOR THE FINAL act of revolution and war against centralism in the northeastern frontier states of Mexico during the period 1838–1840, though the spirit of rebellion to advance the interests of the region continued through the next two decades. And, indeed, norteños also played prominent roles in the great revolution of 1910. As for the regional revolt of 1838–1840, the forces of rebellion had achieved fleeting victories flanked by triumphs of the Supreme Government that also invariably proved inconclusive. During the last scenes of this drama, the Republic of Texas supplied essential and only slightly covert support for sustaining the rebel cause in the form of manpower, funding, and supplies. When the Anglo Texans finally fled back to their homeland with the tacit compliance of the government of the Republic of Mexico, the states of Coahuila, Nuevo León, and Tamaulipas became entirely free of the norteamericanos, who had ostensibly come to serve the cause of freedom and instead earned almost unanimous hatred in Mexico. Leaders from both Mexican factions in the civil conflict sought peace, if for no other reason than their mutual weariness. Only one obstacle stood in the way of an actual accord—the thorny matter of the treason of rebel leader Lic. Antonio Canales Rosillo.

Military, civil, and journalistic leaders alike had repeatedly and vehemently castigated Canales as a traitor, but words could be retracted.[1]

What of his actions? Had he agreed to surrender Mexican territory in exchange for support from the Republic of Texas? That question in turn boiled down to one of definition, specifically (once again): what about the border? The government of Mexico refused to recognize Texas independence but simultaneously asserted the Nueces River as the proper boundary. Thus, the controversy reduced itself to one issue that carried both real and symbolic significance—the Nueces or the Rio Grande?

Canales set out to prove his patriotism on this vital litmus test by producing documents showing his unstinting support for the Mexican stance on the boundary. Specifically, he brought forward copies of letters to and from Col. Henry W. Karnes. Canales could not have chosen a better correspondent, for Karnes had a vital connection to President Lamar and had served in the role of emissary, linking up Canales, the Navarros of the city of Bejar, and the Lamar administration. Furthermore, Karnes could not dispute the accuracy of what had been attributed to him because he had succumbed to either typhoid or yellow fever on August 18, 1840.[2]

Two pieces in this alleged correspondence became available to the public, published as a supplement to the *Semanario del Gobierno de N. León* on November 4, 1840. The letters supposedly came from copies supplied by Canales, who stated that the originals had been lost.[3] According to a document dated July 26, Karnes informed Canales from Bejar of plans to set out for Laredo at the head of volunteers from Texas as soon as they arrived in greater numbers, though he also awaited orders from Lamar and a more favorable turn in his health. Further, the letter stated that Karnes needed assurances from Canales, specifically in regard to "the pretensions of the federalists to the country between the Nueces and the Rio Grande," a matter that had "damaged the favorable sentiments of the president." The document then portrayed Karnes as threatening to plant the Texas flag himself on the east bank at the terminus of the Rio Grande if Canales failed to agree to that boundary. In what he presented as his own return letter, Canales pleaded his outrage at the dishonorable behavior attributed to him by Karnes, showing further "how little understanding you have of me and my countrymen," who would "never take up arms in order to sell, cede, or give up our territory to any foreigners. . . . How[,] Colonel[,] can you propose that we engage in treason against our country? Could you believe us capable of such vile acts? . . . A thousand times to you and to the president I gave my opinions" on the boundary matter. This purported response, dated August 4 from the Nueces River, also contained a belligerent threat that any Texas forces seeking the Rio Grande would have to pass through Canales first.[4]

Closer analysis of the context of this exchange indicates the bogus nature of the correspondence. Canales at the date of the dubious letters had already agreed to another joint expedition to the Rio Grande, specifically starting at Laredo, planned and carried out by Samuel Jordan and Luis López on the day prior to the date of the "Karnes letter" to Canales. Further, as a correspondent, the barely literate Karnes had nowhere near the eloquence of phraseology or the attention to legal niceties outlined in the document attributed to him. For his part, Canales could not have gained support in Texas while proclaiming the views set forth in this correspondence, and in fact he had been widely quoted during his period of sanctuary there as to his willingness to disregard boundary disputes in order to receive the assistance he desperately sought.[5] Given this rather transparent ruse, how could this exchange have been accepted as legitimate by Mexican centralists? Essentially, government officials needed to find a way to exonerate Canales in order to consummate an accord. The time for peace had come, and representatives of the Supreme Government found it preferable to swallow hard and agree to a face-saving formula excusing Canales of the charge of treason if thereby civil war would finally yield to peace.[6]

In the span of only two days in early November 1840, the war of two years not only came to an end but also erased internal discord to a large extent. That remarkable outcome occurred for one basic reason—the Anglo Texans after the Saltillo engagement became the common enemy of all Mexicans on the frontier. The mechanics of peace also contributed to the swift resolution of internal differences in that the chieftains on both sides delegated authority to capable, like-minded subordinates. Canales relied on the cerebral Cárdenas to a certain extent, but Arista turned the enterprise of peace almost entirely over to General Isidro Reyes, who in turn found a useful second in the person of another centralist officer, Lt. Col. José María Carrasco, a cousin of Canales. Messages flew back and forth from the Olmitos River on the left bank of the Rio Grande, where the Canales faction had set up camp, to Mier, the headquarters of Reyes, who gave updates to Arista, who in turn kept his distance. A critical dimension of the peace negotiations occurred when Carrasco, Cárdenas, and Canales all gathered at Los Olmitos, thus speeding communications. None of these processes, though, compared to Arista's decision to accept the fiction of the authenticity of the letters that Canales had forged demonstrating his Mexican patriotism as opposed to his treason.

After only minimal preliminaries, the negotiations began in earnest on November 1, 1840. For his part Canales wrote candidly that fears of reprisals by the centralists had been set aside and that he trusted Reyes to proceed in the manner of friends. He also acknowledged that his goal (whether he meant the restoration of the 1824 constitution or the independence of the three northeastern states) "can no longer be achieved," so the most important remaining obstacle to peace became the continued ability of his supporters to inflict damage on the forces of the government. Thus, to dispel that potential he gave a full accounting of all his military assets and agreed to relinquish them. He acknowledged having 659 troops, 495 being Anglo Texans, 121 Mexicans, and 43 Bejareños. He stated that he had given orders to start a crossing to the eastern bank of the Rio Grande but required twenty or twenty-five additional cargo mules in order to turn over all his armaments. Canales suggested that all Mexican residents should be relocated for a while to one side of the river, removing them from the sight of the Anglo Texans and thus avoiding revengeful retribution for what had occurred in the Saltillo campaign. With the cooperation of Reyes, the artillery pieces could be secured, reducing the potential for resistance from the "Americans" so that "it will not be necessary to fight them." He assured the centralist general that the essential written agreement would easily be crafted soon, but the spirit of that arrangement existed already since "I place in your control my total materiel of war, myself, and all the

Mexicans who accompany me." Once the exchanges had been accomplished, then the two sides together could proceed to the mutually compelling business of "avenging the outrages against the Mexican people ... [including] forcing the foreigners to regret their behavior," especially having the temerity to raise and toast their flag on Mexican soil, along with other actions "despoiling the nation that enrolled their services." Canales added harsh words as well for "the haughty chief from Bejar [probably Juan Seguín] who had attempted to read my correspondence" and to commit other affronts. Canales also promised to attempt to deliver naval vessels and other military assets that he had left behind in the Corpus Christi bay and to assist in maintaining Mexican authority on the Nueces.[7]

In keeping with his self-identified role as "the primary political authority during the revolution," Cárdenas took on the responsibility of communicating directly to Arista. This message offered assurances that the rebel leaders not only accepted defeat but favored the return of all the frontier people "to obedience of the government" as well. Cárdenas himself now subscribed to "reconciliation" out of a commitment to the "highest interests" of national well-being, and he assured Arista that the principle stumbling block, ridding the region of all remaining Anglo Texans, would be quickly resolved since they "have quit us."[8] Carrasco wrote on the same day and confirmed the newfound unity of the frontier and the sincerity of the former rebel leaders. He asserted that the error of recruiting soldiers from outside Mexico had actually unified everyone on the northeastern frontier by "educating" Mexicans as to the duplicity of the foreigners. He described the Anglo Texas volunteers as men without a country who "write laws with the cannon and the pistol." Mexicans now trusted only other Mexicans, and among all of them the "grito de Guerra" had died in the face of the events surrounding the expedition against Saltillo. Instead, all voices had now agreed to the essential "principles of peace" consummated in the form of a detailed agreement.[9]

A man of many words, Canales of course joined in by also writing to Arista. He repeated the themes of the other communications and added some inflammatory allegations against the Anglo Texas volunteers.

Motivated primarily by their constant "thought only of fixing their standard everywhere on the north side of the Rio Bravo," their behavior demonstrated that they had "ceased not only to be federalists but Christians" as well. He declared that from this day forward he would devote himself to fighting those who had committed such "horrible misdeeds" in his beloved country. In the face of this hostile enemy, the time for constitutional debate had come to an end. Canales also wrote to Reyes, confirming his decision to accept the armistice.[10]

Carrasco signed the peace agreement on November 1 along with Canales and Reyes and forwarded four copies to Arista the very next day. Its six provisions suspended hostilities and provided for a temporary boundary of the Rio Grande, giving all former rebels eight days to move to their side, the right bank. Any act of resumption of hostilities would annul all the terms of the armistice. Henceforth, Canales and his forces would recognize the government of the Republic of Mexico unconditionally and in addition would rally to its standard in the case of the necessity of serving as auxiliaries "against the Americans." The accord also intended to cover any remaining forces formerly in rebellion who had served under Molano or who remained encamped on the Nueces.[11] Missing no opportunity to express his newfound loyalty, Canales provided assurances that he had accepted peace "in his heart" and that henceforth nothing could "win us over to the Americans, who always must be our enemies." Reyes in turn also sent word to Arista expressing his optimism that "a new era of felicity and happiness begins to rein [sic] from this day on this frontier." He expected that the eight-day peace period would extend indefinitely, except in the case of war against the "usurpers of Texas," now recognized as the "common enemy" of every Mexican, regardless of previous internal disagreements. The editor of the government newspaper in Monterrey added his hope that civil accord would produce even greater rewards. He foresaw a time of unity so great that Mexico would "wrest away the fertile territory of Texas from the hands of those perfidious pirates who now possess it."[12]

Before the eight-day grace period of the armistice expired, representatives of both sides gathered again, this time at Camargo, where they prepared and ratified a somewhat more elaborate agreement. Its nine articles began with a formal statement of surrender by the federalists, who disavowed all their previous political "pretensions" or "enactments" dating forward from November 3, 1838. The losing side agreed to contribute to the "war against the foreign enemy" by organizing a regiment from the villas del norte under the complete direction of Mariano Arista. The agreement provided for the release of all remaining prisoners and the peaceful expulsion of foreigners from Texas, though Europeans could stay in Mexico by promising to refrain from violence. For his part Arista agreed to respect personal freedom of expression and property rights and to assist Mexicans from outside the frontier in safe passage home. The Supreme Government would receive all remaining matériel of war, specified as follows: 200 rifles, 700 muskets with bayonets, 153 barrels of powder, trenching and carpentry tools, a four-pound artillery piece, and two "estimbotes" that had been partially refurbished and paid for. Canales, Reyes, and Arista all ratified the agreement two days later with but minor qualifications in wording.[13]

In the days ahead the erstwhile rebels fulfilled the terms of the agreement, including the transmission of military equipment to the government.[14] Arista contributed to the newfound expression of good feelings by writing a carefully constructed letter explicitly accepting the authenticity of the forged Karnes documents and thus absolving Canales from treason. "Federalists and centralists, all are acting in concert and affirm this moment of reconciliation," Arista proclaimed. The new order of unity would continue in perpetuity if Canales would "embrace" the feelings of peace moving forward. Arista went so far as to express concern for the safety of Canales in light of the ferocious, cruel, and immoral Anglo Texans, whom he expected to be disposed to seek "cruel revenge" for what had occurred outside Saltillo. Insofar as any reprisals that Canales might face, Arista offered to "assist you in purifying yourself in the eyes of your compatriots; however, much still depended on the former rebel, who would have to use his "influence and relationships" to extend the "peace that currently favors the frontier."[15]

Arista did his part by informing civic officials in the departments of Tamaulipas, Nuevo León, and Coahuila and in Mexico City about the good news of peace and by ordering the publication of the accords. Authorities in the nation's capital approved all the agreements on November 25, and the minister of war suggested that Canales travel there to provide additional insights and information about Texas. Though Canales did not make that trip, he did go to Monterrey to share his knowledge of future "plans of the adventurers of Texas." His assessment found ready acceptance as he described the weakness of the Republic of Texas, especially its financial challenges. He also indicated considerable sentiment there favoring return to obedience to the Republic of Mexico. These views possibly influenced Mexico City to take a hopeful approach concerning reconciliation with Texas and thus the decision not to recognize its independence.[16]

Throughout the states of Tamaulipas, Nuevo León, and Coahuila, once again the war weary took time to rejoice. The citizens of Mier, Saltillo, and Monterrey joined together in public celebrations of what General Reyes proclaimed as a "bloodless victory." Citizens and soldiers, adults and children all began crowding around his house in Mier even before official word came that the rebels had submitted to the central government. As he wrote, he heard not only the bugles of his corps but also the pealing of church bells, and he saw the glare of a thousand rockets, all in a display of "patriotic effusion" that "the blackness of discord has been removed forever from the frontier," replaced by a new standard of "amity and union." Reyes concluded his letter by congratulating Arista for an accomplishment that had not been achieved by "the Canalizos and the Filisolas."[17] In a kind of final testimony, Arista in turn recognized the accomplishments of his troops but actually attributed this "time of jubilee" to the work of "reason and conviction" rather than to the triumph of arms.[18] At the end of the month, Reyes wrote glowingly to "the inhabitants of the frontier," proclaiming November 6 as worthy to be remembered "for all eternity," in heaven and on earth as a great day of "reconciliation."[19] Newspapers chimed in by proclaiming a new era: "compared to a year ago, when all was misery, confusion, and terror, now the watchwords are progress, satisfaction, and confidence."[20] Acts of reconciliation continued to be celebrated in various parts of Nuevo León well into the year 1841. These events included a solemn symbolic joint entry into Monterrey by Canales and Arista and a reunion of veterans on the battlefields at Morelos and San Fernando replete with formal tributes to those who saved Mexico from further territorial dismemberment.[21]

In his most important gesture to assure the end of one epoch and the transition to another, Canales officially cut his lifeline to Texas. He sent the federalist-centralist peace accord to Jordan along with his own unequivocal exclamation point. Never one to worry about distortion mixed with hyperbole, Canales claimed that "we have never thought to rebel against the nation, much less to acknowledge the independence of Texas. . . . We hate the occupiers of that fertile department [Texas] and in proof of this, we offer our persons to combat them" in the next expedition against "the ungrateful colonists of Texas."[22]

Only one voice, that of Juan Pablo Anaya, called out in the old language of liberal idealism. On December 6, 1840, from San Juan Bautista de Tabasco he issued a new meditation defending his well-intentioned behavior. Anaya explained that he had continued to contribute to the cause of freedom among the northeastern states by making peace with the Republic of Texas, seeking aid in the United States, and looking for other states to sustain the federalist cause against the tyrants of Mexico. He defended his support for "the always gallant, loyal, and patriotic D. Antonio Canales" even as other areas surrendered to lethargy. Anaya described the involvement of Anglo Texan freedom fighters as a well-intentioned error but insisted that they sympathized with civil liberty and resistance to despotism. In all his dealings in the Republic of Texas, Anaya claimed, he had opposed "pernicious ideas" such as dividing Mexico into two republics, north and south, and he cited previous publications to that end. He also took credit for reviving federalist principles among the Yucatecans and the Tabascans and for keeping alive the fight against "the usurpers of the one true Mexican political order" as expressed in the Constitution of 1824.[23]

Anaya's impressive commitment notwithstanding, the time had passed when liberal but ineffectual sentiments made a significant difference. Instead, many others very soon added their voices to the open exchange of national rather than ideological animosities. It began as expected with Texas newspaper accounts of Mexican perfidy and cow-ardice during the engagement outside of Saltillo contrasted with the heroic tale of Jordan's escape, equal on a small scale to the "memorable retreat of ten thousand Greeks, of olden time."[24] Many voices in Mexico also took up the theme of irreconcilable conflict between their country and Texas. According to a Matamoros-based correspondent of Arista, even the possession of the Nueces River Valley by the forces of the Texas government threatened Mexico in a "life or death" manner.[25] Though to some extent the words fired off in Texas mirrored the nationalistic views from Mexico, soon the emphasis focused not only on bad behav-ior but also on ethnic and cultural characteristics. Peace with Mexico, wrote correspondent X. Y. Z. to the *Austin City Gazette*, had become a dream, an "hallucination!" that ignored "the origin of this people . . . utterly ignorant in their character, which is a mixture of the sullen stub-bornness of the Indian, with the haughtiness of the Spaniard . . . agra-vated [*sic*] by prejudice and jealousy, in their worst forms." Mexicans, he argued, view Texans "with the most deadly hatred . . . toward whom they have no other feeling than the most bitter resentment and [desire for] revenge." To seek a lasting peace with such people, he concluded, "is to disregard all the laws of human nature."[26]

By the end of the year, Texas newspapers had translated the pub-lished correspondence in Mexico that not only set forth indisputable evidence of the peace accords but also of plans for future invasions. "In almost every document," according to the *Austin City Gazette*, "there is some bitter denunciation of the Texians." The editor argued that, moti-vated by "atrocious vengeance" against foreigners, Mexico would have little choice other than to launch a "glorious march" to "wash out their offences on the plains of Texas."[27] The Matagorda newspaper concurred with the prophecy of ongoing warfare and also attributed its causes to a clash of cultures. "Debased" and "superstitious" Mexicans, with-out schooling in "the merest rudiments of civil and religious liberty, indolent by nature and unsusceptible of all the wholesome restraints of social and moral obligations," would inevitably make war to wipe away the "tarnish" of losing Texas. Not only the leaders of Mexico but the people as well had suffered blows to their pride that produced a "mortal hatred of the Anglo-Saxon blood, warmly nurtured by her national religion." From that perspective, even a meagre prophet could see a future filled with ongoing retribution. The newspaper in the old capital of Houston spiced similar rhetoric with bluster. Interim President Burnet, it wrote, would seek congressional endorsement of a new offensive, not only to affirm the Rio Grande boundary but also to "extend the Texian frontier to the ranges of the Sierra Madre" and thereby reap "a rich harvest of wealth and glory."[28]

Lamar recovered from the nervous breakdown that had forced him to temporarily surrender executive authority to Burnet and proceeded to act on his imperial vision for Texas.[29] Despite failing to gain congressional approval, in June 1841 he dispatched 320 men from Austin onto the Great Plains with the object of taking control of Santa Fe and its lucrative trade route. They meandered northwestwardly amid scorching heat, scarcity of water, and Comanche harassment before a final surrender in October without reaching their destination. Lamar had based his expedition on the illusion that Texans would be received so warmly that the territory would voluntarily affiliate with the Lone Star republic. In reality, nuevomexicanos had over the years developed a wholehearted hatred of Anglo Texans, viewing them as drunken scum, "corrupted" and "depraved," "vomited up" from Europe and North America to Texas, where they became "famous criminals." Furthermore, these views had been spread through government edicts and harangues from the pulpit in a manner designed to reach not only the wealthy but also the masses. Subsequently, publication of a narrative by George Kendall detailing the entire Santa Fe episode, including the subsequent forced march and the harsh imprisonment of the survivors, spread anti-Mexican feeling in the United States as well.[30] Thus, ugly stereotypes laced with ethnic invective spread throughout the borderlands and beyond after the end of the federalist wars.

The failed Santa Fe aggression by the Republic of Texas sparked retaliatory raids and vengeful responses in 1842 and 1843. Shortly after his return to power, Antonio López de Santa Anna dispatched a force under Rafael Vásquez to Béxar in February 1842, occupying the town for two days in early March before retreating. Four months later another Mexican force under Canales defeated outnumbered Texians at Lipantitlan on the Nueces River, and Adrian Woll commanded a larger unit that took San Antonio once more in September 1842, but again it stayed only briefly before being pursued by Texas Rangers and then defeated by hastily gathered volunteers in a battle at nearby Salado Creek. If Mexico proved incapable of sustaining a reconquest, Sam Houston, having begun a second term as president on December 12, 1841, had no answer as to how to prevent such incursions, much less how to make good the Texas claim to the Rio Grande boundary. Under intense pressure to retaliate, he placed Alexander Somervell at the head of a group of volunteers too small in number and too undisciplined in disposition to prevail along the border. Though officially furloughed by their inept leader after they reoccupied Laredo on December 8, 1842, many of them mutinied and traveled downriver to pillage Ciudad Mier. They found themselves instead forced to surrender to a force of nine hundred soldiers under Ampudia and Canales on Christmas Day.

The Texans subsequently attempted to break free of their captivity, but once recaptured the authorities forced every man to draw a bean out of a jar, with a black one (one of every 10 beans) signifying immediate execution. All these futile military responses and reprisals contributed to the increasing bitterness that prevailed in Texas-Mexican relations, but these acts also gave President Houston more evidence that the Republic of Texas had failed in its attempt at nationhood. In 1843 and 1844 he found but little opposition throughout the realm to his public and private campaign for annexation to the United States, but clearly Texas had failed to validate its title to the Rio Grande boundary by actual occupation and defense of that line.[31] Undeterred by that reality, the US government, following its acquisition of Texas in 1845, stood firmly behind that same boundary claim,[32] occupied the disputed territory south of the Nueces, and proceeded to the Rio Grande.

Not surprisingly, Antonio Canales thought that this tense military situation provided him another opportunity to hatch one last, inscrutable scheme in which he attempted to work both sides, avoid or minimize the clash of arms, and possibly advance his own political fortunes as well. First, he approached US commander Zachary Taylor with a request for aid in establishing a new separatist republic in the north-eastern region of Mexico, attempting to lure the United States with a suggestion that he could bring Mexican troops in support of his plan. Taylor went so far as to contact the State Department in Washington, DC, and gained authorization to enlist disaffected Mexican troops but without any formal endorsement of the separatist scheme. Once again, the boundary had become an immovable obstacle to serious negotiation since the Canales initiative proposed the Nueces River. Military events moved ahead in the absence of further peace talks—the US and Mexican armies clashed first at Palo Alto on May 8, 1846, and again the next day at Resaca de la Palma. In that engagement Canales actually commanded the left wing of the Mexican army under none other than Mariano Arista,[33] who suffered both a tactical and strategic loss and soon retreated, an action that amounted to the surrender of Matamoros.

Almost immediately after that fabled prize changed hands, the irrepressible concept of a Republic of the Rio Grande appeared once again. There had been no public notices for years, but many schemers remained at work even as late as 1845, when the British ambassador to the Republic of Texas, Charles Elliott, wrote his superiors in London regarding a revival of both the notion and title of a Republic of the Rio Grande. He cited the involvement of Canales, Molano, and Cárdenas with rumored support from Arista himself.[34] The separatist concept remained alive, too, in the form of a propaganda campaign by a bilingual newspaper bearing the title *The Republica del Rio Grande y Amiga de los Pueblos*. It appeared in Matamoros beginning June 6, 1846, issuing propaganda about the superiority of US political culture.[35]

A short time after Arista's defeat, Canales proceeded with the second phase of his scheme. On June 28, 1846, he sent a postal express to Mexico's president Mariano Paredes y Arrillaga, suggesting a way to mitigate the inevitable and negative impact that would be produced by a US invading force numbering seventeen thousand men. Since Mexico did not at that moment have sufficient strength to defend itself, why not pursue a delaying ploy? He proposed to turn Anglo American racism into Mexico's advantage. "You can be certain of one thing. I know the disdain in which the norteamericanos hold the Mexican race and their certainty of conquest." Canales offered himself as a mediator "utilizing a revival of ideas that they find attractive," namely proposing the creation of a form of government similar to their own in a new, separate nation among the borderlands. "Why not conduct such talks even as they advance?" In the meantime, the leaders of Mexico could use a possible delay to assemble a force more sufficient to meet the enemy.[36]

Once again Canales's plan did not mature, and the US armies inexorably moved south and west to battlegrounds familiar to the Texans, first at Monterrey, followed by another engagement on the craggy grounds of Buena Vista. The Texas Rangers, made up either of cowboys or the same kind of men as those who fought on the side of the rebels during the federalist wars, contributed as scouts and other kinds of cavalrymen. They carried a new and deadly weapon, the Colt revolver, and conducted themselves in a manner that seemed familiar to the peoples of the northeastern states of Mexico but brutally shocking to the sensibilities of norteamericanos unaccustomed to border warfare. In the words of an Ohio officer, "As a mounted soldier [the Texas Ranger] has no counterpart in any age or country. . . . Chivalrous, bold and impetuous in action, he is yet wary and calculating, always impatient of restraint, and sometimes unscrupulous and unmerciful. He is ununiformed and undrilled, and performs his active duties thoroughly, but with little regard to order or system." Others who served alongside the Rangers noted their outlandish appearance, unwashed but well-mounted habits, and brave if merciless character. They earned the name "los sangrientos Tejanos" from Mexican civilians wherever they rode, including in the national capital where they engaged in murderous, vengeful behavior.[37]

Once the US Army moved beyond the Rio Grande, it faced hit-and-run attacks aimed at supply lines by guerrillas experienced in that manner of warfare from their days as rebels in the earlier federalist wars. Prominent names among these raiders included rebel veterans Juan Seguín, José Urrea, and Antonio Canales. Nothing if not a survivor, Canales remained active in governmental affairs. After the war he sought and won office as a senator and also governor of Tamaulipas in 1851. In that capacity, ironically, he fought against separatist filibusters from Brownsville the next year.[38] In Texas former president Lamar had also volunteered for war duty, serving in the battle for Monterrey and then winning promotion to the rank of lieutenant colonel in charge of Texas volunteers stationed in Laredo. From that location he filled his idle time recording the narratives of former participants in the federalist wars, part of a projected but never finished history of Texas.[39] Ironically, the annexation that he had opposed actually resulted in the fulfillment of his imperialist visions since by force of arms the United States compelled Mexico to cede a vast territory all the way to California.

Many of the Anglo Texans who had served with Jordan found it difficult to lay down their arms, including the leader himself. After brazenly seeking payment from the Republic of Mexico for his service in the wars against it, he returned to Austin, where his most memorable act was to threaten Sam Houston by wielding an axe. Soon Jordan sought more adventure in New Orleans by enlisting in another federalist expedition, this time to the Yucatan. He literally missed the boat and died from an overdose of the opiate laudanum on June 22, 1841.[40] Others of Jordan's compatriots also continued their martial ways by joining Ranger companies. John Reagan Baker volunteered for Trans-Nueces warfare that included the ill-fated Mier expedition, but he did not draw the black bean. Neither did another leader of that "band of brothers," Ewen Cameron, but Canales reputedly fulfilled a long-standing grudge by having him executed anyway. Brother Hugh Cameron also lost his life in border warfare. John T. Price and other "cowboys" enlisted as "spies" along the Texas frontier in 1841. Another of them, Lt. Col. Richard Roman, ended his military career until the US war with Mexico but then joined a Ranger unit and in that capacity returned to fight again in the northeastern states of Mexico and beyond.[41]

For years it seemed that the spirit of separatism simply would not die. In 1851 José María Carbajal launched another revolution aimed at creating a new "republic of the Sierra Madre." Once again, this affair centered upriver from Camargo and Mier and drew support in part from continuing complaints by merchants regarding Mexico's enforcement of a crippling tariff policy. And once again leadership of the separatist movement, according to its opponents, came not only from Carbajal but also from the likes of Antonio Canales, Jesús Cárdenas, and even

Tamaulipas governor Francisco Vital Fernández.[42] Quickly defeated in the field, this uprising failed to gain support because it evoked bitter memories by recruiting a number of Anglo Texans, including the ever more hated "Rinches" (Rangers). In fact, a company of "Free Rangers" under John S. "Rip" Ford fought a three-day pitched battle at Matamoros, an engagement that included setting fire to the town and killing those who attempted to extinguish it.[43]

With regard to larger issues of Mexican politics, the legacy of the days of war and rebellion in the northeastern region persisted into the future. What had begun in 1838 as a revolution attracting the support of the masses in the cause of federalism had by 1840 become but another example of caudillo politics in the person of Antonio Canales. As he fought on, even this grand schemer could not conjure up anything resembling a powerful outcry other than the omnipresent spirit of localism. On the other hand, the centralists who crushed the rebellion did so by relying on naked fear generated by military might, with their views largely bereft of ideology to sustain it and therefore receding when their army of occupation departed. However, this regional revolt actually helped to produce nationalistic consequences. By introducing foreign volunteers from the territorially avaricious Republic of Texas, the rebels had inadvertently stimulated a wave of patriotic defense against further dismemberment by a hated neighbor. In that sense the revolt served as a kind of precursor to the wave of nationalism that occurred as a consequence of the humiliating 1846–1848 war against the United States.

During the next decade the forces of liberal nationalism finally overwhelmed the caudillo tradition as centralizing authority at last successfully confronted disorder and regionalism. The movement of reform that ultimately produced an end to the era of government by local caciques began as yet another pronunciamiento in 1854 known as the Plan of Ayutla. Once again, this revolt proclaimed the principles of federalism against a government headed by Santa Anna. In Nuevo León the initial standard bearer of this plan, Santiago Vidaurri, persisted in defending his regional authority in opposition to all forms of concentrating power at the national level. Soon he attempted to extend his influence by combining his state with Coahuila, a move that echoed the regionalism of the past while clearly violating the plan's goal of national unity. It took almost another decade to resolve this renewed regional-national dynamic. For the next few years Vidaurri continued to dominate in what amounted to his fiefdom while providing but minimal support for La Reforma under the liberal nationalizer, President Benito Juarez. When the president's struggle against France led him to flee northward to Vidaurri's domain in the 1860s, his relations with the Nuevo León–Coahuila caudillo became more tense. Rumors even swirled around yet another separatist endeavor by Vidaurri using the revived name "republic of Sierra Madre." The conflict between the two leaders continued until Juarez prevailed militarily in 1864, and thereby the northeastern region submitted at last to a more compelling cause redefined as liberal nationalism. The reform movement also produced a new political order under the Constitution of 1857, a document that generated a far greater consensus of support than had occurred in the earlier instance of the Constitution of 1824.[44]

Back in Texas bitter struggles over land, power, and justice between Anglos and Tejanos dominated the Trans-Nueces region for many years. What one historian describes as a "cycle of violence" based on a "barbaric code of conduct . . . prevailed along the Rio Grande in the nineteenth century." The government of the state of Texas in 1850 appointed a commission to validate land titles in the Rio Grande Valley and Nueces strip, but various sides staged ongoing protest meetings, one of which in Brownsville proposed the creation of a new territory for the region under US authority. Separatists raised the prospect of revolt any time they objected to a ruling or other outcome and even dabbled in the secessionism that would eventually erupt in the US Civil War. Alienated Tejanos found a champion in Juan Cortina, who pronounced a revolution against the United States in 1859 as retribution against the exploitation of Mexicans along the border. It attracted hundreds of supporters who took up arms and provided shelter for their heroes.[45]

So, what had begun in 1838 as a cause of liberty, opportunity, and justice for the fronterizos of the northeastern states produced instead a legacy of acrimonious conflict. Memories of Mexicans and Anglos united as freedom fighters faded amid open displays of ethnic prejudice and virulent hatred. Many generations passed before a descendant of those who survived could tell another side of the story, one of people in the valley engaged in a sometimes heroic, sometimes more commonplace struggle for dignity. In her "personal history of the place and the people" of the region, Beatriz de la Garza, under the title *From the Republic of the Rio Grande*, detailed the existence of a "strong, independent spirit among the inhabitants of the river settlements" emerging out of a struggle for "self-sufficiency" and an abiding love of their land. In her view "the people of the lower Rio Grande settlements and their neighbors struggled to assert their autonomy against two countries— the Republic of Mexico and the newly declared Republic of Texas." Though acknowledging the role of Canales for having the intellectual acumen to launch a movement, she and her people over the years celebrated instead the entire region as the "kingdom of Zapata." Thus, in the warp of time, there lives on a remembrance of bravery, steadfastness, and loyalty.[46]

CAST OF CHARACTERS

NOTE ON SOURCES

Most of the following biographical profiles are drawn from a database of names, information, and sources compiled during the course of the research for this book. *The New Handbook of Texas* provided a considerable amount of detail, especially on individuals with a background from Texas. Another useful reference work, Frazier's *The United States and Mexico at War: Nineteenth-Century Expansionism and Conflict*, contains biographies of figures from both sides. Other secondary sources also yielded some of the information cited herein, but the bulk of the material derives from research in the primary sources cited throughout the manuscript.

Pedro Ampudia (b. 1805 in Havana, Cuba): He joined the Mexican Independence movement under Agustín de Iturbide. As a centralist officer he took on negotiations with rebel leaders on behalf of the government. He was the field commander of the government forces that defeated the federalists under Antonio Canales at San Fernando near Morelos on March 25, 1840, the most decisive engagement of the federalist wars.

Juan Pablo Anaya: A longtime federalist ideologist with deep roots in the United States as well, having fought in the battle of New Orleans in 1815. He went to Texas and the United States late in the summer of 1839 in search of assistance for the rebellion.

Mariano Arista: Became influential by joining with Iturbide in favor of Mexican independence in 1821. As a centralist general he was destined to become the most important military figure during the 1838–1840 rebellion, having risen to the command of all forces in the northeastern states in May 1839, with his field command delayed until December of that year.

John Reagan Baker (b. August 6, 1809, in Tennessee): Came to Texas in time to volunteer in the federalist wars. He continued to be active in military matters during subsequent Trans Nueces warfare that included the ill-fated Mier expedition, but he avoided drawing a black bean by being hospitalized and remained imprisoned until 1844, after which he returned to Refugio County and later Matagorda and Goliad County, where he established mercantile ventures. He served in the home guard during the US Civil War and survived until January 19, 1904.

Jesús Barera: A resident of the Rio Grande River towns, he fought with Antonio Zapata and surrendered with his leader at Morelos on March 24, 1835, but survived and left an oral interview conducted on behalf of M. B. Lamar, former president of the Republic of Texas, in 1847.

José Lasaro Benavides: Turned down offers to become the federalist governor of Coahuila y Tejas in January 1839 but remained politically active and warned the government that the rebellion continued to be a threat later that year.

Santos Benavides: The nephew of Laredo federalist politician Basilio Benavides, he was among the followers of Antonio Zapata who surrendered to centralists following the battle at Morelos on March 24, 1840; in 1847 he provided an oral interview to a historical project organized by Lamar regarding that engagement and other events of the federalist wars.

Miguel Blanco: In the capacity of adjutant general, he supervised the trial of Bennett McNeil and Victor Loupy, two of those captured with Antonio Zapata on March 25, 1840, leading to a verdict of guilty for "piracy" and their subsequent execution at Monclova, Coahuila, on April 13, 1840.

David G. Burnet: Former empresario who became the interim president of the newly declared Republic of Texas during its war for independence and served a stint as acting secretary of state for the Lamar administration in the late summer of 1839. He then filled in as interim president when Lamar suffered his nervous breakdown the following year. He and Lamar held a common hatred for their political rival Sam Houston.

Anastasio Bustamante (b. July 27, 1780, in Michoacán; d. February 6, 1853): The child of Spanish parents, he studied both theology and medicine before joining the independence movement. He rose to become vice president in 1829 and served as president of Mexico, 1839–1841. Exiled 1841–1844.

Ewen Cameron: Along with his brother Hugh, a native of Scotland, he came to Texas after the fighting phase of its war for independence. The two volunteered on many occasions and were among the "cowboys" who fought in the federalist wars. They later fought against Canales in defense of the Republic of Texas. Ewen drew a white bean to escape execution after the Mier expedition of 1842 but died during another escape effort.

Antonio Canales Rosillo: Often using the legal title "licenciado," he played a critical role in the revolt from its inception through its conclusion. Canales was the major figure in a tightly woven group of federalist leaders since he married the sister of Juan N. Molano who, in turn, married the daughter of J. M. Carbajal, with all three men serving as officials in the so-called Republic of the Rio Grande. He engaged in peace talks with centralists in the spring of 1839 but ascended to become the primary leader a few months later as he outmaneuvered his rival, Pedro

Lemus, for control of the federalist cause. He emerged as the leading federalist general by the summer of that year and remained at the center of the federalist rebellion. His army suffered a major defeat at San Fernando near Morelos on March 25, 1840. He continued to recruit soldiers and fight intermittently until his surrender near the end of 1840. A figure of boundless ego and aspiration, he attracted repeated criticism from other federalists for his duplicity, a function of his endless taste for intrigue and manipulation.

José María Carbajal: A native of San Antonio de Béxar, he received both technical and religious training in Kentucky and Virginia during the 1820s where he became an ardent Protestant. Returning to Texas, he worked as a surveyor and gained support from Stephen F. Austin. He participated in struggles against the national government of Mexico as early as 1831, winning election in 1835 as delegate to the federalist-leaning Coahuila y Tejas legislature. His activities in support of the Texas rebellion led to his arrest later that year, but he escaped and won election to the convention that declared Texas independence (March 1836), though he did not attend. As a federalist leader, he accompanied his father-in-law, Antonio Canales, in the summer of 1839 on his journey to Texas in search of assistance. That fall he fought under Zapata in warfare on the river towns. According to the *Texas Sentinel* (Austin), he was the secretary of the federalist provisional government in 1840, known in Texas as the Republic of the Rio Grande. After the federalist wars he remained politically active and continued to attempt a separatist movement for the northeastern states under what he called the "republic of the Sierra Madre" in 1851. He survived this failed venture, even becoming governor of Tamaulipas in 1865, and never renounced his federalist leanings. He settled in the Matamoros region, where he resided at the time of his death in 1874.

Bartolomé de Cardenas: Federalist governor of Tamaulipas in the spring of 1839.

Jesús Cárdenas: He claimed authority as the federalist political chief in northern Tamaulipas in the summer of 1839, and in that capacity he endorsed Anaya's mission to gain support in Texas. He remained active in federalist politics throughout the rebellion of 1838–1840, including support for separatism as head of a government of the northeastern states known in Texas as the Republic of the Rio Grande.

José María Carrasco: A lieutenant colonel in the centralist army, bilingual, and a cousin of Antonio Canales, he served as an apt negotiator of the peace accord that resolved the federalist wars in November 1840. He later participated in both the Rafael Vásquez and the Adrian Woll expeditions into Texas.

Mauricio Carrasco: Federalist military leader sent to seek aid in Texas by Pedro Lemus, he was arrested by centralists near the Rio Grande in the summer of 1839.

Vicente Córdova: A Nacogdoches, Texas, resident who led a revolt along with a few Indian allies against the Republic of Texas in 1838 as a loyalist to Mexico. Failing to gain sufficient support in what amounted to a hopeless cause given the overwhelming numbers against him, Córdova led a small number of followers in an escape journey through the Texas frontier that cost at least half of his fifty men. Though wounded, he managed to make it all the way to Matamoros. The centralists dispatched him in repeated forays against the Texas government, and he died in that cause at the battle of Salado (Texas) on September 18, 1842.

Juan Nepomuceno Cortina (b. May 16, 1824, in Camargo, Tamaulipas): A Mexican folk hero, he served with Arista at the outset of Mexico's war with the United States in 1846. Subsequently, he was repeatedly indicted for rustling but escaped prosecution under the protection of local citizens. In retribution against the exploitation of Mexicans in the region of the Rio Grande border, he pronounced a revolution against the United States in 1859 but then fought against the Confederacy and in support of Juarez in the war against France. By moving back and forth across the Rio Grande and retaining his status as a hero to the Mexican people of the region, he lived free until his death on October 30, 1894.

José de Jesús Davilo y Prieto: Appointed the centralist governor of Nuevo León in September 1839.

Eugenio Fernandez: The federalist political chief in Coahuila in the summer of 1839.

Francisco Vital Fernández: A Tamaulipas governor and supporter of the failed rebellion on behalf of a republic of the Sierra Madre in 1851.

Vicente Filisola (b. Italy, 1789): Served in the Spanish army in Mexico before making a late reversal in favor of independence. Commander of government forces stationed at Matamoros, 1838–1839.

George Fisher (b. April 1795, in Hungary, as Djordje Ribar): As a merchant and veteran observer of Mexican affairs living in Texas, he advocated for commercial ties with federalist rebels. His incredibly varied background included studies for the Orthodox priesthood and service as an eighteen-year-old in Serbia's failed revolution. Coming to the United States in 1814, he changed his name and soon joined intrigues for the independence of Mexico, where he moved in 1825 and became active in the Yorkino political faction. He managed to receive an empresario contract for the Galveston region but soon moved to Matamoros where he was for a short time a liberal newspaperman, incurring the animus of the government. From New Orleans in October 1835, he supported another filibustering expedition against the centralists but settled in Houston from 1837 to 1840. His later adventures took him to Panama and Greece before he moved to San Francisco, where he died on June 11, 1873.

William S. Fisher: A veteran fighter and adventurer from Virginia, he emigrated to Texas in 1834, settling in Gonzales. He represented that municipality at the Consultation that sought to gain unified resistance to the centralists in November 1835. He served at the battle of San Jacinto and was a perennial volunteer thereafter. He commanded the frontier detachment stationed at Mission San José outside of San Antonio, on April 4, 1840, and later that month became an intermediary with Antonio Canales, who had fled his defeats at the hands of the centralists and once again sought aid in Texas. Fisher left his post to recruit a company that joined Canales in August 1840. After the end of the federalist wars, he continued fighting against the centralists, including as a volunteer in the Somervell expedition of 1842, during which he led those who refused to disband, was captured and sent to Perote prison until his release in 1844. He died in Texas the following year.

Juan José Galan: A centralist who opposed the federalist takeover in Coahuila in March 1839. He led government forces to victory in a battle for Gigedo (Coahuila) on January 7, 1840, with further successes later that month. His most notable accomplishment occurred on March 23–24, 1840, at Morelos where his cavalry unit, numbering eighty-eight men, trapped Antonio Zapata, leading to his surrender and subsequent execution.

Joaquin Garcia: A centralist native of Nuevo León, rising to the post of governor in the fall of 1838. He remained a staunch nationalist until his death in the fall of 1839.

Francisco Garcia Conde: A centralist governor in Saltillo (Coahuila) in early 1839.

Valentín Gómez Farías (b. 1781 in Jalisco): A resident of Zacatecas, he served in the national congress, 1824–1830, and briefly as vice president under Santa Anna. A nationally prominent federalist political figure, he favored disestablishment of the church, republicanism, progressive taxation, and civic militias in place of the regular army. He was exiled from 1834 to 1838 before returning to support the federalist uprising under Urrea in 1838. He escaped from prison but remained in hiding throughout 1839, coming out to stage a failed coup on July 15, 1840, after which he returned to exile but remained a staunch liberal ideologist.

C. José Gonzales Cuellar: Editor of the newspaper *El Correo del Rio Bravo del Norte* advocating for the separatist government for the northeastern states of Mexico in 1840.

José M. Gonzalez: A native of Laredo, he served the federalist cause as early as June 1839, under Antonio Canales in his contest for power with Pedro Lemus, and he participated in missions to seek further support in Texas. During the October 1840 battle at Buena Vista outside Saltillo, he led a defecting unit of cavalry but did not join the centralists.

Bernardo Gutiérrez de Lara (b. August 20, 1774, in Guerrero): A member of a prominent family of hacendados and political leaders in Tamaulipas. A leader in the movement for Mexican independence, he sought assistance in the United States and even had conversations with Secretary of State James A. Monroe in that effort. He helped organize a failed filibustering expedition that set off from Louisiana in April 1812 but returned to New Orleans in time to serve in the battle against British forces in 1815. Elected as governor of Tamaulipas in 1824, he held various important posts thereafter. A federalist supporter of Anaya in his contest for influence against Pedro Lemus, he took over command of the centralist troops in Guerrero only a few days before the federalists attacked and captured him in 1839.

James Hamilton (b. Charleston, May 8, 1786): As governor of South Carolina and a member of the United States Congress, he advocated an extreme states'-rights position in the nullification crisis during the administration of Andrew Jackson. Hamilton won admiration in Texas for his early support, not only recognizing its independence but also securing a loan from the Bank of the United States in Philadelphia. Based on this success, he agreed to seek further financial aid from various European governments but instead gained credit for securing diplomatic recognitions. However, upon his arrival in Texas, he learned that political leadership had veered back to Sam Houston (a Jacksonian and unionist), who repudiated both Hamilton's loan agreements and the personal financial debts that he claimed. He moved back and forth before settling in east Texas in the 1850s. On a trip in 1857 his ship sank, and he died heroically by giving up his place in the lifeboat to a woman and her child.

George Washington Hockley: Generally a supporter of Sam Houston and a critic of both Lamar and the federalist rebels, he was born in

Philadelphia in 1802 and worked for a time in the commissary division of the war department of the United States government, where he met Houston and later followed him to Texas. He fought at San Jacinto in command of the artillery known as the Twin Sisters. Hockley went on to serve on diplomatic missions on behalf of the Texas government, including an effort in 1843 to arrange a peace with Mexico. He made his home in Galveston but died in Corpus Christi on June 6, 1854.

Robert Anderson Irion (b. July 7, 1804, in Tennessee): He worked variously as a physician (having graduated from medical school at Transylvania University in Kentucky in 1826) and a surveyor before becoming first a senator representing Nacogdoches and then secretary of state of the Republic of Texas in the administration of Sam Houston in 1837. He traveled in the United States and Europe discharging his diplomatic duties until Lamar appointed a new secretary on December 13, 1838. Irion returned to his medical practice in Nacogdoches until his death on March 2, 1861, the anniversary of the Texas declaration of independence.

Albert Sidney Johnston: He served the Republic of Texas both as a brigadier general and as secretary of war in 1839. A graduate of the United States Military Academy at West Point, he was one of the few Texas leaders with formal military training. Most famously, he went on to become commander of the western forces of the Confederacy and died of wounds suffered at the battle of Shiloh in 1862.

Samuel Jordan: Once labelled by Houston as "the abandoned man" because of his mysterious past, he was still in his twenties during the time of the federalist wars. Jordan deserted the Texas army with Reuben Ross to attack Guerrero in the fall of 1839 and replaced him through an election by the volunteers in December of that year, leading to a clash and Ross's departure to Texas. Jordan returned again at the head of another company of volunteers in the summer of 1840 and fled back to Texas following nearly disastrous engagements near Saltillo in October. His subsequent clash with Sam Houston included a thwarted attempt to kill the Texas president with an ax, but he left for New Orleans, seeking other filibustering expeditions and died there of an overdose of laudanum on June 22, 1841.

H. W. Karnes: A frontiersman born in Tennessee on September 8, 1812, he fought at the siege of Béxar in December 1835 and joined volunteers raised to relieve the siege of the Alamo. Learning of its fate, he carried the news east and then continued with Houston's army, primarily in scouting duties. Imprisoned when he went to Matamoros at the behest of the Texas government to seek the release of prisoners held there during the winter of 1836, he escaped and returned to military duty the next year, remaining in charge of frontier units from 1838 to 1840, many of which he raised himself while holding the rank of colonel despite being barely literate. He contracted what was variously described as yellow fever or typhoid and succumbed to it in San Antonio on August 16, 1840.

George Kendall: A journalist who published a narrative detailing the fate of the Santa Fe expedition of 1841.

Mirabeau Buonaparte Lamar: A native of Georgia, he arrived in Texas in time to lead a company at the battle of San Jacinto on April 21, 1836, and went on to become president of the Republic of Texas for a three-year term commencing in December 1838. His extensive literary activities later included an unfinished history of Texas. Stationed at a post in Laredo during the US–Mexico war (1846–1848), he compiled memories of veterans of the federalist wars. As president he avoided formal participation in that conflict but, in violation of the principles of neutrality, he allowed rebels to recruit manpower and supplies while they took refuge in Texas.

Pedro Lemus: A native of Cuba, he participated in Mexico's war for independence and developed a friendship with Stephen F. Austin; as a federalist caudillo, he was named to command the third division of the "Army of Liberation" by Urrea in early 1839 but was widely distrusted by both sides for excessive personal ambition; he fled from Mexico in 1839.

Abner S. Lipscomb: A native of South Carolina (b. February 10, 1789), he studied law in the office of John C. Calhoun before emigrating to Alabama where he became chief justice in the state supreme court from 1823 to 1835. In Texas he was secretary of state during most of the Lamar administration (1838–1841). After Texas achieved statehood, he became a member of the state supreme court beginning in 1846. He resided in Austin at the time of his death on December 8, 1856.

Manuel M. de Llano: The interim federalist governor of Nuevo León in March 1839, a post he had held before the rebellion broke out; in that capacity he authorized federalist representatives to solicit aid for the rebellion in Texas and the United States in the summer of 1839. According to the *Texas Sentinel*, he was a delegate to the federalist provisional government in 1840, known in Texas as the Republic of the Rio Grande.

Luis López: A follower of Pedro Lemus during the early days of the federalist wars, he commanded the Mexican branch of rebel cavalry along with Samuel Jordan in the summer of 1840; his unit went over to the centralists during the battles outside Saltillo in October.

Jorge López de Lara: As alcalde of Matamoros in fall 1839, he supported the centralist government and warned against continued revolt.

Victor Loupy (b. ca. 1794, in France): A former sailor, he served for a time in the role of interpreter for Zapata. He was one of two volunteers from Texas captured with Zapata on March 25, 1840, tried as a mercenary, and subsequently executed. During his trial he confessed to having previously participated in military actions as far back as October 1839, including battles at Guerrero, Matamoros, Monterrey, and Talayotes. Judged guilty of "piracy" by a military tribunal, he was executed at Monclova, Coahuila, on April 13, 1840.

James Love (b. May 12, 1795, in Kentucky): He entered the law and politics, including a twelve-year stint in the state legislature and a term in the US Congress from 1833 to 1835. Settling in Galveston, he joined the group that included Lamar and Burnet known for its extreme hatred of Sam Houston. He held a variety of judicial posts there and for a time joined Houston in opposing secession but then served two years in the Confederate cavalry. He was hampered by ill health in his later years and died at his home on June 12, 1874.

Hugh McLeod (b. August 1, 1814, New York City): He graduated from the United States Military Academy at West Point in 1835 but quickly resigned his commission in order to emigrate to Texas, where in the summer of 1836, he volunteered for the Army. The next year McLeod accepted the role of Texas adjutant general and then left to become an aide to T. J. Rusk during the fight against Vicente Córdova and the Cherokees in 1838. He commanded the Santa Fe expedition at Lamar's request in 1841, resulting in his capture and imprisonment at Perote in Mexico City until securing release in 1842. Eventually he married into the Lamar family and earned a living as a planter, lawyer, and politician in the legislature of the republic. Something of a perennial volunteer, McLeod served as Texas adjutant general during the war between the United States and Mexico (1846–1848) and joined the Confederate Army with the rank of colonel but soon contracted pneumonia and died on January 3, 1862.

Bennett McNeil (b. ca. 1804 in Philadelphia): One of two volunteers from Texas captured with Zapata on March 25, 1840. Judged guilty of "piracy" by a military tribunal, he was executed at Monclova, Coahuila, on April 13, 1840.

José Antonio Mejia: The federalist leader of assault against Tampico in the winter and spring of 1839. Although victorious at Tuxpan, he was defeated by Valencia on May 3, 1839, captured, and executed.

Manuel Menchaca: As centralist company commander he arrested federalist leaders as they sought to escape across the Rio Grande in the late summer of 1839. In March 1840, he fought as a centralist in the crucial battle at Morelos that led to the capture of Antonio Zapata.

Juan Nepomuceno Molano: A brother-in-law of Antonio Canales and married to the daughter of fellow federalist leader J. M. Carbajal, he was listed by the Austin newspaper *Texas Sentinel* as vice president of the "provisional government" for the northeastern states in 1840 headed by Jesús Cárdenas and known in Texas as the Republic of the Rio Grande. Previously he had been lieutenant governor of Tamaulipas, and as alcalde of Matamoros in 1836 he earned gratitude from Anglo Texans by intervening in favor of the prisoners brought there by the centralist forces as they retreated following the battle of San Jacinto. In the summer and fall of 1840, he led a company in the expedition headed by S. W. Jordan but became disenchanted and surrendered his unit of rebels to the centralists during the battles for Saltillo, thus gaining the hatred of the Anglo Texas survivors of that engagement.

José Cayetano de Montoya: He commanded a regiment of cavalry under Pedro Ampudia at the battle in and around Morelos in March 1840, in which Antonio Zapata was captured; he then led the centralist defenders of Saltillo in October. He represented the interests of the government when Arista negotiated the surrender of the federalists under Antonio Canales at Camargo in November 1840.

Juan Morales: A veteran of the campaign in Texas that included the Battle of the Alamo, he commanded government forces in the engagements at Buena Vista outside Saltillo in October 1840.

Manuel Musquiz: Brother of Ramón Musquiz, former political chief in Texas and official of the Coahuila y Tejas state government, he carried out the federalist takeover of local government at Candela in January 1839.

José Antonio Navarro (b. February 27, 1795): From a leading family in San Antonio de Béxar, he advocated for Mexican independence and became a friend of Stephen F. Austin. As a delegate, he signed the Texas Declaration of Independence in March 1836, and remained friendly with Anglo Texans thereafter. He participated as a commissioner from Texas in the disastrous Santa Fe expedition of 1841, was declared a traitor by Mexico, and sentenced to death, a punishment commuted to life imprisonment from which he escaped after three years. Returning to

Texas, he served as a delegate to the convention for annexation to the United States and used his influence to advocate for Tejanos, including as a member of the state legislature combating efforts to disenfranchise them. He died on January 31, 1871.

Benjamin F. Neal: Veteran of the May 1839 battles for Monterrey, he returned with the Texas volunteers later that year and participated in actions in early 1840. A native of Virginia, he had acquired some legal training prior to emigrating to Texas in 1838. He served as a justice in Refugio County in the early 1840s before moving to Corpus Christi in 1846 and becoming its first mayor. Later he made his fortune in the Arizona gold rush, but he returned to become an ardent advocate of states' rights and fought as a Confederate artilleryman. He lived until 1873.

Andrew Neill [Neal]: A native of Scotland, he had studied law in Virginia and served as a judge in Mississippi. He emigrated to Texas with the rank of captain of volunteers under Felix Huston in 1836. He was recruited from the town of Houston for service in the federalist wars in September 1839. Subsequently, he served in various campaigns against the Indians before being captured by forces from Mexico under Adrian Woll. He escaped to write a narrative of his misadventures and lived for a time in Galveston before joining the Confederate Army. He later moved to the town of Seguin, where he resided at the time of his death in 1875.

José María de Ortega: A veteran of military engagements in and around Monterrey since 1838, he became governor of Nuevo León in the summer of 1840.

Francisco G. Pavón: Veteran of military service dating back to 1809. As centralist company commander he pursued federalists when they escaped across the Rio Grande into Texas in the summer of 1839 and commanded the garrison at Mier that fought against Texas-laden federalist forces in November of that year.

Santana Penalbes: Alcalde in the Department of the Rio Grande who called for the militia to turn out in favor of the federalist rebellion in February 1839.

Antonio Pérez: A native of San Antonio de Béxar and a veteran on the side of Texas independence, he attempted to warn Jordan about the potential for betrayal by Juan N. Molano. Frustrated that his advice was not heeded, he left at the head of Tejano cavalrymen during the battle outside Saltillo in October 1840 and reputably became loyal to the Mexican government in subsequent conflicts on the Texas frontier during the latter days of the Republic of Texas.

S. A. Plummer: Lamar's personal attorney and representative dispatched to explore matters in the Victoria (Texas) area in the spring of 1840. Instead of confronting those with aggressive intent, he supported their talk of conquests in Mexico.

John T. Price: Selected as a "commissioner" to represent the Cárdenas government in Texas in February 1840. He led a company of "cowboys" in the unit initially serving with Reuben Ross in the late summer of 1839. He then returned for the final military phase with S. W. Jordan in the summer of 1840. Subsequently, he remained active in frontier service for the Republic of Texas.

Benito Quijano: Given the title of brigadier general and commander of a small unit of centralist forces by President Bustamante in March 1839.

José Antonio Quintero: Tamaulipas governor starting in 1837.

Mateo Quiroz: Became the centralist governor of Nuevo León in the summer of 1839.

Miguel Ramos Arizpe (b. February 15, 1775, in Coahuila): Ordained as a priest in 1803, he later earned a doctorate in law in Mexico City. Beginning in 1811, he served in Spain's Cortes (parliament), where he first began to advocate for liberal ideas, including federalism, which led to his imprisonment. Freed in 1820, he became a member of the new Cortes formed as a consequence of a revolution that year. Back in Mexico in 1823, Ramos Arizpe represented Coahuila in Congress and then led the commission that established the Constitution of 1824. Thereafter he held a variety of cabinet and diplomatic posts.

He became dean of the Puebla Cathedral and died there on April 18, 1843.

Isidro Reyes: He commanded the centralist forces numbering 650 that captured Antonio Zapata and a handful of followers at Morelos on March 23–24, 1840, followed by a rapid move to engage federalists under Antonio Canales that evening and a major clash the next day on a battlefield at San Fernando, the bloodiest and most significant engagement of the entire conflict. In November 1840 he assisted the government's negotiations with Antonio Canales to end the federalist wars. In 1844 he served as minister of war under Santa Anna.

Pedro Rodriguez: As military commander at Guerrero, he acceded to federalist demands for cooperation in order to avoid bloodshed there in February 1839.

Richard Roman (b. 1811, in Kentucky): He attended medical school at Transylvania University without finishing. He fought in the Black Hawk War in 1832 and emigrated to Texas in January 1836, later participating in the battle of San Jacinto. Resigning from the Army, he settled around the Victoria/Refugio area and won election to the first Congress of the Republic of Texas. As a "major" in command of volunteers in the Republic of Texas, he threatened to lead a company of cowboys to intervene in the federalist wars of northeastern Mexico in 1839. His varied career later included service as a Texas Ranger under John C. Hays in the 1846–1848 war between the United States and Mexico.

Reuben Ross: A native of Kentucky, he first came to Texas in April 1836 and attached himself to Felix Huston between then and June of 1837. In 1839 he led a company of volunteers from Gonzales, Texas, known loosely as "rangers." He commanded a company of regular troops of the Republic of Texas who participated in the assault that began at Mier in the fall of 1839. Returning to Texas in disgust at the slow pace of activity, his turbulent trajectory included a duel that wounded Ben McCulloch, whose brother Henry fatally shot Ross on Christmas Eve, 1839.

Severo Ruiz: An ally of the prominent Tamaulipas federalist Bernardo Gutiérrez de Lara. Operating under the authority of Urrea, he led federalist forces in and around Monterrey at the outset of hostilities in February 1839. Pedro Lemus dispatched him to seek aid in Texas in August 1839.

José María Salinas: A Guerrero judicial official who in mid-October of 1839 warned of the coming of an army reinforced in Texas and bent on bringing about renewed rebellion.

José Juan Sanchez: Holding the rank of colonel, he led a cavalry company against Samuel Jordan's invaders in engagements at Buena Vista in October 1840.

Manuel Sánchez Navarro: A member of a prominent Coahuila family of ranchers and public officials, at Candela he resisted the federalist takeover of local government in January 1839.

Antonio López de Santa Anna (b. February 21, 1794, in Jalapa, Vera Cruz): He rose to become the major political and military figure of Mexico for a twenty-year period beginning in the mid-1830s. He is generally seen as the ultimate caudillo in that his personal self-interest mostly overshadowed policy. His ignominious legacy included the loss of Texas (1836) and the cession of another large chunk of Mexico's territorial domain to the United States as a result of the disastrous 1846–1848 war, both of which occurred after he personally commanded the Mexican Army. He likewise lost most of his huge personal fortune. In and out of power at least eleven times during the decades of the 1830s, 1840s, and 1850s, he generally gained support from financiers, elements of the army, and centralist politicians but had little interest in the actual exercise of governmental policy; even his dictatorships invariably collapsed. During the 1830s he shared the presidency with Bustamante but stayed in the background of the federalist wars in the northeastern states. Often exiled, including for a twenty-year period following the success of the Plan of Ayutla (1854), he was allowed to return to Mexico and died there on June 21, 1876.

Juan Nepomuceno Seguín (1806–1890): The most famous Bejareño of the era before and after Texas independence, his political activity included a stint as political chief at the age of twenty-eight. His military career commenced in 1835 when he raised a company in support of what began that year as a federalist revolt in Texas against centralist rule, and he participated in the assault that forced the capitulation of his native city in December 1835. His cavalry unit served at San Jacinto and shadowed the retreat of the Mexican Army afterward. As commander of a military company in 1837, he oversaw the burial of the men who fell at the Battle of the Alamo. Seguín won election to the senate of the Republic of Texas, resigning in 1840 to follow federalist Antonio Canales. Though he returned to become mayor of his city, he found himself embroiled in many disputes with Anglo Texans, suffering accusations of disloyalty and threats so great that in 1842 he fled to Mexico with his family and fought against the United States during the 1846–1848 war. He eventually returned to his native land and ended his days in the residence of his son in Laredo.

Alexander Somervell (b. June 11, 1796, in Maryland): He came to Texas in 1833 under the auspices of one of the land grants of Stephen F. Austin. He fought at both the siege of Béxar and San Jacinto and served in the Congress of the Republic of Texas before he was tapped by President Sam Houston to lead a retaliatory expedition against Mexico in 1842. This ill-fated and poorly led venture resulted in the infamous "black bean" episode at the town of Mier, leading to the execution of 10 percent of those recaptured following a prison break. He survived but was murdered in February 1854.

Valentín Soto: A federalist rebel volunteer from Laredo, he was among those serving under Antonio Zapata and was captured on March 25, 1840. In 1847 he provided oral testimony at the behest of M. B. Lamar, former president of the Republic of Texas, describing his leader's execution.

James Treat: A veteran investor who had long resided in central America, he received appointment as special agent to Mexico based on persuading President Lamar of a high probability of success in gaining the recognition of the Republic of Texas. Arriving in Mexico City in December 1839, Treat attempted a variety of approaches without closing in on an agreement and departed a year later but succumbed to consumption while at sea.

Domingo Ugartechea: A colonel commanding centralist forces at Monterrey in February 1839, he was previously known as the commander of the government forces in San Antonio that surrendered to the rebels there in December 1835. He commanded centralist forces in Saltillo in the spring of 1839, where he was killed in battle on May 24 of that year.

Rafael Ugartechea: A captain in charge of the government forces at Agualeguas in the fall of 1838, as head of a small unit of centralists he was defeated by Pedro Lemus at the villa of Serraldo on April 22, 1839.

Rafael Uribe: As a federalist official, he urged cooperation with other communities in carrying out a takeover of the government in 1839, but he later reconciled to the centralists under Arista.

José Urrea (b. 1797 in Tucson, Sonora): He rose in influence by supporting the cause of independence and became a major federalist caudillo. After being denied appointment as governor, he launched a rebellion in Sonora in March 1838 and gained wide recognition as a rebel general-in-chief in early stages of the conflict. By early 1839 he bore the title "liberator and general-in-chief" of the rebel cause in the northeastern region. Along with Mejia, he commanded the failed federalist campaign against Tampico, during which he was defeated by Valencia on May 3, 1839, captured, and imprisoned. From prison in April 1840, Urrea wrote a thoughtful analysis of the tragedy that the federalist wars represented. However, he continued to be repeatedly arrested after many more failed pronunciamientos (including an aborted coup with Gómez Farías on July 15, 1840), but he managed to avoid long-term imprisonment and even held executive power in Sonora, from 1842 to 1844, and lived to fight against the United States during its invasion, 1846–1848.

Gabriel Valencia: A centralist general who defeated the federalists under Mejia and Urrea at San Miguel Lablanca near the Tampico–Puebla Road on May 3, 1839.

Cornelius Van Ness (b. 1803 in Vermont): He had accompanied his father's diplomatic mission to Spain sometime after 1820, moving to San Antonio where he practiced law beginning in 1837 and served as district attorney there from 1838 to 1842, the year of his death from an accidental gunshot wound. His brother George took part in the Santa Fe expedition sponsored by President Lamar and was imprisoned for a time in Saltillo.

Rafael Vásquez (b. 1804 in Mexico City; d. 1854): He served as an officer during the wars for independence. Following the centralist defeat at Béxar in December 1835, he commanded the rear guard during that army's subsequent retreat. He fought at the head of a company of centralist cavalry at the engagement at Buena Vista outside Saltillo in October 1840 and remained in the army, returning to Texas in command of the expedition that temporarily captured Béxar in March 1842. He became the military governor of Coahuila in 1845, and during the war between the United States and Mexico (1846–1848), he returned to the Buena Vista battleground, where he fought with distinction against the army under Zachary Taylor. He ended his career as a commanding general in several states of Mexico during the 1850s.

Santiago Vidaurri (b. July 25, 1809, in Lampazos, Nuevo León): He rose to become the chief assistant to the governors of his state. In the 1840s and early 1850s he remained a staunch conservative until leading a revolt against Santa Anna under the banner of federalism. He then became military caudillo over the states of Nuevo León and Coahuila between 1855 and 1864. Upon losing power there he joined the French imperialist government and for that was executed as a traitor without a trial by Porfirio Díaz in 1867.

Francisco Vidaurri y Villaseñor: The federalist governor of Coahuila y Tejas in 1834, he sought aid for the federalist cause in Texas in July

1839. He led some 270 rebels in attacking the villa of Gigedo on January 7, 1840, where they were defeated by a smaller force under Juan José Galan. According to the *Texas Sentinel*, he was a delegate to the federalist provisional government in 1840 known in Texas as the Republic of the Rio Grande.

Agustín Viesca: A federalist, former Coahuila governor, and thus a leading political figure during the early stages of the rebellion.

Adrian Woll (b. December 2, 1795, in France): Mexican centralist general, educated in France for a military career. He served in Mexico's Wars for Independence beginning in 1817, became a naturalized citizen, and married in Mexico. His career advanced through association with Santa Anna and Bustamante. He fought in Texas in 1836, participating in the retreat that followed the Battle of San Jacinto in April. He returned to carry out a brief expedition that captured San Antonio in the summer of 1842, and later back in Mexico he fought against Juarez both before and during the French occupation, after which he returned to his native land where he died in 1875.

Antonio Zapata (b. 1800): He became a successful rancher headquartered in Guerrero, Tamaulipas, but suffered financial losses from centralists as they sought provisions during their war in Texas, 1835–1836. Known as a ferocious fighter against Comanche raiders, he became an ardent federalist rebel military figure, leading his followers to proclaim total commitment to that cause in the summer of 1839, a position that he maintained throughout the wars up to and including his death by execution at Monclova on March 29, 1840, following his capture resulting from a battle at Morelos on March 23–24.

NOTES

INTRODUCTION

1. Catherine Andrews, "The Rise and Fall of a Regional Strongman: Felipe de la Garza's Pronunciamiento of 1822," in *Malcontents, Rebels, and Pronunciados: The Politics of Insurrection in Nineteenth-Century Mexico*, ed. Will Fowler, 22–40 (Lincoln: University of Nebraska Press, 2012).

2. Charles A. Hale, *The Transformation of Liberalism in Late Nineteenth-Century Mexico* (Princeton, NJ: Princeton University Press, 1989), 79, 81, 84. José María Luis Mora, the ideological father of Mexican liberalism, himself felt concern over the evil influences of Mexico City, but by 1830 he also worried over the disruptive tendencies of factional splits and general instability, 103, 107. On the absence of a clear sense of nationhood in the 1820s and 1830s, see Richard N. Sinkin, *The Mexican Reform, 1855–1876: A Study in Liberal Nation-Building* (Austin: Institute of Latin American Studies, University of Texas at Austin, 1979), 24–25.

3. Donald Fithian Stevens, *Origins of Instability in Early Republican Mexico* (Durham, NC: Duke University Press, 1991), 82; Timothy Anna, *Forging Mexico, 1821–1835* (Lincoln: University of Nebraska Press, 1998), 263.

4. Michael T. Ducey, "Municipalities, Prefects, and Pronunciamientos: Power and Political Mobilizations in the Huasteca during the First Federal Republic," in *Forceful Negotiations: The Origins of the Pronunciamiento in Nineteenth-Century Mexico*, ed. Will Fowler, 74–100 (Lincoln: University of Nebraska Press, 2010), 79.

5. Anna, *Forging Mexico*, 263; Michael P. Costeloe, *The Central Republic of Mexico 1835–1845* (New York: Cambridge University Press, 1993), 49; Andrés Reséndez, *Changing National Identities at the Frontier: Texas and New Mexico, 1800–1850* (Cambridge: Cambridge University Press, 2004), 175–77; Brian DeLay, *War of a Thousand Deserts: Indian Raids and the U.S.-Mexican War*

(New Haven, CT: Yale University Press, 2008), 166.

6. Will Fowler, ed., *Malcontents, Rebels, and Pronunciados: The Politics of Insurrection in Nineteenth-Century Mexico* (Lincoln: University of Nebraska Press, 2012), vii, xxii, xxiv.

7. Will Fowler, "'I Pronounce Thus I Exist': Redefining the Pronunciamiento in Independent Mexico, 1821–1876," in *Forceful Negotiations: The Origins of the Pronunciamiento in Nineteenth-Century Mexico*, ed. Will Fowler, 246–65 (Lincoln: University of Nebraska Press, 2010), 249.

8. Fowler, "I Pronounce," 246.

9. Ibid., 262.

10. Antonio Annino, "The Two-Faced Janus: The Pueblos and the Origins of Mexican Liberalism," in *Cycles of Conflict, Centuries of Change: Crisis, Reform, and Revolution in Mexico*, ed. Elisa Servín, Leticia Reina, and John Tutino, 60–90 (Durham, NC: Duke University Press, 2007), 88.

11. François-Xavier Guerra, "Mexico from Independence to Revolution: The Mutations of Liberalism," in *Cycles of Conflict, Centuries of Change: Crisis, Reform, and Revolution in Mexico*, ed. Elisa Servín, Leticia Reina, and John Tutino, 129–52 (Durham, NC: Duke University Press, 2007), 134; see also Sinkin, *Mexican Reform*, 11.

12. For more details on the Texas rebellion, see Paul D. Lack, *The Texas Revolutionary Experience: A Political and Social History, 1835–1836* (College Station: Texas A&M University Press, 1992).

13. Shara Ali, "The Origins of the Santiago Imán Revolt, 1838–1840: A Reassessment," in *Forceful Negotiations: The Origins of the Pronunciamiento in Nineteenth-Century Mexico*, ed. Will Fowler, 143–61 (Lincoln: University of Nebraska Press, 2010), quotations, 146–48.

14. D. A. Brading, *The Origins of Mexican Nationalism* (Cambridge: Centre of Latin American Studies, 1985), 70; D. A. Brading, *The First America: The Spanish Monarchy, Creole Patriots and the Liberal State, 1492–1867* (Cambridge: Cambridge University Press, 1991), 601; Costeloe, *Central Republic*, 92.

15. Brading, *First America*, 640.

16. Timothy Anna, "Demystifying Early Nineteenth-Century Mexico," *Mexican Studies* (Winter 1993): 135; Stevens, *Origins of Instability*, 59.

17. Will Fowler, "The Forgotten Century: Mexico, 1810–1910," *Bulletin of Latin American Research* 15 (1995): 3.

18. Brading, *Origins*, 68; Stevens, *Origins of Instability*, 59.

19. Anna, "Demystifying," 130. See also the pioneering study by David Weber, *The Mexican Frontier 1821–1846: The American Southwest under Mexico* (Albuquerque: University of New Mexico Press, 1982).

20. Timothy Anna, "Inventing Mexico: Provincehood and Nationhood after

Independence," *Bulletin of Latin American Research* 15 (1996): 7; Armando
C. Alonzo, *Tejano Legacy: Rancheros and Settlers in South Texas, 1734–1900*
(Albuquerque: University of New Mexico Press, 1998).

21. Reséndez, *National Identities*, 146–49.

22. Omar S. Valerio-Jiménez, *River of Hope: Forging Identity and Nation in the Rio Grande Borderlands* (Durham, NC: Duke University Press, 2013), *passim*.

23. Vito Alessio Robles, *Coahuila y Texas desde la Consumación de la independencia hasta el Tratado de Paz de Guadalupe Hidalgo* (México: Biblioteca Porrua, 1979), 2: 180.

24. DeLay, *Thousand Deserts*, 145.

25. Costeloe, *Central Republic*, 86–103, quotation from 92.

26. Ibid., 8, 303.

27. William Ransom Hogan, *The Texas Republic: A Social and Economic History* (Austin: University of Texas Press, 1969), 267–90.

28. Paul D. Lack, "The Córdova Revolt," in *Tejano Journey 1770–1850*, ed. Gerald E. Poyo, 89–109 (Austin: University of Texas Press, 1996).

29. Fowler, *Malcontents*, xvii–xxii.

CHAPTER 1

1. Linda Arnold, "José Ramón García Ugarte: Patriot, Federalist, or Malcontent?" in *Malcontents, Rebels, and Pronunciados: The Politics of Insurrection in Nineteenth-Century Mexico*, ed. Will Fowler, 91–110 (Lincoln: University of Nebraska Press, 2012); Sergio A. Cañedo Gamboa, "Ponciano Arriaga and Mariano Ávila's Intellectual Backing of the 14 April 1837 Pronunciamiento of San Luis Potosí," in *Malcontents, Rebels, and Pronunciados: The Politics of Insurrection in Nineteenth-Century Mexico*, ed. Will Fowler, 111–28 (Lincoln: University of Nebraska Press, 2012).

2. De Lay, *Thousand Deserts*, 175; Germán Martínez Martínez, "Inventing the Nation: The Pronunciamiento and the Construction of Mexican National Identity, 1821–1876," in *Forceful Negotiations: The Origins of the Pronunciamiento in Nineteenth-Century Mexico*, ed. Will Fowler, 246–65 (Lincoln: University of Nebraska Press, 2010), 240.

3. William A. Depalo, *The Mexican National Army, 1822–1852* (College Station: Texas A&M University Press, 1997), 65, 68–69.

4. Anna, *Forging Mexico*, 256–57.

5. Don M. Coerver, "The Sonora Revolt of 1837," in *The United States and Mexico at War: Nineteenth-Century Expansionism and Conflict*, ed. Don Frazier, 391 (New York: Macmillan Reference, 1998).

6. *The generals and other leaders of the Army of the North to their subordinates and*

all fellow citizens, Broadsheet, March 6, 1838, Streeter Collection, Archives, Briscoe Center, University of Texas at Austin; Juan Gimala Cabofrana to the Governor of the Department of Coahuila, January 19, 1838, Guerrero Archives, Instituto Estatal de Documentación de Coahuila. Ramos Arizpe, Coahuila, Mexico; hereafter cited as GA.

7. Bernard Bee to Brig. Gen'l [Albert Sidney] Johnston, January 20, 1838; Johnston to Bee, February 8, 1838, Albert Sidney and William Preston Johnston Collection. Special Collections, Tulane University, New Orleans, Louisiana, hereafter cited as ASJ.

8. Costeloe, *Central Republic*, 137.

9. A. Viesca to Valentín Gómez Farías, March 9, 1838; April 18, 1838, Valentín Gómez Farías Papers, Nettie Lee Benson Library Latin American Collection, University of Texas at Austin, hereafter cited as VGF.

10. Valentín Canalizo [broadside] *To the Individuals Composing the Second Division*, April 3, 1838, Streeter Collection.

11. Santiago Galván to Valentín Gómez Farías, October 5, 1838, VGF.

12. Filisola to residents of this region, October 13, 1838, in *Gaceta del Gobierno de Coahuila* (Saltillo), October 27, 1838.

13. *Gaceta de Coahuila*, December 1, 1838.

14. Josefina Z. Vazquez, *La Supuesta Republica del Rio Grande* (Victoria, Tamaulipas, Mexico: Instituto de Investigaciones Históricas, 1995), 8–9.

15. Joaquin Garcia, Governor of Nuevo León to the Governor of the Department of Coahuila, November 30, 1838, in *Gaceta de Coahuila*, December 1, 1838.

16. *Gaceta de Coahuila*, November 24, 1838; Joaquin Garcia to the Governor of the Department of Coahuila, November 25, 1838, in *Gaceta de Coahuila*, December 1, 1838.

17. Charles Adams Gulick et al. (eds.), *The Papers of Mirabeau Buonaparte Lamar* (Austin, TX: A. C. Baldwin & Sons, 1922), 5: 223.

18. Valentín Gómez Farías to Vicente Lara, December 23, 1838 (first quotations), Gómez Farías to [unknown in Guadalajara], December 25, 1838, VGF.

19. F[elix] Huston to M. B. Lamar, December 31, 1838, Gulick (ed.), *Papers of Lamar*, 2: 376–83.

20. Ayuntamiento to the Citizens of this Municipality, GA, November 30, 1838; Matias Ramirez to justices in Camargo, January 10, 1839, Laredo Archives (microfilm in St. Mary's University Library, San Antonio, Texas), hereafter cited as LA.

21. [Vicente Filisola] Proclamation, January 6, 1839, in *El Ancla* (Matamoros), January 12, 1839, Matamoros Archives, Dolph Briscoe Center for American History, University of Texas at Austin, 32: 66, hereafter cited as MA; A. Neill to Albert Sidney Johnston, ASJ; *Telegraph and Texas Register* (Houston), January

16, 1839.

22. Elustiano Mendez, Circular, January 7, 1839, LA.

23. [Report] by J. M. Fernandez, January 20, 1839, LA.

24. [Declaration by] the Ayuntamiento Constitucional de Monclova, January 19, 1839; Proceedings of a meeting of Coahuilenses, January 19, 1839, GA.

25. Manuel Sánchez Navarro to Francisco Garcia Conde, January 24, 1839, GA.

26. Plan adopted by the Ayuntamiento Constitutional of the Villa of Gigedo, January 25, 1839; Pedro Rodriguez to the Constitutional Alcalde of this villa [Guerrero], January 26, 1839; Eugenio Hernandez to the President of the Legal Ayuntamiento of 1834 in the villa of Guerrero, January 27, 1839 (quotations), all in GA.

27. Rafael Uribe [report], January 29, 1839, LA.

28. Antonio Arranagas and Julian Salinas to the Ayuntamiento of the Villa of Guerrero, January 28, 1839; Guerrero Ayuntamiento meeting minutes, January 28, 1839, GA; Eduardo Davila to the Ayuntamiento of the Villa del Laredo, January 29, 1839, LA.

29. Minutes of a meeting in the villa of Santa Ana de Nava, January 27, 1839; José Lozano Benavides to the Ayuntamiento of Guerrero, February 1, 1839, both in GA.

30. Santana Penalbes to the Ayuntamientos of the six villas of this Department, February n.d., 1839; Pedro Rodriguez to the Constitutional Ayuntamiento of this villa [Guerrero], February 2, 1839, both in GA.

31. Anastasio Bustamante, *El Gabinete Mexicano* (Mexico: J. M. Lara, 1842), 1: 159; Alessio Robles, *Coahuila y Texas*, 2: 205.

32. Urrea letter, February 4, 1839, copied by Eugenio Fernández, March 3, 1839, GA; Jesus Cárdenas to the villas of the border, February 16, 17, 1839, LA.

33. [Joaquin Garcia] to the Commanding General of Tamaulipas and Head of the Auxiliary Division of this Department, February 16, 1839; [Joaquin] Garcia to the Governor of Coahuila, February 18, 1839, Militares Caja 26, Archivo General del Estado de Nuevo León, Monterrey, Mexico, hereafter cited as AGNL.

34. Vazquez, *Supuesta*, 8–10; Costeloe, *Central Republic*, 28.

35. Francisco G. Conde, General in Command of Coahuila and Texas to the President and General in Chief of the army of operations, March 2, 1839, in Anastasio Bustamante, *Manifesto que el Ciudadano Anastasio Bustamante dirige a Sus Compatriotas* ... (Mexico: Impreso por Ignacio Cumplido, 1839), document 40, 74.

36. Anastasio Bustamante to the Ministry of War, March 4, 1839, Archivo Histórico [Militar Mexicano] Digital, record group 1418, fojas 163–67, hereafter cited as AHD.

37. "Printed circular" of the government of the free and sovereign state of Nuevo León, March 4, 1839, in AHD, record group 1465, foja 20.

38. Juan Leandro to the Minister of War, March 18, 1839, in AHD, record group 1355, foja 7.

39. Pedro Ampudia to Pedro Lemus, March 27, 1839, AHD, record group 1355, fojas 49–51.

40. [Armistice arbitration proposal], April 4, 1839, AHD, record group 1355, fojas 64, 70.

41. *El Mosquito Mexicano*, April 9, 1839.

42. Pedro Lemus [report], March 6, 1839; Eugenio Fernandez to the ayuntamiento of Guerrero, March 7, 1839 (quotations), both in GA; David M. Vigness, "The Republic of the Rio Grande: An Example of Separatism in Northern Mexico" (PhD. diss., University of Texas at Austin, 1951), 122.

43. Vazquez, *Supuesta*, 10–12, Policarpo Velarde copy of Mejia letter, April 10, 1839, GA.

44. [—] Gomez to the Governor of the Department of Coahuila and Texas and reply by [Francisco] Garcia Conde, March 13, 1839, GA.

45. *Joaquin Garcia* [circular] *to his fellow citizens*, March 17, 1839, Streeter Collection, 946.

46. Joaquin Garcia to the Minister of War, March 22, 1839, AHD, record group 1355, fojas 9–11.

47. Domingo Ugartechea to the Minister of War, March 19, 22, 1839, AHD, record group 1355, fojas 4–5, 17–18.

48. Ministry of the Interior to Francisco Garcia Conde, March 5, 1839, GA.

49. H. W. Karnes to Albert Sidney Johnston, March 27, 1839, ASJ.

50. *Telegraph and Texas Register* (Houston), April 10, 1839.

51. José Lazaro Benavides to the Justice of the Peace of Guerrero, March 11, 1839; Eugenio Fernandez to the ayuntamiento of Guerrero, March 15, 16, 23, 1839, both in GA.

CHAPTER 2

1. José Antonio Quintero [proclamation], March 29, 1839, MA, Vol. 31, 152.

2. Pedro Ampudia to Pedro Lemus, March 24, 29, 1839, AHD, record group 1355, fojas 52–53, 71–72.

3. Costeloe, *Central Republic*, 123–26; Daniel S. Haworth, "Anastasio Bustamante," in *The United States and Mexico at War: Nineteenth-Century Expansionism and Conflict*, ed. Don Frazier, 62–63 (New York: Macmillan Reference, 1998); Ducey, "Municipalities," 78.

4. José María Tornel to Anastasio Bustamante, April 8, 1839; Francisco G. Conde

to Anastasio Bustamante, April 11, 1839; Anastasio Bustamante to José María Tornel, April 12, 1839; Anastasio Bustamante to the commanding general of Coahuila, April 23, 1839, all in Bustamante, *Manifesto*, 45–48, 73–74.

5. Domingo Ugartechea to the Governor of the Department of Nuevo León, [April] 26, 1839, AGNL; Valentín Canalizo to [Anastasio Bustamante], April 27, 1839, in Bustamante, *Manifesto*, 51–53; Domingo Ugartechea to the Minister of War, April 15, 18, 1839, AHD, record group 1346, fojas 6–9.

6. Anastasio Bustamante to the Minister of War, April 17, 1839, AHD, record group 1465, fojas 3–5, Bustamante to Domingo Ugartechea, April 26, 1839, record group 1418, foja 168.

7. Mariano Arista to Anastasio Bustamante, April 23, 1839; Anastasio Bustamante to Valentín Canalizo, April 25, 1839, both in Bustamante, *Manifesto*, 50–51; Domingo Ugartechea to Joaquin Garcia [April] 26, 1839, AGNL.

8. Valentín Canalizo to Anastasio Bustamante, April 27, 1839, in Bustamante, *Manifesto*, 51–53.

9. Eugenio Fernandez, list of individuals in the villa of Nava assisting in the escort of ammunition and artillery to the capital, April 5, 1839, GA; *Telegraph and Texas Register* (Houston), April 10, 1839; *El Mosquito Mexicano* (México), May 28, 1839.

10. Political Chief of the Department of the Rio Grande to the Ayuntamiento of Morelos, April 8, 1839, and to the Villa of Guerrero, April 26, 1839, GA.

11. Eugenio Fernandez to the Ayuntamiento of Guerrero, April 26, 1839; Pedro Lemus [communication] April 30, 1839, forwarded by Eugenio Fernandez to the ayuntamientos of the villas of the Department of the Rio Grande; Pedro Lemus to the Governor of Coahuila and Texas, May 1, 1839, all in GA; Bustamante, *Manifesto*, 71–72.

12. Anastasio Bustamante to the Minister of War and Naval Affairs, May 16, 1839, in Bustamante, *Manifesto*, 71–72.

13. Anastasio Bustamante, The PRESIDENT of the Republic [and] General in Chief of the Army of Operations to the Inhabitants of the Departments of Tamaulipas, Nuevo León, and Coahuila, May 4, 1839, in *La Concordia: Semanario del Gobierno Departamental de Tamaulipas* (Ciudad Victoria), May 18, 23, 25, 1839.

14. Bartolomé de Cardenas to the Political Chief of the Department of the Rio Grande, May 11, 1839, GA.

15. Valentín Canalizo to Anastasio Bustamante, May 2, 1839, Anastasio Bustamante to the Minister of War and Naval Affairs, May 6, 1839, Anastasio Bustamante to Valentín Canalizo, May 6, 1839, Valentín Canalizo to [Antonio Canales], May 12, 1839, all in Bustamante, *Manifesto*, 54–56, 61, 64–67.

16. *La Concordia: Semanario del Gobierno Departamental de Tamaulipas* (Ciudad Victoria), May 11, 1839; Depalo, *Mexican National Army*, 71–72.

17. Depalo, *Mexican National Army*.

18. Anastasio Bustamante to the Minister of War, May 15, 1839, in Bustamante, *Manifesto*, 67.

19. Bustamante, *Manifesto*, 68, 70–72.

20. Domingo Ugartechea to the Minister of War, May 9, 1839, AHD, record group 1357, fojas 3–4.

21. Santiago Vidaurri, notes regarding an "extraordinary notice" of Pedro Lemus, May 15, 1839 (quotation); Eugenio Fernandez to the Ayuntamiento of the Villa of Nava [communication ordered by the Governor], May 16, 1839, GA; Domingo Ugartechea to the Minister of War, May 9, 1839, AHD, record group 1357, fojas 6–7.

22. Bustamante, *Gabinete Mexicano*, 1: 188–93; Alessio Robles, *Coahuila y Texas*, 2: 205–6.

23. Anastasio Bustamante to the Minister of War, May 24, 1839, AHD, record group 1418, fojas 124–26.

24. *La Concordia: Semanario del Govierno Departamental de Tamaulipas* (Ciudad Victoria), May 11, 1839; Anastasio Bustamante to the Governor of the Department of Tamaulipas, May 17, 1839, in *La Concordia*, June 15, 1839.

CHAPTER 3

1. Eugenio Fernandez to the Ayuntamiento of the Villa of Guerrero, June 1, 1839, GA.

2. *El Mosquito Mexicano* (México), April 9, 1839.

3. Anastasio Bustamante to the Commanding General of Nuevo León, AHD, April 4, 1839, record group 1355, fojas 37–38.

4. *El Mosquito Mexicano*, April 26, 1839, citing reports dated April 14 from Ciudad Victoria; Anastasio Bustamante to Valentín Canalizo, May 6, 1839, AHD, record group 1540, fojas 90–99; Pedro Ampudia [notation], March 29, 1839, AHD, record group 1355, fojas 71–72.

5. *El Mosquito Mexicano* (México), June 14, 1839, quoting *La Concordia* (Ciudad Victoria), May 27, 1839.

6. Bustamante, *Gabinete Mexicano*, 192–93.

7. John Milton Nance, *After San Jacinto: The Texas-Mexican Frontier, 1836–1841* (Austin: Texas State Historical Association, 1963), 167.

8. [M. B. Lamar] Historical Notes, in Gulick, *Lamar Papers*, 6: 114–15, 120, 155–61; Manl. M. de Llano to Juan Pablo Anaya, June 10, 1839, Juan Pablo Anaya Papers, Nettie Lee Benson Library, University of Texas at Austin,

hereafter cited as JPA.

9. Eugenio Fernandez to the Ayuntamiento of Guerrero, July 23, 1839, GA.

10. Juan Pablo Anaya to Valentín Gómez Farías, July 22, 1839, JPA.

11. Melchor Lobo to the Constitutional Alcalde [of San Buenaventura], August 2, 1839, GA; Lic. [Antonio] Canales to Juan Pablo Anaya, August 3, 1839, JPA.

12. Agreement made by the First Division of the Federal Army in the villa of Aldama, August 4, 1839, JPA.

13. Lic. Antonio Canales and José M. Carvajal [affadavit], August 8, 1839, JPA.

14. Jesús Cárdenas to [Juan Pablo Anaya], August 15, 1839, JPA.

15. Bustamante, *Manifesto*, 72–73; *La Concordia* (Ciudad Victoria), June 15, 1839.

16. "Citizen Mariano Arista Commanding General of the Department of Tamaulipas to its Inhabitants," June 17, 1839 [broadside], MA, XXX, 116.

17. *La Concordia* (Ciudad Victoria), June 8, 1839.

18. [Proclamation] from Mateo Quiroz, June 23, 1839, *La Concordia* (Ciudad Victoria), July 13, 1839, MA, XXX, 129.

19. Valentín Canalizo to the Governor of this Department, June 28, 1838, AGNL; Nance, 169.

20. Eugenio Fernandez to the Ayuntamiento and alcalde of the villa of Guerrero, July 1, 15, 16, 1839; José Andres Cervera to José María Salinas, July 19, 1839; Antonio Arrañagas to the Political Chief of this Department, July 21, 1839, all in GA.

21. Anselmo María Marichalano to the Governor of the Department of Coahuila, July 1, 1839, Valentín Canalizo to the Governor of the Department of Coahuila and Texas, July 17, 1839, both in GA; *La Concordia* (Ciudad Victoria), July 6, 13, 1839.

22. Valentín Canalizo [report], August 7, 1839, AHD, record group 1367, foja 39.

23. Valentín Canalizo, Noticia Extraordinaria, August 19, 1839, broadside, Streeter 944; José D. Romero [notation] August 20, 1839, AGNL; Eugenio Fernandez to the Ayuntamientos of Guerrero, Morelos, and Rosas, August 15, 1839; Eugenio Fernandez to the Ayuntamiento of Guerrero, August 16, 1839, Manuel Menchaca and José María Salinas [report], August 16, 1839 (quotations), all in GA.

24. Valentín Canalizo to the Minister of War, August 20, 1839, AGNL; Blas de la Barreda to the Governor of the Department of Coahuila, August 23, 1839, GA; Valentín Canalizo, Noticia Extraordinaria, August 26, 1839, Broadside, Streeter 949.

25. Eugenio Fernandez to the Ayuntamientos [of the villas del norte], August 9, 1839, GA; Nance, 168–71.

26. Valentín Canalizo to the Governor of the Department of Nuevo León, August 19, 1839, AGNL. Canalizo also attempted to quell concerns about retribution.

27. *La Brisa* (Matamoros), August 30, 1839, MA, Vol. 32, 26.

28. *La Concordia: Semanario del Gobierno Departamental de Tamaulipas* (Ciudad Victoria), August 31, 1839, MA, XXX, 153–54.

29. Valentín Canalizo to the Governor of Coahuila, September 4, 1839, GA.

30. Valentín Canalizo, "measures that it is my duty to take to assure peace and tranquility," September 10, 1839, AGNL.

31. There was even talk of renewed pursuit of the Comanches. Francisco G. Pavón to the Governor of the Department of Nuevo León, September 30, 1839, AGNL.

32. *La Brisa* (Matamoros), September 30, 1839, MA, XXXII, 34.

33. *La Concordia: Semanario del Gobierno Departamental de Tamaulipas* (Ciudad Victoria), June 1, 1839.

34. *La Concordia: Semanario del Gobierno Departamental de Tamaulipas* (Ciudad Victoria), June 1, 1839, quoted in *El Mosquito Mexicano* (México), June 14, 1839.

35. "Circular to the Chief Justice of the county of Goliad," June 13, 1838, Andrew Jackson Houston Collection, Texas State Archives, Austin, Texas, hereafter cited as AJH.

36. *Telegraph and Texas Register* (Houston), February 20, 1839; Proclamation Opening a trade with the Mexican citizens on the Rio Grande, February 21, 1839, Gulick, *Lamar Papers*, 2: 457–58; H. W. Karnes to Albert Sidney Johnston, March 27, 1839, ASJ.

37. *Telegraph and Texas Register* (Houston), April 10, 1839, see also April 24, 1839.

38. Since he had lived among Anglo Americans for several years previous to his return in 1830, Carvajal no doubt believed that he understood the culture that Anaya would have to parlay with. However, much of Carvajal's time in Kentucky and Virginia had been spent with deeply religious and fundamentalist (Protestant) families, and he and Anaya would find themselves with but few of those kind of people during their mission in Texas. Quintellen McMillan, "Surveyor General: The Life and Times of José Maria Carvajal" (Austin: Briscoe Center for American History, University of Texas at Austin, 1990), 6, 72, 73, 75; José M. J. Carvajal to Juan Pablo Anaya, August 9, 1839, JPA.

39. José M. Carvajal to H. W. Karnes, August 9, 1839, Gulick, *Lamar Papers*, 5: 304.

40. Anson Jones to John Forsyth, Diplomatic and Military Copy Book, 1836–1839, Texas State Archives, Austin, Texas; James Webb to Richard G. Dunlap, March 14, 1839 (quotations), AJH.

41. Letter from the Louisianan, August 13, 1839, quoted in *Telegraph and Texas Register* (Houston), October 23, 1839.

42. *Telegraph and Texas Register* (Houston), August 14, 1839.

43. *El Mosquito Mexicano* (México), July 2, 1839.

CHAPTER 4

1. *Telegraph and Texas Register* (Houston), September 4, 1839.
2. C. Van Ness to Albert Sidney Johnston, September 8, 1839, ASJ.
3. *Telegraph and Texas Register* (Houston), September 11, 1839.
4. *Telegraph and Texas Register*, September 18, 1838.
5. Juan Pablo Anaya to the editor, September 20, 1839, *Telegraph and Texas Register*, September 25, 1839.
6. [Decree from Houston, December 14, 1839], in folder entitled "Legal documents, decrees, and orders, 1833–1835" [*sic*], JPA.
7. H. S. Foote to M. B. Lamar, September 15, 1839, in Gulick, *Papers of Lamar*, 3: 168–69.
8. J. Browne to A. S. Johnston, September 13, 1839, in Gulick, 3: 106–7.
9. [Richard Roman recollection], in Gulick, 6: 136.
10. Recapitulation [by Lamar]," in Gulick, 6: 114–15.
11. Valentín Canalizo to the Governor of Coahuila, September 4, 1839, GA.
12. Valentín Canalizo, "Measures that it is my duty to take to assure peace and tranquility," September 10, 1839, AGNL.
13. Valentín Canalizo to the Governor [of Nuevo León], September 10, 1839, AGNL; José Vicente Miñon, letter dated September 13, 1839, quoted in *La Concordia* (Ciudad Victoria), October 12, 1839, MA, XXXII, 73; José Vicente Miñon to the Minister of War, September 13, 1839, AHD, record group 1367, fojas 48–49.
14. Beatriz de la Garza, *From the Republic of the Rio Grande: A Personal History of the Place and the People* (Austin: University of Texas Press, 2013), 14. On the background of Gutiérrez de Lara, see *The New Handbook of Texas* (Austin: Texas State Historical Association, 1996), 3: 392–93.
15. José Lasaro Benavides to the Jues de Paz of Guerrero, October 1, 1839, GA.
16. Francisco G. Pavón to J. de Jesús Davila y Prieto, October 7, 1839, AGNL.
17. Vazquez, *Supuesta*, 27–28.
18. Valentín Canalizo to Francisco G. Pavón, October 11, 1839, in documents 3 and 4, Francisco G. Pavón, *Manifestación que hace de su conducta militar, a la Nación, el Coronel del 1st Regimiento de Caballeria* (Mexico: Imprenta del Mosquito, 1841), 6–7.
19. *La Concordia* (Ciudad Victoria), October 12, 1839, MA, XXXII, 73.
20. Rafael de Lira to Lic. D. Antonio Canales, October 12, 1839, in *La Concordia* (Ciudad Victoria), November 10, 1839, MA, XXX, 171–72.
21. [Public resolutions in the villa de Mier], October 13, 1839, in *La Concordia*

(Ciudad Victoria), November 10, 1839, MA, XXX, 171.

22. Governor of Nuevo León to Francisco G. Pavón, October 17, 1839; [José María de] Ortega to the Governor of Nuevo León, October 17, 20, 24, 1839, all in AGNL.

23. José María Salinas to the Governor of Coahuila, October 14, 1839, GA.

24. *Telegraph and Texas Register* (Houston), October 30, 1839.

25. [Testimonial] of Mariano Martinez de Lejarza, July 9, 1840, in Pavón, *Manifestación*, 9–11.

26. Vigness, "Rio Grande," 150–51.

27. This account comes from the summary of events provided in the military court martial of Pavón by the prosecutor, who had read many reports of the engagement. See Martín Martínez de Navarrete [trial affidavit], October 16, 1840, in Pavón, *Manifestación*, 11–16.

28. Additional details of the engagement come from the oral testimony of the Texas volunteers recorded in 1847 and printed in Gulick, (ed.), *Papers of Lamar*, 6: 99–103, 118, 134–38. See especially the narratives of Benjamin Hill, Richard Roman, Thomas Hancock, and Andrew J. Neal.

29. Milton Lindheim, *The Republic of the Rio Grande: Texans in Mexico, 1839–1840* (Waco, TX: Morrison, 1964), 2–4.

30. Nance, *After San Jacinto*, 221–23.

31. "El general en Gefe De la Division del Norte, a sus Subordinados" [broadside], n. d., MA, XXXII, 63.

32. J. de Jesús d. y Prieto to the Governor of Coahuila, November 1, 1839, GA; [José María de] Ortega to the Governor of Nuevo León, November 4, 5, 9, 1839; Juan José Elguesaba to the commanding general of Nuevo León, November 5, 1839, all in AGNL.

33. *Telegraph and Texas Register* (Houston), November 6, 1839.

34. *La Brisa* (Matamoros), November 8, 1839, MA, XXXII, 52. *La Concordia* (Ciudad Victoria), November 10, 1839, also accused Pavón of duplicity for treating with Canales prior to battle. See MA, XXX, 171.

35. Sinkin, *Mexican Reform*, 30.

36. Jorge López de Lara [to the inhabitants of Matamoros], Matamoros, November 8, 1839, Streeter 942.

37. [Handwritten Proclamation by Antonio Canales], November 10, 1839, LA.

38. Antonio Canales [Statement against the failures of the Supreme Government], November 11, 1839, AHD, record group 1378, fojas 151–52.

39. [José María de] Ortega to Governor of Nuevo León, November 18, 1839, citing letter of José Zevallos dated November 16, 1839, regarding an expedition through the countryside in the area of Cadereyta. AGNL.

40. Maria de la Fuente to General [Juan Pablo] Anaya, December 13, 1839, JPA.

41. Lic. Antonio Canales to Valentín Canalizo, November 20, 1839, quoted in letter from Canalizo to the Senior Commanding General of Nuevo León, December 24, 1839, AHD, record group 1378, foja 40.

42. *Telegraph and Texas Register* (Ciudad Victoria), December 25, 1839.

43. Valentíin Canalizo to the Minister of War, November 15, 1839, AHD, record group 1378, foja 72; José Antonio Quintero, [circular under the heading] "EL GOBERNADOR Del Departamento, November 15, 1839, Streeter 948.

44. J. de Jesús D. y Prieto to the Minister of War, November 20, 1839, AHD, record group 1378, fojas 163–64.

45. Ramon de Cardenas [open letter], December 1, 1839, in *La Concordia* (Ciudad Victoria), December 7, 1839, MA, XXX, 175–76.

46. J. de Jesús D. y Prieto to the Governor of the Department of Coahuila, December 1, 1839, GA; J. de Jesús D. y Prieto to Commanding General of this Department, December 11, 1839, AGNL.

47. Governor of Nuevo León to Mariano Arista, December 11, 1839, AGNL.

48. Michael P. Costeloe, "The British and an Early Pronunciamiento, 1833–1834," in *Forceful Negotiations: The Origins of the Pronunciamiento in Nineteenth-Century Mexico*, ed. Will Fowler, 125–42 (Lincoln: University of Nebraska Press, 2010).

49. "Ciudadano Mariano Arista General en Jefe de la División del Norte, a los Habitantes de los Departamentos de Tamaulipas, Coahuila y Nuevo León," December 12, 1839, Streeter 943.

50. Juan José García, [report], December 7, 1839, AHD, record group 1378, fojas 51–52; Juan N. Almonte [in Mexico City] to the Governor of Coahuila, December 13, 1839; J. de Jusús D. y Prieto to the Governor of the Department of Coahuila, December 29, 1839, both in GA.

CHAPTER 5

1. For different accounts of the withdrawal of Ross and others, see the narratives of Benjamin Hill, Thomas Newcomb, and Basilio Benavides, in Gulick, *Papers of Lamar*, 6: 123, 130, 134.

2. Jesús de Prieto to the Minister of War, December 22, 1839, record group 1378, fojas 130–41.

3. John F. Henderson and Thomas Jamison, letter to the editor, January 8, 1840, in *Colorado Gazette and Advertiser* (Matagorda), January 18, 1840.

4. Mariano Arista [report] December 13, 1839, AHD, record group 1378, fojas 100–106.

5. J. de Jesús D. y Prieto to the Governor of the Department of Coahuila, December 29, 1839, GA.

6. Narrative of Anson G. Neal, in Gulick, *Papers of Lamar*, 6: 101–4. He also told a story that Canales outside of Matamoros refused to allow a local baker to provide bread out of fear that it had been poisoned.

7. See, for example, the Henderson and Jamison letter cited above.

8. [—] Ortéga to the Governor [of Nuevo León], January 14, 1840, AGNL.

9. *Gaceta del Gobierno de Tamaulipas* (Ciudad Victoria), January 25, 1840.

10. J. A. Navarro to [—], January 29, 1840, in Gulick, *Papers of Lamar*, 3: 321.

11. *Richmond Telescope*, January 25, 1840.

12. Justin H. Smith, "La Republica de Rio Grande," *American Historical Review* 25 (July 1920): 660–75; Hobart Huson, *Iron Men: A History of the Republic of the Rio Grande and the Federalist War in Northern Mexico* (Austin: Texas State Archives, 1940); Vigness, "Rio Grande"; Nance, *After San Jacinto*; and de la Garza, *Rio Grande*.

13. [Letter to the editor] from the Louisianan, *Telegraph and Texas Register* (Houston), October 23, 1839. Interestingly, Anaya had associates such as Francisco Vidaurri y Villaseñor and Jesús Cárdenas who bore the title of vice president and president, respectively, of this provisional government.

14. *Telegraph and Texas Register*, August 14, 21 (quotations), 1839.

15. [Proclamation] by Lic. Canales, November 10, 1839, LA. It should be noted that this document makes no mention of establishing a separate nation.

16. Jorge L. de Lara, "Proclamation to the Inhabitants of [Matamoros]," November 8, 1839, Streeter 942.

17. Minister of the Interior to the Governor of the Department of Coahuila, November 26, 1839, GA.

18. Anson Neal narrative, in Gulick, *Papers of Lamar*, 6: 100.

19. *El Ancla: Periodico Semanario del Puerto de Matamoros*, January 17, 1840, MA, XXXV, 61. Months later ridicule still accompanied virtually every centralist mention of the provisional government. See also Mariano Arista to Valentín Canalizo, May 6, 1840, AHD, record group 1542, fojas 28–33. Many of the leaders of the federalist rebellions were related by marriage. Canales married the sister of Juan N. Molano and he, in turn, married the daughter of J. M. Carbajal.

20. The details of the process of creating a separate provisional government are elusive. According to de la Garza, another scholar, J. J. Gallegos, in his thesis states that the delegates withdrew to Casa Blanca on the Nueces River to complete the work of crafting a government after holding a convention in Guerrero on January 18, 1840. De la Garza, *Rio Grande*, 16.

21. Lic. Canales to Mariano Arista, January 28, 1840, *El Ancla: Periodico Semanario del Puerto de Matamoros*, February 28, 1840, MA, XXXV, 68.

22. Mariano Arista to D. Antonio Canales, January 31, 1840, *El Ancla*, 68–69.

23. Prospectus of *El Correo del Rio Bravo del Norte*, in Gulick, *Papers of Lamar*, 5: 463.

24. Narrative of Anson G. Neal, in Gulick, *Papers of Lamar*, 5: 104.

25. Lic. Antonio Canales in Gulick, February 8, 1840, 3: 330–31. An inexplicable confusion of dates exists in that the prospectus appeared on February 2 but contained the Canales letter dated February 8.

26. *Correro del Rio Bravo del Norte* (Ciudad Guerrero), February 16, 1840, printed in Vásquez, *Supuesta Republic* [frontispiece].

27. Jesús Cárdenas to José Antonio Navarro, February 29, 1840, *Austin City Gazette*, May 18, 1840.

28. Jesús Cárdenas to John T. Price, March 1, 1840, *Colorado Gazette and Advertiser* (Matagorda), March 28, 1840.

29. Address of Jesús Cárdenas . . . to the Citizens of Victoria, Texas, March 8, 1840, *Colorado Gazette and Advertiser* (Matagorda), April 20, 1840.

30. José Antonio Navarro to the President of the Free Frontier States of the Mexican Republic, March 15, 1840, *Austin City Gazette*, May 13, 1840.

31. Juan Pablo Anaya to *Le Courrier de la Louisiane*, March 20, 1840 [in printed materials], JPA.

32. Mariano Arista [from Monclova] to Joaquin Garcia, April 12, 1840, AGNL.

33. *El Ancla: Periodico Semanario del Puerto de Matamoros*, March 20, 1840, MA, XXXV, 77.

34. *El Ancla*, 75.

35. *Brazos Courier* (Brazoria), March 3, 1840.

36. To be more precise, the name Republic of the Rio Grande does not appear in any *extant* Mexican record. Josefina Vásquez made this point in her excellent study, *La Supuesta Republic del Rio Grande*.

37. *Texas Sentinel* (Austin), March 18, 1840. The officials of this provisional federalist government were a close-knit group—Canales tapped both his brother-in-law Molano and son-in-law Carbajal as among the small group of officeholders.

38. J. Antonio Navarro to Geo. Fisher, March 23, 1840, *Austin City Gazette*, May 13, 1840.

39. *Texas Sentinel* (Austin), April 1, 1840.

40. Geo. Fisher to J. Antonio Navarro, April 17, 1840, *Austin City Gazette*, May 13, 1840.

41. *Houston Star*, quoted in *Brazos Courier*, April 21, 1840.

42. Jesús Cárdenas to M. B. Lamar, April 8, 1840, in Gulick, *Papers of Lamar*, 3: 364. He continued to be toasted and supported in Victoria well into the month of April 1840. *Telegraph and Texas Register* (Houston), April 29, 1840; *Colorado Gazette and Advertiser* (Matagorda), April 20, 1840.

43. "Mirabeau B. Lamar to Soldiers," March 14, 1840, Broadside 1840, Streeter

426.

44. Abner S. Lipscomb to Barnard E. Bee, February 8, 1840, in Garrison, *Diplomatic Correspondence of the Republic of Texas* (Washington, DC: Government Printing Office, 1908), 2: 545.

45. David G. Burnet, Acting Secy of State, to James Treat, March 12, 1840, in Garrison, 2: 582.

46. H. McLeod, Adjt & Inspt. Genl. to Lt. Col Wm. S. Fisher, April 4, 1840, folder 14, Adjutant General Army Papers, TSA.

47. Harriet Smither, *Journals of the Fourth Congress of the Republic of Texas, 1839–1840*, vol. 1: *Senate Journal*, 1: 8, 31, and *Secret Journal*, 156–58 (Austin: Von Boeckmann Jones, n.d.).

48. Mirabeau B. Lamar, Address at a Public Dinner [n.d. 1840], in Gulick, *Papers of Lamar*, 3: 479–80.

49. Anastasio Bustamante [orders to the Matamoros commander], May 28, 1839, AHD, record group 1418, fojas 39–40; Lack, "Córdova Revolt," 89–109.

CHAPTER 6

1. J. de Jesús de Prieto [report] to Mariano Arista, January 22, 1840, AHD, fojas 19–21; Felipe de la Peña to Jesús Garcia Gomez, January 23, 1840, fojas 22–23; Valentín Canalizo [report], February 7, 1840, fojas 166–69; Mariano Arista to the Minister of War, February 19, 1840, fojas 455–57 (all in record group 1540).

2. Mariano Arista letter, March 20, 1840, AHD, record group 1540, fojas 251–53.

3. Bustamante, *Gabinete Mexicana*, 2: 41; [unattributed note to Canalizo and Arista], January 25, 1840, AHD, record group 1540, foja 585.

4. Narrative of Agustín Soto, in Gulick, *Papers of Lamar*, 6: 116.

5. Narrative of Jesús Barera, in Gulick, 131. Prisoner quotation from "Report of legal proceedings against foreigners Bennett McNelly [McNeil] and Victor Loupy . . ." April 14, 1840, in GA.

6. Isidro Reyes to [Mariano] Arista, March 24, 1840, in *El Ancla* (Matamoros), April 24, 1840, MA, XXXV, 94.

7. Mariano Arista, "Extraordinary Notice," March 26, 1840, *El Ancla* (Matamoros), Supplement 14, Streeter; Manuel Reducindo Barragan Report, March 24, 1840, *El Ancla* (Matamoros), MA, Vol. XXXV, 94.

8. See the Soto, Santos Benavides, and Barera narratives for speculations about Canales's failure to effect a rescue of Zapata, in Gulick, *Papers of Lamar*, 6: 116, 128–29, 132. Anson Neill [Neal] asserted that Zapata had been "betrayed by his own men," but he provided no further details of the alleged betrayal (see 104).

9. For Arista's most complete accounts, written on the day after the battles (March 26, 1840), see *El Ancla* (Matamoros), April 24, 1840, MA, XXXV, 91–93 and

in AHD, record group 1489, fojas 2–16. Some details vary even in accounts written hours apart. For example, Arista elsewhere indicated that the attack began at 1:30 p.m., rather than 11:30 a.m. The narrative constructed here comes from the broadside cited in note 5 above, from the fuller account in *El Ancla*, and from the manuscript account by Arista, as cited in this note. The list of weapons picked up after the battle also came from Arista's account to his superiors in Mexico City. See also Juan N. Almonte to the Governor of Coahuila, April 21, 1840, GA.

10. Narrative of Jesús Barera, in Gulick, *Papers of Lamar*, 6: 131.

11. Narrative of Agustín Soto, in Gulick, 116; Mariano Arista to the Minister of War, March 29, 1840, AHD, record group 1489, fojas 75–78.

12. Mariano Arista to the inhabitants of the Villas of the North, March 29, 1840, AGNL.

13. *El Ancla* (Matamoros), April 10, 1840, MA, XXXV, 86.

14. J. Cayego de Montoya to the Governor of this Department, March 30, 1840, Governor of Nuevo León to the commander of the armies of Nuevo León & Coahuila, April 1, 1840; Governor of Nuevo León to the commanding general of the auxiliary division of the north, April 3, 1840, all in AGNL.

15. Mariano Arista to Joaquín Garcia, April 8, 1840, AGNL.

16. Ibid.

17. "Report of legal proceedings against foreigners Bennett McNelly [McNeil] and Victor Loupy . . ." April 14, 1840, GA.

18. Mariano Arista circular issued from Saltillo, April 1840, GA.

19. Arista statement of April 8, 1840, quoted in Marcos Hernandez to the Justice of the Peace of the Villa Guerrero, April 30, 1840, AGNL.

20. Governor of Nuevo León to Commanding General of the Auxiliary Division of the North, April 22, 1840, AGNL.

21. Editorial of *El Ancla* (Matamoros), April 3, 1840, accompanying "Noticia Extraordinaria," in Streeter, 952.

22. Letter to W. D. Wallach, March 24, 1840, *Colorado Gazette* (Matagorda), March 28, 1840; C. Van Ness to Inspector General McLeod, April 7, 1840, *Colorado Gazette*, April 20, 1840.

23. C. Van Ness to Inspector General McLeod, April 7, 1840, *Colorado Gazette*, April 20, 1840.

24. *Texas Sentinel* (Austin), April 29, 1840.

25. Antonio Canales to M. B. Lamar, April 29, 1840, Gulick, *Papers of Lamar*, 5: 424.

26. Sam[ue]l A. Plummer to [Lamar], April 25, 1840, Gulick, 3: 381.

27. Proceedings and Resolutions of a Citizens Meeting of Western Texas, April 23, 1840, Gulick, 3: 376–77.

28. Miguel Benavides [report], April 24, 1840, in *Gaceta de Tamaulipas* (Ciudad Victoria), May 16, 1840, MA, XXXII, 123.
29. *El Ancla* (Matamoros), April 17, 1840, MA, XXXV, 88.
30. José Urrea to Valentín Gómez Farías, April 6, 1840, VGF.

CHAPTER 7

1. Costeloe, *Central Republic*, 162.
2. José María Ortega, "Extraordinary News" [proclamation], July 23, 1840, in *Gaceta de Tamaulipas* (Ciudad Victoria), MA, XXII, 164.
3. José Lasaro Benabides to the Justice of the Peace of Guerrero, August 12, 1840, GA; Mariano Arista [report], July 2, 1840, AHD, record group 1549, fojas 59–61; Vázquez, 27.
4. Mariano Arista to Joaquín Garcia, August 1, 1840, AGNL.
5. Philip Dimitt letter to the editor, August 8, 1840, *Colorado Gazette* (Matagorda), August 29, 1840.
6. *El Ancla* (Matamoros), August 7, 1840, MA, XXXV, 131–32.
7. Pedro Ampudia to the Justice of the Peace of the Villa of Laredo, May 3, 1840, LA.
8. Subprefect from Montemorelos to the Commanding General of this Department, May 8, 1840, AGNL.
9. Mariano Arista [regulations], May 9, 1840, in *Gaceta de Tamaulipas* (Ciudad Victoria), May 16, 1840, MA, XXXII, 132.
10. [Edict] by Miguel Benavides et al., April 24, 1840, in *Gaceta de Tamaulipas* (Ciudad Victoria), May 10, 1840, MA, XXXII, 123.
11. *Gaceta de Tamaulipas* (Ciudad Victoria), MA, XXXII, 127.
12. Manuel Quinto de Lima to the Governor of the Department of Coahuila, May 29, 1840; Marcos Hernandez to the Governor of the Department of Coahuila, May 29, 1840, both in GA.
13. Editorial, *Gaceta de Tamaulipas* (Ciudad Victoria), June 13, 1840, MA, XXXII, 142.
14. *Gaceta de Tamaulipas* (Ciudad Victoria), July 25, 1840.
15. Mariano Arista to Joaquín Garcia, August 1, 1840, AGNL.
16. *Texas Sentinel* (Austin), May 16, 1840.
17. *Texas Sentinel*, May 23, 1840.
18. *Colorado Gazette* (Matagorda), June 6, 1840.
19. *Telegraph and Texas Register* (Houston), July 1, 1840.
20. *Telegraph and Texas Register*, July 24, 1840.
21. *Colorado Gazette* (Matagorda), July 4, 1840.
22. Nance, *After San Jacinto*, 238–39.

23. M. B. Lamar, Address at a public dinner, n. d. [1840], Gulick, *Papers of Lamar*, 3: 479–80.

24. Abner S. Lipscomb to James Hamilton, May 4, 1840, in Garrison, *Diplomatic Correspondence*, 2: 633.

25. Abner Lipscomb to James Treat, June 13, 1840, in Garrison, 2: 644.

26. Antonio Canales to M. B. Lamar, May 31, 1840, Mirabeau Buonaparte Lamar papers, TSA. At least one of the Canales to Lamar documents (number 1841) is missing in this collection.

27. James Love to Albert Sidney Johnston, June 4, 1840, ASJ.

28. Antonio Canales to M. B. Lamar, July 21, 1840, in Gulick, *Papers of Lamar*, 3: 423.

29. G. W. Hockley to A. Clendennin, July 30, 1840, Adjutant General Army Papers, TSA.

30. A. S. Johnston to M. B. Lamar, August 6, 1840, Gulick, *Papers of Lamar*, 3: 427.

31. Jas. Love to A. Sidney Johnston, May 20, 1840, ASJ.

32. Henry J. Jewett to M. B. Lamar, June 21, 1840, Gulick, *Papers of Lamar*, 3: 414.

33. James Love to Albert Sidney Johnston, July 22, 1840, ASJ.

34. J. M. J. Carbajal to M. B. Lamar, July 27, 1840, Gulick, *Papers of Lamar*, 3: 424–25.

35. Luis Lopez to Antonio Canales, July 26, 1840, in *Telegraph and Texas Register* (Houston), August 26, 1840; narrative of Anson Neal, Gulick, *Papers of Lamar*, 6: 106.

36. Rafael Vásquez to Mariano Arista, July 31, 1840, AHD, record group 1550, fojas 160–63.

37. "Quintoques" could also be translated as "soldiers of fortune." See *Gaceta de Tamaulipas* (Ciudad Victoria), September 12, 1840, MA, XXXII, 190.

38. Luis Perez to Mariano Arista, October 11, 1840, in *El Ancla* (Matamoros), October 19, 1840, MA, XXXV, 179.

39. Narrative of Anson Neal, Gulick, *Papers of Lamar*, 6: 107 (quotations); Mariano Arista to Juan Nepomuceno Molano, October 11, 1840, in *El Ancla* (Matamoros), December 7, 1840, MA, XXXVI, 2; *El Ancla*, October 19, 1840, MA, XXXV, 178; *Gaceta de Tamaulipas* (Ciudad Victoria), October 13, 1840, MA, XXXIX, 152; Alessio Robles, *Coahuila y Texas*, 2: 220.

40. Narrative of J. A. Wilkinson, Gulick, *Papers of Lamar*, 6: 130; Nance, *After San Jacinto*, 346–48.

41. These derisions come from *El Ancla* (Matamoros), October 19, 1840, MA, XXXV, 178 (ingrate) and Pedro Ampudia, quoted in *El Ancla*, October 5, 1840, MA, XXXV, 172 (el estúpido).

42. Juan Nepo. Molano and Luis Lopez to Mariano Arista, *El Ancla* (Matamoros),

October 12, 1840, MA, XXXVI, 2.

43. The Jordan/Molano march went through the pueblos of Bargos, Cruillas y San Fernando, Villagra y Hoyos Hidalgo, Jaumava, Padilla, and Palmillas. *Gaceta de Tamaulipas* (Ciudad Victoria), November 7, 1840, MA, XXXIII, 16; José Antonio Bejanso [report from Padilla], October 9, 1840, AHD, record group 1548, foja 104.

44. Narrative of Anson Neal, Gulick, *Papers of Lamar*, 6: 108–9. The narrative of Basilio Benavides, 6: 129, contains a summary of the secret plan to take the expedition to San Luis Potosí. Some battle details, including casualty numbers, come from P. F. Bowman to M. B. Lamar, n.d. [1840?], Gulick, 4: 238–39. The source for numbers that seems most reliable and that is used here is Jordan's report, made immediately upon his return to Texas. See *Brazos Courier* (Brazoria), December 22, 1840.

45. Narrative of [José María] Gonzales, Gulick, *Papers of Lamar*, 6: 114, 132–33.

46. The Military Commander of Saltillo to his troops, October 20, 1840, AHD, record group 1548, foja 10.

47. José Cayetano de Montoya [Published Report] to Mariano Arista, October 30, 1840, in Streeter 960.

48. *San Luis Advocate* (Brazoria County), December 10, 1840.

49. This description of the battle comes from several sources. Two members of the expedition left somewhat extensive accounts of the events, but their versions differ on many points. Therefore, the present description sacrifices some detail in favor of central areas of agreement in these narratives (of Anson Neal and Thomas Newcomb). See Gulick, *Papers of Lamar*, 6: 109–11, 124–27 respectively. The Gonzales narrative provides some battlefield numbers (see 114), as does a narrative left by P. F. Bowman in an 1840 letter to Lamar, Gulick, 4: 238–39, and the description of historian Vito Alessio Robles, *Coahuila y Texas*, 221–23. An account in the *San Luis Advocate* (Brazoria County), December 10, 1840, is the source for the artillery demolition of the stone wall. Other Texas newspapers covered the story based on direct testimony from Jordan, with emphasis, of course, on the heroic behavior of the Anglo Texans, but they also supplied descriptions that are compatible with other accounts and are therefore deemed reliable. See *Texas Sentinel* (Austin), December 12, 1840, and *Brazos Courier* (Brazoria), December 22, 1840. The present description also comes from the excellent post-battle report of José Cayetano de Montoya, [Published Report] to Mariano Arista, October 30, 1840, Streeter, 960.

50. José Cayetano de Montoya [Published Report] to Mariano Arista, October 30, 1840, Streeter 960.

51. *Gaceta de Tamaulipas* (Ciudad Victoria), November 7, 1840, MA, XXXIII, 13, 16.

52. Central Prefectura of the Department of Tamaulipas [report], October 16, 1840, *Gaceta de Tamaulipas* (Ciudad Victoria), November 7, 1840, MA, XXXIII, 14.

53. Mariano Arista to Pedro Ampudia, October 27, 1840, *Gaceta de Tamaulipas* (Ciudad Victoria), MA, XXXIII, 13, 16.

54. Mariano Arista to Antonio Canales, October 12, 1840, *Austin City Gazette*, December 2, 1840.

CONCLUSION AND EPILOGUE

1. Many fine scholars have accepted the version of events put forth by Canales to demonstrate his patriotism as a defender of Mexico's right to the Rio Grande against boundary claims of the Republic of Texas. See, for example, de la Garza, *Rio Grande*, 127; and Vázquez, *Supuesta*, 30–34.

2. At the battle of San Jacinto in April 1836, where Texas volunteers overwhelmed Mexico's army under Antonio López de Santa Anna, Karnes served as second-in-command in Lamar's cavalry corps, and he followed up with a heroic escape from a Matamoros prison and with service in frontier defense as a leader of Rangers. Nance, *After San Jacinto*, 322–25.

3. Historian John M. Nance also expressed doubts as to the authenticity of this correspondence and noted that the memoir of Mary Maverick described Karnes as "uneducated" (317). However, Nance also printed additional polished excerpts attributed to Karnes but from a published, secondary source and not from Karnes's own hand (320).

4. H. W. Harnes [Karnes] to General Canales, July 26, 1840; Canales to H. W. Harnes [Karnes], August 4, 1840, both in *Supplement of the Semanario del Gobierno de N. León*, 4–5, Streeter 961. For sake of comparison of the published letter that Canales attributed to Karnes, consider the text of this handwritten manuscript document penned by Karnes and preserved in the papers of Albert Sidney Johnston. Karnes wrote Johnston on March 27, 1839, with notable absence of skill in grammar, spelling, and syntax: "He feel in with the federal party commanded by General Lemos on his way to attack Saltillias [*sic*]. He got only all his horses but prest him also," ASJ.

5. In a quotation cited in the *Colorado Gazette* on May 23, 1840, Canales stated unequivocally: "We are not anxious about boundaries but are willing to allow Texas any line she may choose; we are fighting for liberty . . ." See Nance, *After San Jacinto*, 304–5.

6. Professor Josefina Vázquez, though accepting as genuine the Karnes-Canales correspondence, also acknowledges that Arista and others needed to foreswear doubts about Canales in order to bring peace to the region. Vázquez, *Supuesta*,

30–31.

7. Lic. Canales to Isidro Reyes, November 1, 1840, *Supplement of the Semanario del Gobierno de N. León*, November 4, 1840.

8. Jesús Cárdenas to Mariano Arista, November 2, 1840, *Gaceta de Tamaulipas* (Ciudad Victoria), November 28, 1840, MA, XXXIII, 2.

9. José María Carrasco to Mariano Arista, November 2, 1840, *Gaceta de Tamaulipas*.

10. Lic. Canales to Mariano Arista, November 2, 1840, *Supplement of the Semanario del Gobierno de N. León*.

11. Armistice declared by Lt. Col. José María Carrasco under the authority of Isidro Reyes, November 1, 1840, *Supplement of the Semanario del Gobierno de N. León*.

12. Isidro Reyes to Mariano Arista, November 2, 1840, *Supplement of the Semanario del Gobierno de N. León*.

13. [Articles of agreement to end the civil war], November 6, 1840, in *Gaceta de Tamaulipas* (Ciudad Victoria), November 14, 1840, MA, XXXIII, 6.

14. Lic. Canales to Isidro Reyes, November 6, 1840, in *Gaceta de Tamaulipas*, 22.

15. Mariano Arista to Antonio Canales, November 6, 1840; Mariano Arista to Isidro Reyes, November 7, 1840; Mariano Arista to Jesús Cárdenas, November 7, 1840; all in *Gaceta de Tamaulipas*, 17–18.

16. Mariano Arista [orders for Antonio Canales], November 25, 1840, AHD, record group 1548, foja 40. Vázquez, 30, also cites an important document: "Informe de A. Canales sobre el estado actual de Texas," written in Monterrey on November 29, 1840, located in the military archives but not detected by my research in the Archivo Historico Digital (AHD).

17. Isidro Reyes to Mariano Arista, AHD, 22–23; Mariano Arista to José María Carrasco, November 7, 1840, in *El Ancla* (Matamoros), November 23, 1840, MA, XXXV, 194.

18. Mariano Arista to the Troops under his command, *Gaceta de Tamaulipas*, November 28, 1840, MA, XXXIII, 2–3.

19. el comandante general y inspector de coahuila y tejas y 2 en gefe del cuerpo de ejército del Norte, á los habitantes de la frontera, Broadside in Streeter 952.

20. *Gaceta de Tamaulipas* (Ciudad Victoria), December 19, 1840, quoting *El Boletín* (Monterrey), December 1, 1840, MA, XXXIII, 24.

21. Nance, *After San Jacinto*, 373; Mariano Arista, [retrospective report on events of March 24–25, 1840, July 13, 1841], AHD, record group 296, fojas 5–7.

22. Lic. Canales to Col. Jordan, November 10, 1840, in *Texas Sentinel* (Austin), December 12, 1840.

23. Juan Pablo Anaya, *Alocucion . . . á sus Conciudadanos* (Tabasco: Impreso por Trinidad Flores, 1840), 1–14. Streeter 950. From the Yucatan Anaya soon

published another verbal attack against the governing powers of Mexico, but he also cast blame on Canales and Molano for permitting the expedition that resulted in pillaging the people in Ciudad Victoria and en route to Saltillo. See *El Progreso ó Anaya en Campaña* (San Juan Bautista de Tabasco), January 3, 1841, JPA.

24. *Austin City Gazette*, December 2, 1840.

25. Cayetino Martínez to my great friend [Mariano Arista], July 24, 1840. See also *El Mosquito Mexicano* (México), September 25, 1840.

26. X. Y. Z. [letter to the editor], November 22 [1840], in *Austin City Gazette*, December 2, 1840.

27. *Austin City Gazette*, December 30, 1840.

28. *Colorado Gazette* (Matagorda), December 5, 1840; *Telegraph and Texas Register* (Houston), December 30, 1840.

29. During his time of recuperation away from public affairs, Lamar received a solicitous note from his friend and advisor James Webb, describing the source of the malady that took the president away from his duties. Webb wrote, "I had hoped that travelling and getting into cheerful society, would, by removing the gloom which seemed to hang around you here, have restored you, if not to entire health, at least to comfort & a comparative exemption from pain, and I still hope, that as you progress farther, you will feel better." J. Webb to M. B. Lamar, January 18, 1841, Gulick, *Papers of Lamar*, 3: 485.

30. Reséndez, *National Identities*, 230–31, 232 (quotations), 233–35; Sam W. Haynes, "Santa Fe Expedition," in *The United States and Mexico at War: Nineteenth-Century Expansionism and Conflict*, ed. Don Frazier, 379 (New York: Macmillan Reference, 1998).

31. Robert Wooster, "Texas: Conflicts with Mexico, 1836–1845," in *The United States and Mexico at War: Nineteenth-Century Expansionism and Conflict*, ed. Don Frazier, 415–17 (New York: Macmillan Reference, 1998); Sam Haynes, *Soldiers of Misfortune: The Somervell and Mier Expeditions* (Austin: University of Texas Press, 1990), *passim*.

32. Years ago, historian William C. Binkley demonstrated the inaccuracy of the claims of the Republic of Texas, and thus subsequently the United States, to the Rio Grande as the historic boundary. See *The Expansionist Movement in Texas 1838–1850* (Berkeley, California: University of California Press, 1925; reprint, New York: De Capo Press, 1970).

33. Vigness, "Rio Grande," 246–55.

34. Vázquez, *Supuesta*, 31, note 100.

35. Ibid., 1.

36. Quoted in ibid., 32.

37. Quotation from Michael L. Collins, *Texas Devils: Rangers and Regulars on the*

Lower Rio Grande, 1846–1861 (Norman: University of Oklahoma Press, 2008), 8, 16.

38. Andrés Tijerina, "The Trans-Nueces," and Octavio Herrera, "Antonio Canales Rosillo," both in *The United States and Mexico at War: Nineteenth-Century Expansionism and Conflict*, ed. Don Frazier, 434 (Tijerina), 75–76 (Herrera) (New York: Macmillan Reference, 1998).

39. Stanley Siegel, "Mirabeau B. Lamar," in *The United States and Mexico at War: Nineteenth-Century Expansionism and Conflict*, ed. Don Frazier, 217–18 (New York: Macmillan Reference, 1998).

40. Don Frazier, "Samuel Jordan," in *The United States and Mexico at War: Nineteenth-Century Expansionism and Conflict*, ed. Don Frazier, 213 (New York: Macmillan Reference, 1998).

41. Huson, *Iron Men*, 77–82.

42. Vázquez, *Supuesta*, 33–34.

43. Nasser Momayezi, "Republic of the Sierra Madre," in *The United States and Mexico at War: Nineteenth-Century Expansionism and Conflict*, ed. Don Frazier, 385–86 (New York: Macmillan Reference, 1998).

44. Sinkin, *Mexican Reform*, 3–5, 62, 97, 102, 105–9, 148–53. Vidaurri eventually allowed his personal ambition to reach the level of supporting France in its conflict with Mexico, and his life ended in execution in the most humiliating of circumstances.

45. Collins, *Texas Devils*; Nance, *After San Jacinto*, 58–68, 108–16.

46. De la Garza, *Rio Grande*, 1 (quotation), *passim*.

BIBLIOGRAPHY

ABBREVIATIONS

AGN: Archivo General del Estado de Nuevo León, Monterrey, Mexico

AHD: Archivo Histórico [Militar Mexicano] Digital

AJH: Andrew Jackson Houston Collection, Texas State Archives, Austin, Texas

ASJ: Albert Sidney and William Preston Johnston Collection. Special Collections, Tulane University, New Orleans, Louisiana

GA: Guerrero Archives, Instituto Estatal de Documentación de Coahuila, Ramos Arizpe, Coahuila, Mexico

JPA: Juan Pablo Anaya Papers, Nettie Lee Benson Library, University of Texas at Austin, Austin, Texas

LA: Laredo Archives. Microfilm in St. Mary's University Library, San Antonio, Texas

MA: Matamoros Archives, Dolph Briscoe Center for American History, University of Texas at Austin, Austin, Texas

TSA: Texas State Archives, Austin, Texas

VGF: Valentín Gómez Farías Papers. Nettie Lee Benson Library, Latin American Collection, University of Texas at Austin, Austin, Texas

BOOKS

Alessio Robles, Vito. *Coahuila y Texas desde la Consumación de la independencia hasta el Tratado de Paz de Guadalupe Hidalgo*. 2 vols. México: Biblioteca Porrua, 1979.

Alonzo, Armando C. *Tejano Legacy: Rancheros and Settlers in South Texas, 1734–1900*. Albuquerque: University of New Mexico Press, 1998.

Anaya, Juan Pablo. *Alocucion . . . á sus Conciudadanos*. Tabasco: Impreso por Trinidad Flores, 1840.

———. *El Progreso ó Anaya en Campaña*. San Juan Bautista de Tabasco, 1841.

Anna, Timothy. *Forging Mexico, 1821–1835*. Lincoln: University of Nebraska Press, 1998.

Binkley, William C. *The Expansionist Movement in Texas, 1838–1850*. Berkeley: University of California Press, 1925. Reprint, New York: De Capo Press, 1970.

Brading, D. A. *The First America: The Spanish Monarchy, Creole Patriots and the Liberal State, 1492–1867*. Cambridge: Cambridge University Press, 1991.

———. *The Origins of Mexican Nationalism*. Cambridge: Centre of Latin American Studies, 1985.

Bustamante, Anastasio. *El Gabinete Mexicano*. 2 vols. Mexico: J. M. Lara, 1842.

———. *Manifesto que el Ciudadano Anastasio Bustamante dirige a Sus Compatriotas*. Mexico: Impreso por Ignacio Cumplido, 1839.

Collins, Michael L. *Texas Devils: Rangers and Regulars on the Lower Rio Grande, 1846–1861*. Norman: University of Oklahoma Press, 2008.

Costeloe, Michael P. *The Central Republic of Mexico, 1835–1845*. New York: Cambridge University Press, 1993.

De la Garza, Beatriz. *From the Republic of the Rio Grande: A Personal History of the Place and the People*. Austin: University of Texas Press, 2013.

DeLay, Brian. *War of a Thousand Deserts: Indian Raids and the U.S.-Mexican War*. New Haven, CT: Yale University Press, 2008.

Depalo, William A. *The Mexican National Army, 1822–1852*. College Station: Texas A&M University Press, 1997.

Fowler, Will, ed. *Forceful Negotiations: The Origins of the Pronunciamiento in Nineteenth-Century Mexico*. Lincoln: University of Nebraska Press, 2010.

———. *Malcontents, Rebels, and Pronunciados: The Politics of Insurrection in Nineteenth-Century Mexico*. Lincoln: University of Nebraska Press, 2012.

Frazier, Don, ed. *The United States and Mexico at War: Nineteenth-Century Expansionism and Conflict*. New York: Macmillan Reference, 1998.

Garrison, George P., ed. *Diplomatic Correspondence of the Republic of Texas*. 2 vols. Washington, DC: Government Printing Office, 1908.

Gulick, Charles Adams et al., eds. *The Papers of Mirabeau Buonaparte Lamar*. 6 vols. Austin, TX: A. C. Baldwin & Sons, 1922.

Hale, Charles A. *The Transformation of Liberalism in Late Nineteenth-Century Mexico*. Princeton, NJ: Princeton University Press, 1989.

Haynes, Sam. *Soldiers of Misfortune: The Somervell and Mier Expeditions*. Austin: University of Texas Press, 1990.

Hogan, William Ransom. *The Texas Republic: A Social and Economic History*. Austin: University of Texas Press, 1969.

Huson, Hobart. *Iron Men: A History of the Republic of the Rio Grande and the Federalist War in Northern Mexico*. Austin: Texas State Archives, 1940.

Jones, Oakah L., Jr. *Spanish Settlers on the Northeastern Frontier of New Spain*. Norman, University of Oklahoma Press, 1979.

Lack, Paul D. *The Texas Revolutionary Experience: A Political and Social History, 1835–1836*. College Station: Texas A&M University Press, 1992.

Lindheim, Milton. *The Republic of the Rio Grande: Texans in Mexico, 1839–1840*. Waco, TX: Morrison, 1964.

McMillan, Quintellen. *Surveyor General: The Life and Times of José Maria Carvajal*. Austin: Briscoe Center for American History, University of Texas at Austin, 1990.

Nance, John Milton. *After San Jacinto: The Texas-Mexican Frontier, 1836–1841*. Austin: Texas State Historical Association, 1963.

The New Handbook of Texas. 6 vols. Austin: Texas State Historical Association, 1996.

Pavón, Francisco G. *Manifestación que hace de su conducta militar, a la Nación, el Coronel del 1st Regimento de Caballeria*. Mexico: Imprenta del Mosquito, 1841.

Reséndez, Andrés. *Changing National Identities at the Frontier: Texas and New Mexico, 1800–1850*. Cambridge: Cambridge University Press, 2004.

Secret Journal, 4th Congress, November 11, 1838, to February 5, 1840.

Servín, Elisa, Leticia Reina, and John Tutino, eds. *Cycles of Conflict, Centuries of Change: Crisis, Reform, and Revolution in Mexico*. Durham, NC: Duke University Press, 2007.

Sinkin, Richard N. *The Mexican Reform, 1855–1876: A Study in Liberal Nation-Building*. Austin: Institute of Latin American Studies, University of Texas at Austin, 1979.

Smither, Harriet, ed. *Journals of the Fourth Congress of the Republic of Texas, 1839–1840*. Vol. 1, Senate Journal. Austin, TX: Von Boeckmann-Jones, n.d.

Stevens, Donald Fithian. *Origins of Instability in Early Republican Mexico*. Durham, NC: Duke University Press, 1991.

Valerio-Jiménez, Omar S. *River of Hope: Forging Identity and Nation in the Rio Grande Borderlands*. Durham, NC: Duke University Press, 2013.

Vázquez, Josefina Z. *La Supuesta Republica del Rio Grande*. Victoria, Tamaulipas, Mexico: Instituto de Investigaciones Históricas, 1995.

Vigness, David. "The Republic of the Rio Grande: An Example of Separatism in Northern Mexico." PhD diss., University of Texas at Austin, 1951.

Weber, David. *The Mexican Frontier, 1821–1846: The American Southwest under Mexico*. Albuquerque: University of New Mexico Press, 1982.

BOOK CHAPTERS AND ARTICLES

Ali, Shara. "The Origins of the Santiago Imán Revolt, 1838–1840: A Reassessment." In *Forceful Negotiations: The Origins of the Pronunciamiento in*

Nineteenth-Century Mexico, edited by Will Fowler, 143–61. Lincoln: University of Nebraska Press, 2010.

Andrews, Catherine. "The Rise and Fall of a Regional Strongman: Felipe De la Garza's Pronunciamiento of 1822." In *Malcontents, Rebels, and Pronunciados: The Politics of Insurrection in Nineteenth-Century Mexico*, edited by Will Fowler, 22–40. Lincoln: University of Nebraska Press, 2012.

Anna, Timothy. "Demystifying Early Nineteenth-Century Mexico." *Mexican Studies* (Winter 1993): 119–37.

———. "Inventing Mexico: Provincehood and Nationhood after Independence." *Bulletin of Latin American Research* 15 (1996): 1–12.

Annino, Antonio. "The Two-Faced Janus: The Pueblos and the Origins of Mexican Liberalism." In *Cycles of Conflict, Centuries of Change: Crisis, Reform, and Revolution in Mexico*, edited by Elisa Servín, Leticia Reina, and John Tutino, 60–90. Durham, NC: Duke University Press, 2007.

Arnold, Linda. "José Ramón García Ugarte: Patriot, Federalist, or Malcontent?" in *Malcontents, Rebels, and Pronunciados: The Politics of Insurrection in Nineteenth-Century Mexico*, edited by Will Fowler, 91–110. Lincoln: University of Nebraska Press, 2012.

Coerver, Don M. "The Sonora Revolt of 1837." In *The United States and Mexico at War: Nineteenth-Century Expansionism and Conflict*, edited by Don Frazier, 391. New York: Macmillan Reference, 1998.

Costeloe, Michael P. "The British and an Early Pronunciamiento, 1833–1834." In *Forceful Negotiations: The Origins of the Pronunciamiento in Nineteenth-Century Mexico*, edited by Will Fowler, 125–42. Lincoln: University of Nebraska Press, 2010.

Ducey, Michael T. "Municipalities, Prefects, and Pronunciamientos: Power and Political Mobilizations in the Huasteca during the First Federal Republic." In *Forceful Negotiations: The Origins of the Pronunciamiento in Nineteenth-Century Mexico*, edited by Will Fowler, 74–100. Lincoln: University of Nebraska Press, 2010.

Fowler, Will. "The Forgotten Century: Mexico, 1810–1910." *Bulletin of Latin American Research* 15 (1995): 1–9.

———. "'I Pronounce Thus I Exist': Redefining the Pronunciamiento in Independent Mexico, 1821–1876." In *Forceful Negotiations: The Origins of the Pronunciamiento in Nineteenth-Century Mexico*, edited by Will Fowler, 246–65. Lincoln: University of Nebraska Press, 2010.

———. "Valentín Gómez Farías: Perceptions of Radicalism in Independent Mexico, 1821–1847." *Bulletin of Latin American Research* 15 (1956): 39–61.

Frazier, Don. "Samuel Jordan." In *The United States and Mexico at War: Nineteenth-Century Expansionism and Conflict*, edited by Don Frazier, 213. New

York: Macmillan Reference, 1998.

Gamboa, Sergio A. Cañedo. "Ponciano Arriaga and Mariano Avila's Intellectual Backing of the 14 April 1837 Pronunciamiento of San Luis Potosí." In *Malcontents, Rebels, and Pronunciados: The Politics of Insurrection in Nineteenth-Century Mexico*, edited by Will Fowler, 111–28. Lincoln: University of Nebraska Press, 2012.

Guerra, François-Xavier. "Mexico from Independence to Revolution: The Mutations of Liberalism." In *Cycles of Conflict, Centuries of Change: Crisis, Reform, and Revolution in Mexico*, edited by Elisa Servín, Leticia Reina, and John Tutino, 129–52. Durham, NC: Duke University Press, 2007.

Haworth, Daniel S. "Anastasio Bustamante." In *The United States and Mexico at War: Nineteenth-Century Expansionism and Conflict*, edited by Don Frazier, 62–63. New York: Macmillan Reference, 1998.

Haynes, Sam W. "Santa Fe Expedition." In *The United States and Mexico at War: Nineteenth-Century Expansionism and Conflict*, edited by Don Frazier, 379. New York: Macmillan Reference, 1998.

Herrera, Octavio. "Antonio Canales Rosillo." In *The United States and Mexico at War: Nineteenth-Century Expansionism and Conflict*, edited by Don Frazier, 75–76. New York: Macmillan Reference, 1998.

Lack, Paul D. "The Córdova Revolt." In *Tejano Journey, 1770–1850*, edited by Gerald E. Poyo, 89–109. Austin: University of Texas Press, 1996.

Lynch, John. "Antonio López de Santa Anna." In *The United States and Mexico at War: Nineteenth-Century Expansionism and Conflict*, edited by Don Frazier, 372–77. New York: Macmillan Reference, 1998.

Martínez Martínez, Germán. "Inventing the Nation: The Pronunciamiento and the Construction of Mexican National Identity, 1821–1876." In *Forceful Negotiations: The Origins of the Pronunciamiento in Nineteenth-Century Mexico*, edited by Will Fowler, 246–65. Lincoln: University of Nebraska Press, 2010.

McDonald, Kerry. "The Origins of the Pronunciamientos of San Luís Potosí: An Overview." In *The United States and Mexico at War: Nineteenth-Century Expansionism and Conflict*, edited by Don Frazier, 101–24. New York: Macmillan Reference, 1998.

Momayezi, Nasser. "Republic of the Sierra Madre." In *The United States and Mexico at War: Nineteenth-Century Expansionism and Conflict*, edited by Don Frazier, 385–86. New York: Macmillan Reference, 1998.

Salas, Carlos Gonzalez. "Miguel Ramos Arizpe." In *The United States and Mexico at War: Nineteenth-Century Expansionism and Conflict*, edited by Don Frazier, 349. New York: Macmillan Reference, 1998.

Siegel, Stanley. "Mirabeau B. Lamar." In *The United States and Mexico at War: Nineteenth-Century Expansionism and Conflict*, edited by Don Frazier, 217–18.

New York: Macmillan Reference, 1998.

Smith, Justin H. "La Republica de Rio Grande." *American Historical Review* 25 (July 1920): 660–75.

Tijerina, Andrés. "The Trans-Nueces." In *The United States and Mexico at War: Nineteenth-Century Expansionism and Conflict*, edited by Don Frazier, 434. New York: Macmillan Reference, 1998.

Wooster, Robert. "Texas: Conflicts with Mexico, 1836–1845." In *The United States and Mexico at War: Nineteenth-Century Expansionism and Conflict*, edited by Don Frazier, 415–17. New York: Macmillan Reference, 1998.

ARCHIVES

Adjutant General Army Papers, Texas State Archives

Albert Sidney and William Preston Johnston Collection, Special Collections, Tulane University, New Orleans, Louisiana

Andrew Jackson Houston Collection, Texas State Archives, Austin, Texas

Archives and Information Services Division, Texas State Library and Archives Commission, Austin, Texas

Archivo General del Estado de Nuevo León, Monterrey, Mexico

Archivo Histórico Digital de México. Militares

Dolph Briscoe Center for American History, University of Texas at Austin

Guerrero Archives, Instituto Estatal de Documentación de Coahuila, Ramos Arizpe, Coahuila, Mexico

Instituto Estatal de Documentación de Coahuila. Ramos Arizpe, Coahuila, Mexico

Juan Pablo Anaya Papers, Nettie Lee Benson Library, University of Texas at Austin, Austin, Texas

Laredo Archives, microfilm in St. Mary's University Library, San Antonio, Texas

Matamoros Archives, vols. 28, 29, 30, 32–38, Dolph Briscoe Center for American History, University of Texas at Austin, Austin, Texas

Mirabeau Buonaparte Lamar papers, Texas State Archives, Austin, Texas

Nettie Lee Benson Latin American Collection, University of Texas at Austin

Spanish and Mexican Manuscript Collection, Catholic Archives of Texas, Austin, Texas

Special Collections, Tulane University, New Orleans, Louisiana

Streeter Collection [imprints], Archives, Briscoe Center, University of Texas at Austin

Valentín Gómez Farías Papers, Nettie Lee Benson Library, Latin American Collection, University of Texas at Austin, Austin, Texas

NEWSPAPERS

El Ancla: Periodico Semanario del Puerto de Matamoros, 1840

Austin City Gazette, 1840

Brazos Courier, 1840 (Brazoria)

La Brisa, 1839 (Matamoros)

Colorado Gazette and Advertiser, 1840 (Matagorda)

La Concordia: Semanario del Gobierno Departamental de Tamaulipas, 1839–1840 (Ciudad Victoria)

Correro del Rio Bravo del Norte, 1840 (Ciudad Guerrero)

Diario del Gobierno, 1839 (México)

Gaceta del Gobierno de Coahuila, 1838–1840 (Saltillo)

Gaceta del Gobierno de Tamaulipas, 1840 (Ciudad Victoria)

El Méxicano, 1839 (México)

El Mosquito Mexicano, 1838–1840 (México)

Richmond Telescope, 1840

San Luis Advocate, 1840 (Brazoria County)

Telegraph and Texas Register, 1838–1840 (Houston)

Texas Sentinel, 1840 (Austin)

INDEX

ABOUT THE AUTHOR

PAUL D. LACK IS A RETIRED PROFESSOR OF HISTORY AT McMurry University in Abilene, Texas, and academic administrator at Stevenson University in Baltimore County, Maryland. He is the author of three books and several book chapters and articles in scholarly journals, mostly focusing on Texas in the context of the southern United States and its Hispanic heritage as part of and in rebellion against Mexico.